Mom

THE BEHAVIOUR OF HORSES

The Behaviour
of
Horses

In Relation to Management and Training

Marthe Kiley-Worthington
B.SC., D.PHIL

J. A. Allen
London

British Cataloguing in Publication Data

Kiley-Worthington, Marthe
  The behaviour of horses: in relation
  to their training and management.
  1. Horses—Training
  I. Title
  636.1   SF287

ISBN 0–85131–397–3

Published in Great Britain by
J. A. Allen & Company Limited,
1, Lower Grosvenor Place, Buckingham Palace Road,
London, SW1W 0EL

Printed in Great Britain by
Butler & Tanner Ltd, Frome and London

To

BAKSHEESH

It was an infinite privilege to have known you. To have shared so many magic moments
Your comprehension, sensitivity, beauty and athleticism will always remain a cherished memory, and source of admiration
Thank you for your patience, forbearance and endurance in teaching me so much, and forgive my clumsy crass insensitivity. You must have found humans to have such terrible bad taste!
I hope this will in a small way help your descendants and their human friends towards a better understanding and a greater mutual respect between the species

Contents

Acknowledgements

Thanks are due to so many, firstly to my mother who encouraged and enabled me to pursue my interest in horses and their behaviour. Then to Mosquito, Kathiawar, her daughter Syringa and her grandson Baksheesh (to whom this book is dedicated) and to his daughters and sons for teaching me so much, and still leaving me wondering.

To George Iwanowski, one of the twentieth century's most accomplished horsemen, who struggled to teach me the elements of equestrian tact and first suggested the idea of this book. Many people have helped with the farm and stud and the collection of data and its analysis over the years. In particular I would like to thank Chris Rendle, Chloe and Tony Carter, Christine and Matthew Nickol, Christina Herup, Bettina von Skerst, Chloe Dear and the many 'clients' who have come to learn about horses and riding, discuss horse behaviour and become my friends. Rosie Brindley typed the manuscript and Lyn and Alan Cody read it critically.

Without the spur from Lucy Rees who asked me to read her book, *The Horse's Mind*, before it was published, I do not suppose I would have gone on to write this book. It will, I hope, feed the appetite of those who have had it wetted by hers and other books.

List of Illustrations

Preface

During the course of various lectures, weekend schools and courses on horse behaviour and its relationship to management and training that I have given over the years in Britain, Australia, the United States and Europe, there has been a constant plea from the audience 'Where can I read all about this, can you recommend a book?'

Although there are books which touch on the subject here and there, these tend to be personalised accounts written by skilled horsemen, but not professional animal psychologists. The reason for this book, therefore, is to remedy this and to present what is known about horse behaviour to date and how this knowledge can be used to improve the husbandry and training of horses. Judging from the attendances and enthusiasm recorded at my lectures, there is a great thirst for knowledge about horse behaviour.

There is a danger when people popularise science and a scientific approach that, firstly, they assume that the reader is of low intelligence and therefore write down in a way which is unnecessary. Secondly, such popularisers of science have a tendency to over simplify and present such an abridged account that what they say ends up far from what we at present think is the truth: that is, it is plain wrong. At the other extreme, scientists often feel they have to blind people with science and jargon and can talk and write some most incomprehensible nonsense.

I firmly believe that any idea can be explained to any interested adult of average intelligence – if you cannot do this then you do not know your subject! Thus, I have tried to tread the tightrope between these two extremes and produce a readable book that teaches (in, I hope, an interesting way), throws out ideas for discussion, and includes a great respect not only for the horse but for many trainers and handlers.

Nowhere is science (as it is interpreted today) more limiting and misguided than where scientists either with a very limited practical experience (confined to a Sunday afternoon hack), or (not uncommonly) none at all, have written papers or books which once translated into a readable language only tell those of us who work with horses what we learnt in our childhood days with horses.

My serious interest in horse behaviour began when I was seven years old. I realised I was unable to understand much of what my Somali pony was saying. I resolved to study animal behaviour and become an animal psychiatrist (a profession that did not exist at the time). After degrees and adventures with horses and other species in Africa and in Europe I found myself studying communication in animals for a doctorate and then realised that there was much that ethologists (animal behaviour researchers) knew which would be useful to farmers, horsemen, veterinarians and zoo keepers. I became one of the first Applied Ethologists trying to help design environments for the animals that would be more in line with their behavioural needs and reduce their behavioural problems.

During the course of the next ten years I held various fellowships to study various aspects of behaviour in cattle, horses, eland and blesbok (another African antelope), and travelled widely in Europe, the United States, Australia and Africa, always looking (among other things) at methods of riding, horse keeping and training and doing consultancy work on behavioural problems. At the same time I realised that I must set up my own stud and riding school to try out different, perhaps rather radical, ideas and to design *ethologically sound* environments.

The founding member of my stud was Baksheesh. He is an Anglo-Arab stallion whose mother and grandmother I owned. For the last twelve years I have been running the stud and riding school along rather unconventional lines breeding 'all round horses', that can be put in a plough one day and win a race on the next. I needed to test my horses in competition so have collected prizes in Arab flat-racing, long distance racing and riding, dressage, cross-country and jumping, as well as driving and giving displays. I now have one international class horse, two nationally competing horses among others, although I can afford to go to very few competitions each year. This indicates progress may be along the right lines and my horses now can more than hold their own in competition; there is still much research to do however.

In October 1983, I moved the stud (including 12 horses and 20 cattle, 2 peacocks, 9 hens, 5 dogs) from balmy Sussex to the cold, wild Isle of Mull. It remains to be seen how things will develop here. One thing I have found is that the horses (like children) are amazingly adaptable and now clamber like mountain goats and swim like fishes where they had no previous experience.

During my research, what has become more and more apparent is that what the present establishment practises and much of the advice available is either plain wrong from a horse's point of view or too doctrinaire; we must reassess our thoughts about horse welfare and ethics in many ways. This is why I have written this book.

With a book of this nature it is important to discriminate between what is actual fact, that which scientists know and agree on, and what is personal opinion, however well informed. I have too often had to contend with having a personal opinion quoted to me as fact so I am very aware of this. To avoid making the same mistake, I have, I hope, made plain where what I say is scientifically known, and where it is my own opinion, however well founded!

The book is highly controversial and it is meant to be. In the light of the knowledge we have of the behaviour of horses and other animals it is becoming increasingly clear that much of modern horse husbandry seems to be designed to cause behavioural problems and so the message throughout this book is 'think and work out what you should do; don't do what you have been told without thinking about it'. Perhaps if we do this and discuss the issues raised by this book then in the end the horse will benefit.

Apart from trying to inform the reader of things he may not know about horse behaviour, the other motive for this book is to try and improve horse welfare. Unlike pigs, chickens or veal calves, the way horses are kept has not as yet come under scrutiny from animal welfare organisations. It is assumed that provided horses are well fed, physically healthy and not abused, that the animal welfare organisations have nothing to investigate. In particular, competition horses and racehorses are so valuable and so pampered that there should be no reason to worry about their welfare. Having spent some 15 years now studying the behavioural problems of horses, and other farm livestock, I have come to the conclusion that this is not so. I think there is much to worry about from the welfare point of view, sometimes just as much in the 'showpiece' of the horse industry as in the factory farm.

I have not referred in detail to scientific papers throughout the text, but have included a Bibliography for those who would like to find out more.

1 The Evolution and Domestication of the Horse

The earliest records of domestic horses are from around 3000 B C and Zeuner (1962) suggests that the centre of their original domestication is Turkestan, north of the Persian mountains. Horses were originally used for draught, and probably not domesticated until after cattle, when the early agriculturalist must have cast an envious eye on the wild horses galloping around cocking a snook at him plodding slowly along with his cattle.

The most likely method of domesticating these relatively large, swift and reactive wild mammals would have been to capture very young foals and raise them, probably nursed by sheep or goats which had been domesticated somewhat earlier in history. The foal would then be imprinted on humans and stay around. If it were a filly, eventually it might attract stallions to mate and so the herd, in association with man, would increase. There is no doubt that horses gave the early agriculturalists much greater mobility which, in the isolated populations in the open savannah of Turkestan, must have been very attractive. However, the first record of the horse being ridden is later. A picture dated at 1560 B C in Egypt shows a boy riding a black horse. From this time the use of draught and ridden horses spread throughout Europe with the movement of peoples and the development of their culture. Horses also became particularly important in war.

Horses have always been the aristocrats of the domestic

animals and, after dogs, have had the closest relationship with people. Their use in war as comrades rather than slaves or servants probably gave rise to the taboo on eating their flesh which today still exists – at least in some Anglo-Saxon countries. In ancient China, for example, there are records of horses buried beside their human 'comrades-in-arms'. With the modern increase in urbanisation of humans and their loss of contact with domestic animals other than house pets, the taboo is less widespread.

Perhaps because of their beauty and swiftness compared to other domestic animals, horses have always been the companions and associates of princes and kings and perhaps too because of the skill required to handle and train them correctly, which requires voluntary co-operation from the horse rather than sheer physical restraint. This association of horses with royalty certainly continues today. Luckily however, in this modern age the ordinary folk can enrich their lives by a close association with the horse.

Very little has been written about the importance of behaviour in the selection of our domestic animals. A horse's value is based more on behaviour than anything else and animals with suitable behaviour have been bred from by people since they started controlling breeding in the hope of 'like breeding like'.

An understanding of the behaviour of horses is vital if one is to become an equestrian. This was understood by one of the first masters, the Greek, Xenophon in about 400 B C. Everyone has their own ideas on how horses behave and what makes them 'tick'. All my life I have wanted to know as much as possible about this, so, apart from practical involvement with horses, I have spent the last 15 years or so studying their behaviour (having first learnt all that seemed to be known at the time about this, and how to study it 'scientifically'). I quickly discovered that very little *was* actually known, but there were an awful lot of opinions among horsemasters. I have tried to sort out fact from opinion in this book, but the central theme which can act as a basis in understanding and explaining how and why horses behave the way they do is a biological one – that horses have evolved to live in a particular environment in a particular way. If we want to manage, keep and train horses and minimise problems associated with so doing, then the closer we can approach to providing conditions similar to those of the environment in which they evolved, the easier it will be.

In the past few years ideas of thinkers and observers such as Darwin and Wallace on how evolution took place have been made popular, and most people today are more or less aware of the evolution of species as a result of natural selection. We will very briefly outline how this works, and the reader is referred to others such as Richard Dawkins (1976) and Darwin (1859) himself for greater detail.

A chance change in the genes (the vehicles that determine the characteristics of individuals by inheritance) may result in an animal being better 'adapted' to its environment, therefore living long and, particularly important, leaving more offspring. These in turn will be more likely to have this genetic change or mutation too (since the offspring inherits its parents' genes). Thus they will have an advantage and also leave more offspring than will their contemporaries who are without this helpful genetic change. In this way the new character will become more frequent in the population. It will be 'selected for'. Animals with this character are described as the 'fittest' and so we have 'the survival of the fittest'. The word *fittest* is usually used to denote *the best adapted to the environment at that time*. So there is a gradual change of the species which helps it to be better adapted to the environment. But of course the environment may change, and then selection for other criteria may lead to better survival. This dynamic process is called evolution – it is never finished – species are always changing because of evolution.

The way species have changed physically over long periods of time is better known in some species than others. It so happens that there is an almost complete record of the physical evolution of the horse (*Figure 1.1*): from a four-toed little skulking creature that looks a bit like the agouti or mouse deer of today to the modern one-toed horse. Many books on horses describe these changes. What is new and interesting about ideas on evolution in the last few years is that these ideas are being applied to the evolution of *behaviour* too. Unfortunately there is little or no record of the behaviour of the ancestors of most species because behaviour does not preserve like skeletons. We can obtain tips on

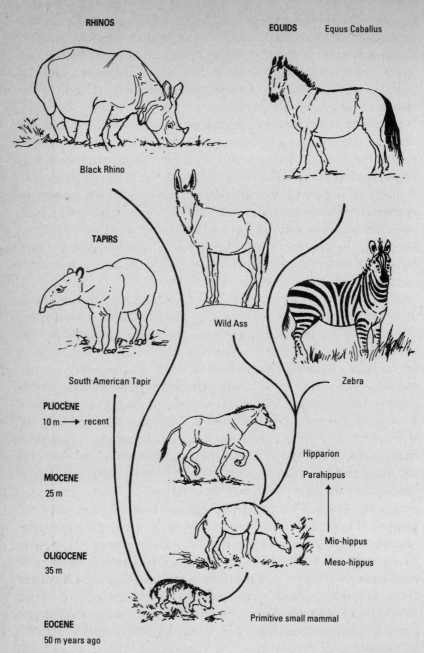

RHINOS

Black Rhino

EQUIDS Equus Caballus

TAPIRS

Wild Ass

South American Tapir

Zebra

PLIOCENE

10 m ⟶ recent

Hipparion

Parahippus

MIOCENE

25 m

OLIGOCENE

35 m

Mio-hippus

Meso-hippus

Primitive small mammal

EOCENE

50 m years ago

Figure 1.1
The evolution of the horse

the animal's behaviour from its skeleton, it tells us what sort of food it ate for example, and quite a lot about its life style, but for the rest we are dependent on working out how and why one species behaves differently from another, and then testing the hypotheses we come up with by studying the behaviour of the species we have around today.

Much of the behaviour is genetically programmed and has evolved through the same processes as physical changes which enable the animal to be better adapted to its environment. It is important to realise that the genes will work to maximise the chances of a particular *individual* surviving, *not* the group or species. For this reason Richard Dawkins called his book, which popularises some of these ideas and relates them to human society, *The Selfish Gene*. The result is that individuals will behave in order to maximise *the survival of their own genes* – this means selfishly.

However, there are exceptions because some humans and animals including horses do behave altruistically sometimes. If we hold the notion that it will be in their interests to behave to maximise their own survival, why, for example, do mares protect their foals when attacked by a predator and thereby put themselves at risk? To explain this various people support what is called 'kin selection'. This theory proposes that altruistic behaviour toward another animal may be programmed into the individual depending on the degree of relatedness of the animal being helped. The more closely related one animal to another, the more similar genes they have. A puppy for example, has half his genes from his mother, half from his father. With a litter of 5 puppies, there will be $2\frac{1}{2}$ sets of the mother's genes around ($\frac{1}{2}$ per puppy). There only needs to be 2 puppies surviving for the same number of her genes as she has to be kept going. Thus it is thought that she will be pre-programmed to sacrifice her life if it will lead to the survival of more than 2 of her puppies. Of course there are many 'costs' and 'benefits' here, and there is no guarantee for example that even if she *does* sacrifice herself at one time, the puppies will survive without her, in fact they may be less likely to do so.

A mare however has only *one* offspring at a time. Thus, at any one lactation, by sacrificing herself she can still at best only have

Figure 1.2
A comparison of the social organisation of several species of equids, including feral and domestic horses

	Source
Asiatic wild horses	Mohr 1971 Kingel 1974 Groves 1974
Plains zebra	Kingel 1974
Mountain zebra	Kingel 1974
New Forest Feral/wild	Tyler 1972
Camargue ponies Feral	Duncan 1976 Goldsmidth– Rothchilde 1980
Pryer mountains Feral horses	Feist and McCullough 1976
Grand Canyon Feral horses	Berger 1977
Domestic horses at pasture	Kiley-Worthingto in prep 1985
Wild asses	Kingel 1974 Groves 1974
Grevys zebra	Kingel 1974
Sable Island Feral horses	Welsch 1973
Shackleford Island Feral horses	Rubenstein 1981

half her genes around. The 'kin selection' theory would predict that if she is a young mare who has the possibility of breeding many more foals, the risk may be too great and she will not sacrifice herself for her foal. If she is an old mare and has little chance of producing many more, then she may defend her foal more strongly.

There are many other aspects to this argument, but suffice it to say that animals will behave *socially* if it is in the interest of each individual and if it will enhance its survival and that of its young.

Family Groups	Permanent Size of Group	Batchelor Groups	Solitary Males	Temporary Groups	Home Range	Solitary Territorial Males
?	5–6	?	?	×	√	×
√	4–7	2–3	?	×	√	×
√	6–7	4–8	?	×	√	×
√	1–5	√ ?	?	×	√	×
√	3–10	?	?	√	√	? ×
√	5	1–2	√	×	√	×
? √	5	?	√	×	√	×
√	√ ?	√	√	×	√	?
√	×	×	–	2–8	√	√
√	×	×	–	2–6	√	√
? √	6	1–2	√	√	√	√
√	12	1–4	√	√	√	√

An animal will behave *altruistically* if it is in the interest of preserving more of its genes. The result is that horses behave the way they do because by behaving in that way, they maximise their own survival and that of their offspring.

Each species has developed rather different strategies and solutions to the problems of survival, and in this book we will look at the behavioural strategy of the horse, not only *how* but *why* they behave the way they do. We must however bear in mind that any species that is around today has played the survival game rather well and got it right. It would be very arrogant and misguided surely to stride in and try and change it all. To a great extent this is what man has tried to do with domestic horses, largely I believe through ignorance. Things in the past have gone very wrong with horse management and continue to do so. This is illustrated by the host of behavioural problems which show that the types of environments which we have developed for the horse are not appropriate to their psychological demands or 'needs'.

There have been a number of studies in the last decade on the social organisation and behaviour of wild or feral equines, and we now have a reasonably good idea of the way the horse behaves and the way its society functions when it has the chance to develop it. Much of this is discussed in the following chapters.

But, you will say, the horse has changed so much during the process of domestication, physically and behaviourally, that wild horse behaviour is of no relevance to modern horse management. It is true that the horse has changed physically in many ways. Some are very much larger than the original *Equus caballus*, the Preswalski horse and the Tarpan – for example, heavy horses – while some, such as the Shetland, are smaller. There is enormous variation in coat colour and indeed in behaviour from the very reactive thoroughbred to the slow heavy horse. Despite all these obvious changes, which we can think of as the dressing on the cake, all horses still have the same structure and physiology. They have the same bones in the same relationship to each other, they have the same teeth and digestive tract and so on. If all these basic systems are still the same, why then should behaviour have changed so grossly – or has it?

The answer is that in the horse, as in any other domestic mammal that has been studied to date, the basic social organisation, communication system and so on has *not* changed. This is illustrated by comparing social organisation in various groups of horses in different habitats (*Figure 1.2*).

One of the problems here is that there are very few truly wild horses which have never been domesticated. The majority of the apparently wild populations of horses around the world are in fact feral, that is, they are domestic animals which have returned to the wild. There are still a few truly wild horses in Mongolia but as yet they have not been studied. However, there are other wild equines around the world, zebras for example, so we can use them too for comparison (*Figure 1.2*). We see that there has been remarkably little change in social organisation in any of these populations although they are living in very different habitats. Thus, the horse's basic behaviour does not appear to have changed during domestication.

Superimposed on this inherited, innate behaviour, is behaviour that is the result of experiences during the horse's lifetime. This is called 'learnt behaviour'. All behaviour we see is to a degree the result of both learning and instinct, intricately interwoven. Some behaviour owes more to instinct, other to learning. The act of suckling in the foal is innate or instinctive behaviour, but exactly *how* the foal sucks is learnt. Much behaviour is the result of innate tendencies that are moulded by experience. If we understand these innate tendencies, then we can use them to help us with our training and management of horses (or similarly in bringing up our own children!). If we do not take them into account, then we may end up with animals which have constant conflicts within their minds, and those are the ones which have behavioural problems. The horse has only been domesticated for around 5,000 years, say 250 generations, which is nothing in evolutionary time and, apart from other considerations, there has not been time enough for large scale genetical changes in behaviour.

There are indeed aspects of behaviour that have changed during domestication, one of them is that we have selected for horses which are very adaptable, as they have had to adapt to every conceivable habitat and almost every type of vegetable food (and even milk and blood when living with certain Middle East tribes) during their sojourn with man.

Why is it that wild animals apparently are more difficult to train even if they have been born in captivity? Is it that there is a basic behavioural difference in terms of, for example, learning – that is, wild animals are slow learners compared to the domestic animals? Or is it rather that many of the people who have tried to train large animals are inexperienced in handling and training them and the lack of success only reflects this?

To test this I obtained a one month old red deer stag, whom I named Rhumba, and, using the normal techniques used to train young horses, such as lungeing and long-reining monitored his progress. Rhumba weighed about one-fifth of one of our young horses, he was well handled and behaved in the field like any friendly horse, coming up to see and nuzzle a person. He would lead and lunge, knew the words of command for the various paces and finally accepted harness. However, he was very unpredictable and would suddenly and for no obvious reason decide that enough was enough and simply take flight. He could easily drag an adult man through a fence and still keep going, despite his small size.

This brought home to me very forcibly how co-operative our domestic horse is. There is no reason why he has to put up with our demands. Even a yearling has a great deal more strength than we have, and if he so wishes could move off dragging us with him. But the horse very rarely does act in this way, despite what must at times be extreme provocation.

Similarly, circus trainers and others maintain that although zebras, for example, can learn apparently as well as a horse, they are unpredictable and not always co-operative. A friend of mine in Africa, Amber May, used to take visitors up Mount Kenya on zebras and zebroids (half zebra and half horse) and she found the same; that they could be taught to be adequate riding or pack animals but they were always somewhat unpredictable.

Thus I am suggesting (we do not have enough evidence to say this is a fact at this stage) that one of the features of behaviour that has changed over the course of domestication of the horse is their co-operation. They not only do what is required a remarkable amount of the time, they also seem to enjoy it! Why? The answer to this question I am not yet clear about, but what is clear is that by so doing they not only survive, but are bred in greater numbers. Thus, within the domesticated situation, it is certainly a normal survival strategy, and may well have become selected for in so far as there has been time during domestication.

Do domestic horses learn faster or are they more 'intelligent' than their wild cousins? To date there is no evidence that this is the case. We know from the work done in experimental psychology laboratories on learning that domestic species in general do not appear to learn faster than wild ones but it may be

fairly safely conclude that the horse is probably not able to feel it!

It is perhaps important for any good horseman to realise how false the commonly held belief is that if there is no response to one aid (or stimulus), this should be repeated and increased in intensity. In fact it is often the opposite that is the case, the smaller the cue, the more sensitive the horse will become and the easier to manage and more pleasant to ride. Always use the *minimum* stimulus on your horse. Increasing the stimulus as a result of a lack of response is like shouting louder when a foreigner does not understand you!

There are different degrees of sensitivity depending on things like the thickness of the coat, the thickness of the skin and the number of receptors at different points in the skin. Moyra Williams (1960) tried a series of mini-experiments to test the relative sensitivity of different areas on the horse's body and concluded that the withers were a very sensitive area. I have done something similar (*Figure 2.2*) using brushes of different hardness. I am sure most people are aware that apart from individual horses varying in their response to degrees of hardness of brush, different parts of the horse also vary.

Horses of course use touch to cement bonds between individuals. Mothers and foals are often seen touching noses and other parts of each others' bodies. Social partners, too, will smell and touch each other, and in sexual situations tactile stimulation is particularly important.

The nose and nostrils in particular are well supplied with whiskers and sensory cells and the nerves to relay the messages to the brain. Like those of a cat they are used to test and 'feel' objects. Surely it is outrageous therefore to cut off whiskers for cosmetic reasons, like showing? The degree of suffering is probably similar to that caused when a horse is docked, now illegal in Britain on welfare grounds.

Another way of finding out about the relative importance of different areas of the body in terms of its tactile sensitivity can be measured by finding out how much of the sensory cortex (the part of the fore brain which analyses the sensory information fed into it) is concerned with that part. The nose and lips of the horse are very well represented, but no one knows the details (*Figure 2.3*).

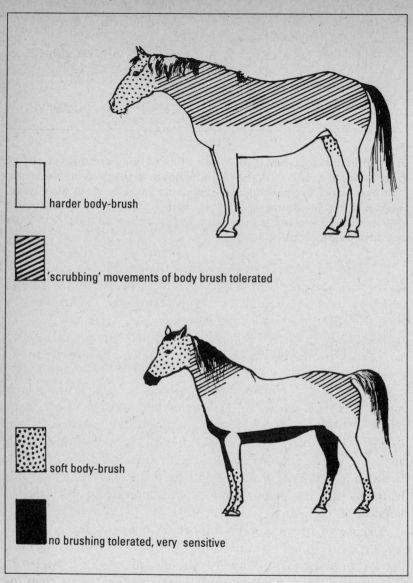

Figure 2.2
The response to tactile stimulation tested in horses which were brushed at different strengths. (*Top*) A less sensitive cob; (*bottom*) An Anglo-Arab who is more sensitive. Each horse has his own idiosyncratic responsiveness as every good groom knows. It is quite interesting and a good student exercise to construct similar diagrams for every horse in the stables

| Rabbit | Cat | Horse | Human |

Figure 2.3
A hypothetical representation of the different body areas in the cortex (fore brain) of a rabbit, cat, horse and human. In the drawing the larger that part of the body, the better represented it may be in the cortex. Thus people's hands are well represented since they use them a great deal. Horses, by comparision, have well represented noses and faces and little body representation.

Because the horse is very good at running fast, co-ordinating movement and keeping upright at speed, it probably has the feet and legs well represented in the sensory cortex. The horse is however *not* good at manipulating things with his feet, as monkeys and men are for example and so the motor system (which sends messages back from the brain to the muscles in the feet and legs) may not be well represented.

I did some pilot (preliminary) experiments with a foal which illustrates this. The idea was to see to what extent he would learn to use his front legs for manipulation. We attempted to teach him to kick a football. This he learnt with difficulty, preferring always to use his nose. He became quite adept though at noseball, but would not have made the village team at football! He also learnt to play the piano, producing an interesting and original version of 'chopsticks' with his nose.

A sense of touch is very important in horses for gathering information about the environment and for communication between horses – and between horses and people (*Chapter 9*): perhaps this sense is almost more important for horses than for people.

TASTE

Considering the importance of understanding the sense of taste in horses from the point of view of getting horses to eat (a frequent problem of management) it is really surprising that so little is known. There is, of course, an enormous amount of folklore about the tastes that horses prefer and recipes to improve appetite. These range from old fashioned feeding of herbs, such as rue, wormwood and feverfew, to injections of modern drugs, both of which seem to have both good and bad results. A sensible approach perhaps is to try and understand as much about taste, what it does and how it works, before believing in any particular remedy.

The function of taste is generally involved with the intake of food. Some people suggest that it encourages nutritional prudence thus preventing animals from poisoning themselves. It is also widely believed that taste provides a cue to the animal as to the nutritional value of food – this is called 'nutritional wisdom'.

There is some evidence that horses when grazing will, if given the option, choose for themselves a nutritionally balanced diet, and, indeed, if it proves deficient in certain minerals will tend to seek out material rich in these and eat them. Eating bark from trees is often ascribed to this and there appears to be some truth in it. Therefore, it is not a bad rule to allow the animal to choose his own diet for his present physiological needs as far as possible. On the other hand this does not always work. For example, Susan Marinier (1982) found in South Africa that in a group of horses at pasture, some of them persistently ate ragwort (*Senecio jacobaea*), a poisonous herb, and subsequently died although there was plenty of non-poisonous and nutrient rich food to eat. It is possible to mask the required food with strong tastes (quinine has been used to test this in several laboratory experiments). The animal does not then eat the food although it may be very rich in a required nutrient or mineral. It is also possible to encourage horses to eat foods that they may not require, or they might normally reject, by giving them a particularly desired taste. Many manufacturers of horse foods use sweet substances to do this. However this will only work if the animal has previously learnt to like sweet tastes! Horses are not born with a sweet tooth, though some of them acquire it through conditioning (*Chapter 9*).

The texture, the ease of chewing and all sorts of other variables as well as taste will also affect selection and intake and to date we do not know enough about this in the horse – or any other species for that matter (*Chapter 7*).

We do know however that taste is very important in having an effect on gastric contractions and this in turn depends on the nutritional state of the horse. There are various things that effect how this works but a simple illustration of what this means is that when you (or a horse) are very hungry food tastes better!

We can conclude that at present the importance of taste in horses is not well understood and there are *no* known wonder drugs or particular substances we can add to feeds to ensure that our animal eats them all and has a balanced diet! We may be better off letting him choose his own diet to a degree.

TASTE RECEPTORS

Taste receptors are groups of chemically sensitive cells which in the horse are found predominantly on the tongue in groups called 'taste buds'. They are also found in other parts of the mouth and at the back of the throat. In the horse they are melon shaped cells. The nerves attached to these cells run to various parts of the brain, particularly the hind brain, but some fibres go to the cortex or 'thinking' brain (*Figure 2.4*).

The taste receptors in humans respond to four major taste types: salt, sour, bitter and sweet. There are wide differences

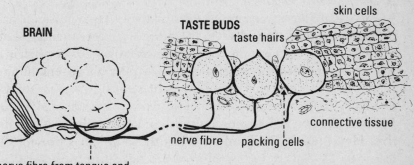

Figure 2.4
A taste bud in the tongue and the connections of the nerve fibres to the brain

between species in responses. All species that have so far been tested, respond to salts and acids, although to different levels of concentration. From everyday experience we know that horses can tolerate, and apparently enjoy, foodstuffs that are much too bitter for humans. They also can pick up sweet, sour and salt tastes, but how sensitive they are to these we do not know.

As everyone who is interested in food and the art of cooking will know, taste, at least in humans, is not that simple. The order in which different taste fibres are stimulated affects their responsiveness. For example, the response of a sweet fibre to sugar can be prevented by washing it with salt, whereas salt fibres are not affected by washing with sugar. The complexity of the taste sensations is considerable and there is not reason to believe that this is less for horses than for humans.

We do not know if horses have a particularly acute sense of taste, or a poor one and the degree to which they can discriminate differences in the strength of tastes. However one would think that because of the inability of horses to vomit (*Chapter 6*), it would be particularly important for them to be able to discriminate good from bad things to eat and one of the major ways of doing this is by taste. We do know from other species, such as the chicken and the rat, that wild animals are much more responsive to the nutritional and physiological consequences of their diet and less to the sensory qualities than their domesticated cousins. Domestic rats, for example, are far more 'self-indulgent' than wild ones. If this is true of the horse, then we might expect that the domestic horse would be less able to select a wise diet than his wild cousin. Katherine Houpt (1979) found that it was particularly difficult to condition *taste aversion* in horses, when, after being fed a particular food, the horses are injected with a drug to make them feel sick. Most animals, including human beings, after only one such experience will avoid that particular food, but horses are slow to learn this. However, there are other factors (*Chapter 9*) which qualify this.

PAST EXPERIENCE AND TASTE PREFERENCE

There is much individual variation in taste preferences in horses. This is probably largely the result of their past experiences.

We have already mentioned that some of the nerve fibres from the taste buds eventually end up in the cortex, or thinking part of the brain. Here the information is analysed and messages sent back via the motor system (the response system) to muscles which result in a particular response (that is rejecting the foodstuff, or, alternatively, eating it).

In the domestic horse learning experiences in relation to taste and eating are probably particularly important. Most people will know that young horses rarely, if ever, voluntarily take sugar, but once they have had the experience of eating it once or twice and in particular seeing other horses eat it, then they will indeed take it willingly and may even work to obtain more. Different horses take different titbits, depending on what they are 'used to' or have been conditioned to take. Thus, certain foodstuffs can have associations of pleasure, or approval. I would suggest that this should be made use of in feeding horses that are inclined to be difficult feeders. It is possible to have the horse associate particular food types with good times, when he is relaxed and happy in his own home with his social partners and so on. This particular food may well then be associated with all being well and therefore more likely to be eaten in a strange place or at a strange time. This may be more or less understood by horse management, but the *reasons* are not often understood.

The temperature can substantially modify the reaction to taste stimulation in man and chickens and probably many other species. This is something worth remembering. In general, cold temperatures tend to reduce the strength of the taste. Thus if unfamiliar but necessary foodstuffs are introduced cold, they are more likely to be eaten. Feeding behaviour and selection is discussed in more detail later (*Chapter 6*).

SMELL

The sense of smell is considered to be one of, if not the most primitive senses and is commonly associated with selecting food, avoiding predators and in particular with social behaviour. It has received most attention in relation to sexual behaviour and the recognition of young by the mother. However, as we learn more about behaviour it is becoming evident that smell plays a role in

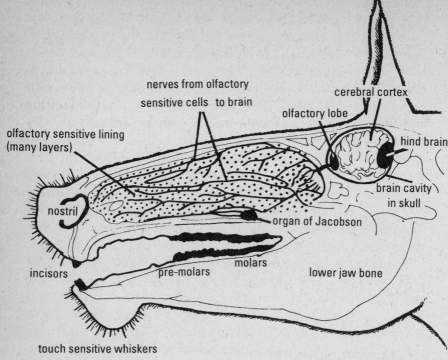

nerves from olfactory
sensitive cells to brain

cerebral cortex

olfactory lobe

olfactory sensitive lining
(many layers)

hind brain

brain cavity
in skull

nostril

organ of Jacobson

incisors

pre-molars

molars

lower jaw bone

touch sensitive whiskers

Figure 2.5
Section through the head of a horse, showing the 'smell sensitive'
membranes and their connection to the brain. Note the 'Organ of
Jacobson' which may be associated with detecting smell messages

almost every type of social behaviour although its importance
varies between species. Smell is also a chemical sense and is
closely related to taste.

One of the *main reasons* why horses have such long faces is
probably because they have to accommodate an enormous area
of olfactory mucosa (membrane capable of picking up smell
cues). The anatomy of the olfactory system consists of paired
external nostrils, leading to internal nostrils which direct the air
flow to the nasal cavities or chambers. The receptor cells are
found in the specialised membranes which line portions of the
cavities. These pick up the messages and relay them to the brain
via the olfactory nerve. The olfactory nerve feeds a particular
part of the brain right at the front . . . the olfactory bulbs.

The nasal cavities are subdivided by a series of rolled bones called 'turbinates' which can be seen in any skull. These are covered by the olfactory sensitive mucosa and respiratory epithelium which warms and filters the air. Because of the structure of the turbinate bones and therefore the area of the olfactory mucosae, the total area is of great size, often more than the whole surface area of the horse! This allows for a great degree of testing and filtering of the air for molecules with a smell.

The air currents in normal breathing short cut the various chambers of the nose, but, when the animal is sniffing, the air is forced in and out of all the chambers and in this way it can be thoroughly screened for smells and at the same time warmed.

There is in the horse an organ called the vomeronasal organ or 'Organ of Jacobsen' which opens into the back of the mouth (*Figure 2.5*). Its function has for long been obscure but recently it has been suggested that it may well be involved in the extra screening of the inspired air for 'pheromones', which are chemical substances secreted by animals which have messages. Estes (1972) suggests that the 'flehmen', or lip curl of the horse (*Chapter 3*) allows the air and pheromones in solution to drop into the organ and they can then be further scrutinised and identified. As we shall see later, flehmen is not just concerned with sex, but it does seem that this organ adds to the olfactory screening which can be performed by the horse. The extent to which the sense of smell is important in locating and discriminating between foods is difficult to test and we know very little about it in the horse. In fact the senses of taste and smell do seem to be very closely related. What is clear is that there is no good scientific evidence that aromatic food additives such as aniseed, fenugreek or onion render the food more appealing and thus increase intake.

We are only just beginning to understand the importance of smells in social behaviour. We humans have a relatively bad sense of smell, so we have tended to neglect the importance of this sense in social organisation. However, recently with the help of chromatography and other modern equipment used for measuring different substances, we are beginning to understand how very important smell is to horses and other domestic animals. There is little doubt that horses recognise each other individually; that they have a complex social structure; that they form long term and close relationships between individuals; that when males mate with females they detect when the female is in oestrus; and that mothers recognise their young and their young recognise their dams. All of this seems to involve smells. They also, no doubt, involve all the other senses as well.

Smell may also be important in recognising areas and home ranges. We think of the dog as following trails, but horses may show every sign of following trails by smell in a similar way at appropriate times. They are notoriously good at homing. This may also involve smell cues.

HEARING

Horses are of course able to hear sounds and interpret them in their environment and make sounds in order to communicate (*Chapter 3*). The ear is the organ which efficiently converts acoustical information from the environment into nerve impulses which are carried to the brain via the auditory nerve (*Figure 2.6*). There is a specific part of the brain whose function is to analyse these messages and interpret their meaning (*Figure 2.7*).

The structure and function of the ear of the horse is similar to other mammalian species and has been well described in many other books. Briefly, the ear is made up of three divisions:

1. The pinna or external ear which collects the sound.
2. The middle ear consisting of the ear drum or tympanic membrane, and the three bones (hammer, stirrup and anvil). Leading off from this area is the eustacian tube which in the horse, uniquely among the domestic animals has a large swelling (diverticulum) on one side called the 'gutteral pouch'. The function of this is obscure.
3. The inner ear containing the cochlea where the auditory sensitive cells are situated. This converts the sound waves to electrical energy. This information is then transferred by the auditory nerve to the higher centres in the brain.

The middle ear amplifies the sound and facilitates its passage through the inner ear and thence to the sound receptors in the cochlea. The external ears of the horse are remarkably mobile,

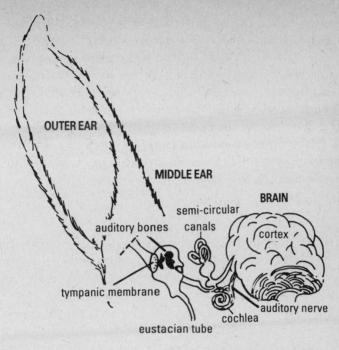

OUTER EAR

MIDDLE EAR

BRAIN

semi-circular
canals

auditory bones

cortex

tympanic membrane

cochlea

auditory nerve

eustacian tube

INNER EAR

Figure 2.6
The ear of the horse and its connection to the brain by the auditory
nerve. Sound is picked up by the tympanic membrane and transfered by
the vibration of the bones in the middle ear to the inner ear and cochlea

moving independently and in any direction and are particularly
good at picking up sound (*Chapter 4*). It has recently been found
that the size and shape of the external ear is very important in
picking up sound and locating its origin. In horses the secondary
function of the external ears, as a result of their conspicuousness
and mobility, is for communication. This we will consider in
detail later (*Chapter 3*).

Sounds differ in their frequency (number of waves per
second), high sounds having a higher frequency and more waves
per second than low sounds. The frequency of the sound gives it
its pitch. They also differ in 'intensity'. The intensity depends on
the frequency and amplitude of the vibrations and it effectively is
the *loudness* of the sound. Finally, sound waves can vary in

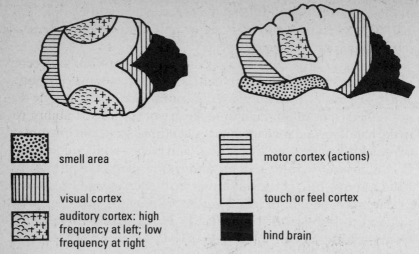

smell area

visual cortex

auditory cortex: high
frequency at left; low
frequency at right

motor cortex (actions)

touch or feel cortex

hind brain

Figure 2.7
The function of different parts of the fore brain, or cortex, of the horse

'timbre'. Thus middle C played on a flute varies from middle C
(the same frequency) played on a cello. The brain, receiving
messages from the ear, enables us to differentiate the note from a
flute or a cello – or indeed individual voices. Exactly *how* we
compute all this information in the brain we still do not know but
it is partly done by the number and pattern of the overtones. If
humans can do it, unless we have evidence to the contrary, we
can assume that horses can too.

RANGE OF HEARING

The most practised way of measuring an animal's range of
hearing is by 'discimination tests'. These involve training the
animal to respond in a certain way to a stimulus (*Chapter 9*). I
have been unable to find any reference to suggest these tests have
been done on horses and therefore believe there is little accurate
knowledge on the extent of the range of hearing in the horse.

ACUITY

How acute or sensitive the hearing of the horse is also remains
largely unknown. However we know they can at least tell

individual horses and human voices apart. A favourite horse will call when he hears his master talking and is expecting to be fed, but will ignore strangers' voices.

Horses can also apparently discriminate between different words. They can be taught to come on command just like dogs and to respond to many other word commands. Many people do not understand this and fail to make use of the horse's ability to make handling and management easier (horses can, for example, be quickly taught 'no' like a dog, and 'stand still' and so on). People instead tend to rely on preventing the horse physically from moving off. The result is that many horses are hung onto, pushed, shoved and dragged around and hence never learn to respond to simple word commands. How much easier it is to have your horse come when he is called and to respond to other word commands.

LOCATION OF SOUND

It is important here to understand how sound is located. This is effectively done by having two ears. The comparison of the sound between the two ears allows for its location. This is done by an analysis of three things:

1. The difference in amplitude (loudness) between the two ears.
2. The difference in the time that the sound arrives at the different ears.
3. Sound travels in waves, it can reach one ear on the trough of the wave, the second on the crest for example. This is called a difference of *phase* between the two ears.

Because horses have very mobile ears, they are able to rotate the ears so that they pick up the maximum amount of sound and use these characteristics to the full.

SIGHT

Sight is probably the most important sense for the horse. Why this may be should become clear when we discuss communication (*Chapter 3*), but let us examine briefly the eyes and how they analyse optical information.

The first thing that strikes one about horses eyes are how

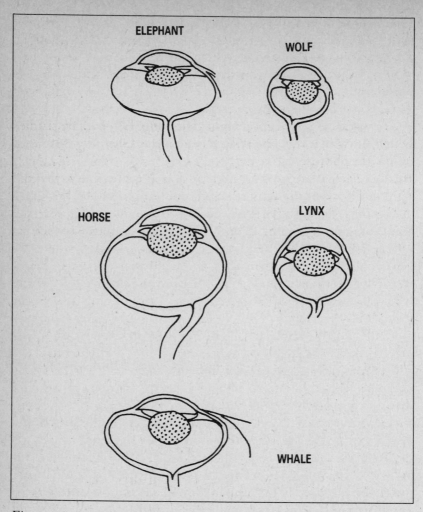

Figure 2.8
The larger the eye, the more light can be picked up. The horse's eye is larger than that in much bigger mammals such as the elephant and the whale. This suggests that night vision may be particularly important to the horse. Nocturnal animals such as the lynx tend to have larger eyes. Does this mean that the horse is to some extent nocturnal?

enormous they are. In fact the eye of the horse is larger than that of a whale or an elephant (*Figure 2.8*). The actual size of the eye is important because a larger eye allows a greater surface available for light receptors. Animals which must make the most of the available light usually have large eyes and they are usually nocturnal, or live in habitats where there is little light. Alternatively, the large eye which allows for more receptors, increases the acuity of sight and the visual field. Thus animals with large eyes may rely more heavily on sight than small eyed animals (such as pigs for example).

Horses do also have good night vision as is indicated by studies which show that they are relatively active at this time. Also, the retina (the photosensitive part of the eye) is rich in rod cells which are the cells that are used for night vision. It is possible to test the sight of a horse at night by riding fast or jumping small obstacles in darkness. Tests I have done indicate that horses are quite good at jumping in very poor light – although it is rather frightening for the almost night blind rider!

The horse, unlike man, has a membranous layer called a *tapetum*, covering the lower half of its eyes (*Figure 2.9*). This is what makes the eyes shine when a light is directed on to them in the dark. It functions as a mirror to double the amount of light on the retina and is another mechanism for improving vision when there is not a great deal of light.

From the retina, where the light sensitive cells are, an optic nerve travels to the brain. The optic nerves are large structures that can be easily seen on the outside of the brain.

An important characteristic of the horse is that, unlike man, his eyes are placed at the side of his head. This means of course that the horse has a much wider visual field than man, but also that the binocular visual field is relatively small (*Figure 2.10*). What this means in practice, is that the horse can see almost all the way around himself. This is especially the case when the animal holds his head up.

It is usually thought that the reason why the horse evolved this position of the eyes was so that he could see predators approaching from the rear and run away. This may indeed have been the case, but since the horse is a social animal, it may have been almost as important to be able to see other members of the group without having to move his head around. In practical terms for horse training, it must never be forgotten that the horse's peripheral field of vision is very large and, in some horses at any rate, if the horse puts his head up he will be able to see the

A

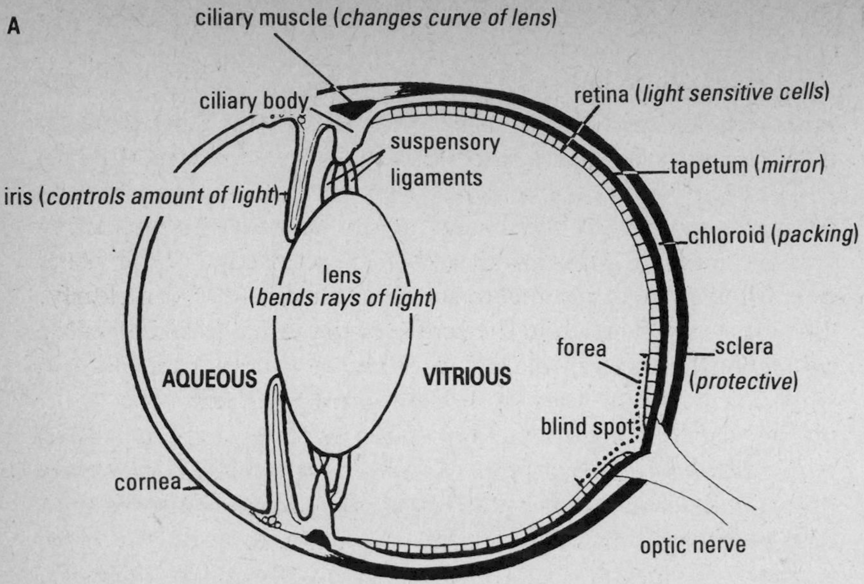

ciliary muscle (*changes curve of lens*)

ciliary body

retina (*light sensitive cells*)

suspensory ligaments

tapetum (*mirror*)

iris (*controls amount of light*)

chloroid (*packing*)

lens (*bends rays of light*)

forea

sclera (*protective*)

AQUEOUS

VITRIOUS

blind spot

cornea

optic nerve

B

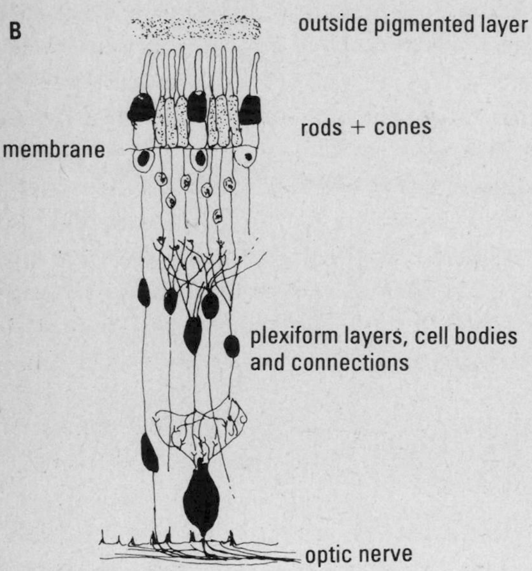

outside pigmented layer

rods + cones

membrane

plexiform layers, cell bodies and connections

optic nerve

C

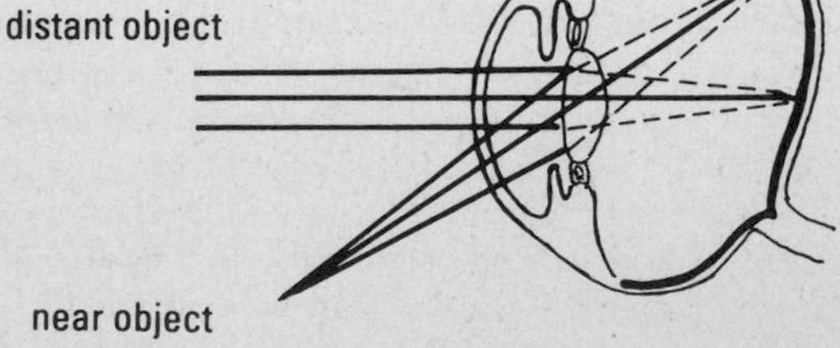

distant object

near object

rider on his back. No wonder a young horse is often hollowbacked and carries his head perpetually high, particularly if he is a sensitive reactive animal such as a thoroughbred or Arab.

The peripheral visual field is in many species, including horses, less acute than the central visual field where the most sensitive area is the fovea. Thus familiar objects on the edge of the visual field often cause the animal to startle as they are not seen clearly. The same object when in the centre of the visual field will cause no response; for example, try moving your arms carefully out sideways when on a young horse – but be careful!

The narrow binocular field of vision indicates that it is wise to have your horse's head pointed forward at a jump if you want him to judge the distance easily and time the take-off correctly. This is because distance judging is usually done by the brain making comparisons between the images presented to it by the two eyes. However it is never so simple and we know that, for example, people who are blind in one eye can still play teninis. It may well be the case that horses are also able to adapt and judge distance with information from the image of only one eye; horses blind in one eye can still jump.

Many people are confused about whether or not the horse can see colours. There is every chance he can see colours almost as well as humans. The reason we know this is from studying the retina which has a large number of *cone* cells in it which are sensitive to colour. If we look at these colour sensitive cone cells, we find that they have a number of colour pigments in them and

Figure 2.9 (OPPOSITE)
A, Diagram of a cross-section of the eye of the horse. B, An enlargement of a small section of the *retina* showing the rods and cones and how their nerve fibres are inter-connected before the *optic nerve* takes the information to the brain for further analysis. Some of the analysis is done at the retina by information being filtered out. C, The squashed eye or 'ramped retina'. This shows how convenient it was for explaining the changes in focusing on far and near objects for horses. But it does *not* exist!

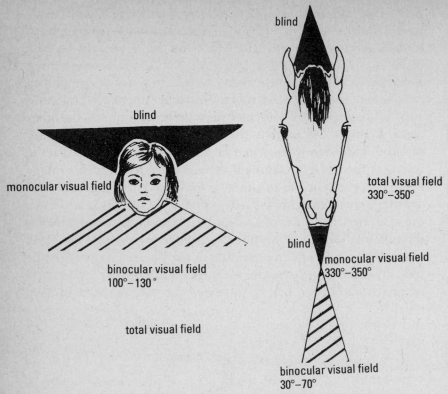

Figure 2.10
The visual fields of a girl and a horse contrasted. Note the much greater
binocular field of vision for a girl, but the much more restricted field of
monocular vision. Some horses can see right around to the person on
their back if they put their head up

it is these which tell us which colours the animal is able to see.
The colour pigments in the eyes of the horse are very similar to
those of man.

The eyes work by the passage of light passing through the lens
(the amount of light is controlled by the iris) and are focussed
(bent) so that the image falls on the light sensitive retina. Each
stimulated retinal cell then relays an electrical message via the
optic nerve. To be in focus, the image must fall on the retina. If
the image falls before it the animal would be short sighted; if

behind it long sighted (*Figure 2.11*). There are small ciliary muscles at the end of the lens whose job it is to stretch the lens to reduce its curvature and thus allow the image of objects at a distance to fall on the retina and *vice versa*. The interesting thing about these muscles, in the horse, is that they are not at all well developed. This may mean that the horse is rather bad at focusing and thus has a poor visual acuity (inaccurate vision). On the other hand it might mean that focussing is done by some other method. Indeed most veterinary textbooks still maintain that the retina of the horse is 'ramped'. This would result in the image being in focus whether the horse is looking down (such as when grazing) when the light rays fall on the part of the retina nearest to the lens; or when the horse is looking at objects at a distance – then they fall on a part of the retina which is further away. This makes a lovely tale but it has unfortunately been shown not to be true, by American researchers (Cornell University), despite the fact that it has been taught to many generations of veterinary

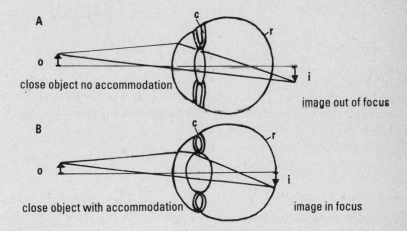

Figure 2.11
How long and short sight works. The effect of increasing the curvature of the lens is to bend the light rays more so that the image (I) falls on the retina (R) when it will be in focus. This is called *accommodation*. The ciliary muscles (C) contract to achieve this, but they are not well developed in the horse. It is as well to remember that some horses may well be long sighted (the image falls behind the retina) as in A; others may be short sighted so that the image falls in front of the retina

students. Early in the century someone (nobody seems quite to remember who) reported the ramped retina presumably as a result of dissecting a rather squashed eye – and it has stayed with us ever since!

We remain with the question then, is it difficult for horses to accommodate (that is to change focus quickly) giving them poor visual acuity? Or do they have some other mechanism by which they focus? It seems as if horses' sight is rather sharp as their perception of very slight visual signals is much superior to humans (*Chapter 3*). It may be, however, that they are not good at very quick change of focus, but at present we do not know.

Something else which is rather remarkable, and which horses have in common with all other mammals, is that the retina is inverted. This means that the light has to travel through a series of packing cells and cell fibres before it reaches the photosensitive cells. This seems a peculiarly inefficient way of organising matters. There are developmental reasons why this should be, but why it has not changed during evolution remains another mystery.

A large area of the fore brain is devoted to analysing visual information – another indicator of the importance of vision to horses. All in all then the sight of horses is, it seems, very good and they are able to see colours and fast movement probably to much the same degree as do humans. However, horses are much better at night vision, they have a different visual field and may be rather slow to accommodate, but we are not sure about the latter.

Brain and Intelligence

As far as we know the brain of the horse works like any other mammalian brain, but we do not know a great deal about this! It used to be thought that there was a little man sitting in the brain, a 'homonculus', who occupied various bits of the brain with different pieces of his anatomy, depending on how important those bits were. Then it was considered that different parts of the brain had very different functions, one bit dealing with aggression, another with sex, another with thought and so on. However, in the last two decades or so, it has become apparent

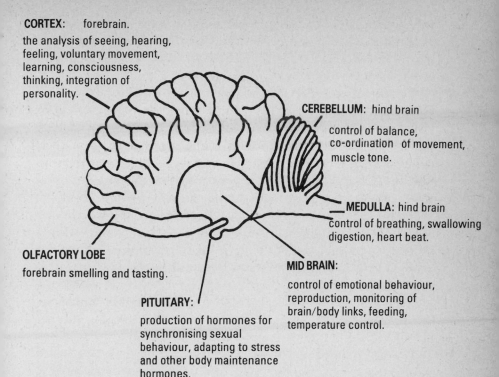

CORTEX: forebrain.

the analysis of seeing, hearing, feeling, voluntary movement, learning, consciousness, thinking, integration of personality.

CEREBELLUM: hind brain

control of balance, co-ordination of movement, muscle tone.

MEDULLA: hind brain

control of breathing, swallowing digestion, heart beat.

OLFACTORY LOBE

forebrain smelling and tasting.

MID BRAIN:

control of emotional behaviour, reproduction, monitoring of brain/body links, feeding, temperature control.

PITUITARY:

production of hormones for synchronising sexual behaviour, adapting to stress and other body maintenance hormones.

Figure 2.12
The most important divisions of the brain, and their function. The cerebellum controls balance, coordinates movement and muscle tone. The medulla, in the hind brain, controls breathing, swallowing, digestion and heart rate. The various parts of the mid-brain control emotional behaviour, and reproduction; they monitor the links between body and brain, control feeding and temperature control. The pituitary produces hormones for sychronising sexual behaviour, adapting to stress and other body maintenance hormones. The olfactory lobes in the fore brain analyse smells and tastes. The cortex analyses seeing, hearing, feeling, voluntary movements, learning, consciousness, thinking and memory, and is responsible for the integration of the personality

from study that there is some localisation of function of different parts of the brain. For example the 'thinking brain' and 'consciousness and self-awareness' is localised in the fore brain. The emotional or 'feeling' part of the brain is in the middle. The hind brain tends to specialise in analysing information concerning the control of many of the bodily functions like breathing, digestion, walking, balance and so on of which we are not often conscious (*Figure 2.12*).

The above description is, of course, a simplified localisation of the *main* functions of the different areas of the brain. However, all the areas also work together so that to a great extent the brain works as a whole. Each part is linked, either directly or indirectly with each other part and some parts can even take over other functions if that particular area is damaged, particularly if this happens when the animal is young. This inter-relatedness of all areas of the brain means that links can constantly be made between intellectual, emotional and physical life through the brain. We can see then how, for example, psychological pressure can result in physical illness, or *vice versa*. There is no reason to believe that this all works differently for horses, compared with man or other species we know more about. The brain has the same structures which appear to have the same relationship with each other.

So little is known about the functioning of the brain of any species that it is not surprising that it is almost impossible to find any information about the brain of the horse as distinct from any other species. Yet it is obviously important to have as much information as is available in order to understand more about the horse and its behavioural potential. On the other hand, in order to find out this sort of thing, it is necessary to do brain surgery, to use drugs and to implant electrodes in the brain and perhaps we must decide whether the results we will get are so fundamentally important that they can justify the suffering and sacrifice of many hundreds, probably thousands, of horses even though the scientist may develop sophisticated techniques as a result. Of what benefit will it be to *the horse*? It is often possible by careful anatomical study and a thorough study of behaviour to obtain as much if not more information without sacrificing animals. Of course, because horses are relatively expensive for laboratories to buy and maintain, they are relatively infrequently used for such neurophysiological work, which is indeed a blessing – for them at least.

If we compare the brain of a horse with that of other species (*Figure 2.13*) there are some interesting points which suggest

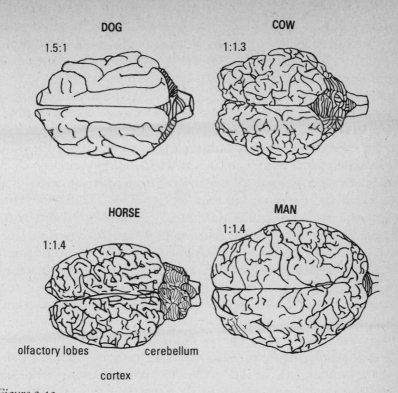

Figure 2.13
A dorsal view (view from the top) of the brains of some different
species. The numbers refer to the scale; thus, the dog's brain is enlarged
by 50 per cent but the others are reduced as marked. Note the size and
convolutions of the cortex of the horse's brain compared with the other
species, in particular the dog. The size and convolutions of brains are
usually indicative of the species' 'intelligence'. The cerebellum, which
co-ordinates movement and pace, is also very well developed in the
horse

certain things which the horse may be more or less able to do than
other species. For example, if we compare the size of the cerebellum (the hind part of the brain which deals with balance, locomo-
tion and so on) we see that it is rather larger and apparently better
developed in the horse than in some other species. We might
indeed expect this, as the horse is particularly good at moving,
and moving fast over rough country. We can do this comparison
for all the various parts of the brain, but it will only tell us about

very gross differences between species. One thing that is obvious is the size and number of convolutions (folds which increase the surface area) of the cortex, or fore brain, of the horse's brain. Compared to the dog, it is much bigger and much more convoluted. In fact it has almost more convolutions than the brain of a human being. Now this is the 'thinking' part of the brain which is supposed to do the reasoning and 'higher intellectual' work. If it is small and undeveloped, then we might suggest that the animal is less intelligent and thinks rather less. This does hold true to a great extent. For example, primitive vertebrates like dog fish have very small cerebral hemispheres; in fact their brain is almost a continuation of the spinal column. Man, who is supposed to be the intellectual giant of the mammals, has a well developed and relatively large cortex. According to this judgement the horse appears to be a great deal more intelligent than the dog, since its cerebral hemispheres are much better developed and the cow more or less equivalent to the horse. But there is a complicating factor here. It is now thought (after much controversy) that the ratio of the brain volume to the body weight is the best measure of intelligence (Jerison 1973). In other words, the bigger the body, the bigger the brain must be just to keep the body running smoothly. To have a surfeit of brain cells to allow the species to spend time being intelligent, thinking and so on, it must have a greater brain size than expected for its body size.

The only problem with this argument is that a tree shrew comes out much brighter than we *Homo sapiens*. But he may be for all we know! Even if this does not always hold sound, nevertheless we would expect a horse to have a bigger brain than us because of its large body. In fact its brain is comparable to ours. The horse does have an extraordinarily well developed cerebral cortex, and we must wonder what goes on there, if the dog (whom we often consider is more intelligent and quicker to learn than the horse) can make do with a very much less developed fore brain.

We shall see that horses are very quick to learn, and retain information as a result often of one trial learning (*Chapter 9*) so we must not underestimate how well they use this fore brain. It may just be also that there are all sorts of other things going on in their heads which we at present do not know or understand. I would suggest therefore that we must be very cautious when dismissing horses as rather stupid animals. Maybe it is we who are stupid in our not being able to understand them. As we shall see (*Chapter 3*), we are very much less proficient at reading their language than they are at ours!

The testing of intelligence is a strange process. Most IQ tests designed for humans simply test the ability to do these tests and that in turn depends on the familiarity of the subject with the tests (you get better at them with practice). When we are trying to design tests to compare the intelligence of different species, this gets very much more difficult because, as we shall see (*Chapter 3*), each species (including humans) has things it can do very well and others it cannot. Each species has its own type of intelligence. How then can one give them all a test that will be equally difficult for all of them? Of course one cannot and so we have to fall back on anecdotal stories, or rather meaningless tests. Katherine Houpt (1979) concluded that horses were really rather stupid because they did not learn and retain a visual discrimination task as well as cattle and were unable to learn not to eat a sweet feed that made them feel ill. It may equally be reasoned that they may not have felt like doing the discrimination test, or that they found it more important to attend to other things in the environment. Or perhaps they could not taste a difference in the sweet feed laced with a sickening substance.

For all these reasons I would suggest that a judgement of the relative intelligence of different species is rather meaningless. On the whole each person will maintain that the species they like best is the 'most intelligent' and they will nearly always mention that their horse is 'very intelligent' implying that everyone else's is not! Let us just assume that horses are very intelligent *at being horses*, and we must try and find out what that means.

3   Horse Language

In this chapter we will examine how horses communicate and also *why* they communicate the way they do and what the meanings of the messages transferred are. In the first place, to communicate there must be:

1. A communicator producing the signal.
2. The means of producing the signal. There must be something to make noises *with* if auditory communication is required; or movements and postures must be possible if there is to be visual communication. If smells are the order of the day, then some method of producing these smells must be there, and so on.
3. A reason for producing the signal. The ultimate reason for interchange, biologists believe, is to benefit the communicator's survival and the chances that he leaves offspring. In the short term however, this is not always easy to see. If we believe that being social benefits the individual horse, then communication that will enhance social living by cementing bonds between individuals, must help with survival. Sometimes it may benefit the individual to be aggressive towards others of the same sex in order to have the chance of leaving more offspring (for example, aggression between stallions); or to be aggressive to other animals (mothers to others, thereby ensuring infant survival).
4. A signal produced, for example, sound, sight, smell, touch, taste, and perhaps extra sensory perception.
5. A receiver of the message, who must have the ability to 'receive the message'! In other words the receiver must have the appropriate receptors to be able to receive it and also the appropriate computer (the brain) to be able to analyse it. We

have examined this to some extent in the last chapter where we have outlined the limits of the various receptors of the horse, as far as we know them today.

6. A 'meaning' for the message, as a result of the analysis by the brain.

It is no good one horse making elaborate visual signals to another horse that is blind, for example, or making noises beyond the other animal's hearing. It is sometimes an advantage to the individual not to respond immediately to a signal – for example, deaf people who do not admit everything they hear.

What is a signal? This is often very difficult to decide in animal communication. One can argue that everything one animal does is potentially of communicative value to other animals. For example, walking over to a particularly good piece of grass and munching it quickly and with 'relish' can convey to a watching horse that there is a nice piece of grass there, but the behaviour was not performed *in order* to have sent a message, nevertheless it has done.

To make it simpler we should try and restrict communication to behaviour that is primarily intended for communication, not for other reasons (such as eating in the above example). In mammals, including man, it is not so easy to tell which actions are performed primarily for communication and which ones for other reasons. If we can isolate the signal produced, then we are in a better position to argue that the behaviour is of obvious communicative value. However this depends on having very obvious signals, such as the flattening back of the ears in horses about to bite. Such behaviour has often been called 'a display'. But very few horse signals are obvious 'displays' so, in order not to miss anything, we must consider practically anything the horse does as having some signal value to others.

How can we decide when a behaviour has transferred a signal? This can be done by measuring the response of another horse to the suspected signal. The type of response will tell us what the meaning of the signal was, or at least help us understand it. But if there is no response at all, does this mean that there has been no message transferred? No, not necessarily so, for, like us, the horse may have received the message but shows no sign.

Alternatively there may be no consistent response, for example slight withdrawal of the ears of the communicator may cause one recipient to withdraw, another to turn around and another to do nothing. By analysing the situation we have some clues as to the meaning of the message. Where the recipient moves away it may mean 'I am slightly bored with your presence, and I might just bite you if you come any nearer' and, if the receiver turns around, 'I think there is something interesting behind me which I am attending to', but the ear position is identical.

We have the added disadvantage here when studying horses that they are really much better than we are at picking up slight muscular changes which may convey messages. Thus we are only recording what we see, but a horse may be seeing much more.

I hope it will be understood that there is much more to communication than meets the eye. It is complicated, but fascinating too. I have been concerned with communication in many mammalian species for some time now and in this chapter will try to illustrate some of the things we now know and the many we do not; and also convey some of the fascination of trying to understand the way horses communicate.

The question that one is always asked is 'Do horses have a language?' This is at present a very controversial issue. A linguist called Hockett (1958) in trying to define language, came up with seven different criteria that had to be fulfilled. These are rather complicated, and this is not the place to discuss them. Fouts and Mellgren (1976), who work with language learning chimps who have learnt American Sign Language (A M S L A N), now believe that several of their chimps can fulfil all Hockett's seven criteria. Thus, chimps at least must be considered to use language. The reason why so many scientists and others find this argument extremely important is that gradually as the uniqueness of man has become undermined by scientific discoveries, one of the few ways in which *Homo sapiens* can (according to some), be separated from the rest of the animal kingdom is because he has a language, whereas no other species does, although they may communicate. If, however, we find that chimps *can* fulfil all the necessary criteria of a language, then perhaps we are not so different from animals after all! (*Chapter 11*).

So what about horses, *do* they have a language? We have begun research to see if they do have a language on the basis of Hockett's seven criteria, by recording the interaction between individuals that we could see or hear. This work has not yet been fully analysed but from the preliminary analysis it appears that at least four of these criteria are fulfilled. This is a complicated subject and for the moment we will leave it there. Reference is given to the relevant scientific papers in the bibliography for those who would like to follow it further.

To me it matters very little whether or not one calls horse communication language or not, the interesting thing is that it is so complex and so highly effective. How nice it would be (and how many of our problems with our horses we could solve), if only we could understand it and even perhaps one day speak it properly and fluently – rather than depending on horses learning our language which is what is done to a large extent today.

We will now examine how horses produce signals, what these signals are and whether we can explain the meaning of the messages by studying the situations in which they occur and the responses they induce. We will consider each type of communication separately.

Communication by smells

Communication by smell (*Chapter 2*) is, as far as we know, a lot more important in horses than it is in man. We as a species are in a difficult position to understand and record this, because our sense of smell is relatively poor for a mammal.

Smell messages, or 'pheromones' as they are called, are produced by skin glands. These are groups of specialised cells that have developed from an out-pushing of the hair follicles; they secrete special substances. They are either distributed over the surface of the skin, or collected together to form identifiable glands. Perhaps one of the easiest of these to spot is the pre-orbital glands (in front of the eye) of many deer and antelope, which often enlarge and have a sticky yellow secretion oozing from them, particularly during the breeding season. Horses have none of these obvious glands that we know of. However, to date, there has been no really thorough study of the skin of horses.

Such collections of secreting cells are not the only producers of pheromones. Scent producing cells, for example, sweat glands or sebaceous glands can be scattered over the body. The sebaceous glands secrete oil for conserving warmth, skin and coat health and are responsible for the 'gloss' on the horse's coat. These secretions may also double as a pheromone. This can be the case for any substances produced by the animal in its normal day-to-day life, as well as at special times. For example, urine and faeces are rich sources of pheromones and convey many messages to other horses, as does the smell of breath, sweat, even burps and so on. At this stage of our knowledge it would be safer to suggest that *any* smell produced by a horse is potentially of communicative value to another.

There are two ways in which pheromones are identified. Firstly, by scanning movements involving head turning; nostril movements (which test the air for possible messages, much like scanning movements of the eyes), or in the horse, ears. The second way involves following gradients of smell, such as following trails. This is perhaps the most studied form of olfactory communication, research into which began in detail with the study of social ants who follow trails. We have some anecdotal evidence to suggest that horses can follow trails. For example, if you separate your horse from his stable companion in the country and leave him on a loose rein, he may well drop his head and follow his companion's trail. We know very little about this in horses, but it may be important for locating the social group and used in 'homing' (finding home) in horses, although they may not be as good at it as are dogs.

An intriguing question here is how do animals who follow trails know in *which direction* to follow the trail? In the case of a very recently laid trail it is probable that they follow the strength of the gradient, but more usually they use orientation to a wind and therefore to the direction of the trail like some fish do to a current in the water.

How do we recognise when a pheromone has been picked up by a horse? There are two divisions here too:

1. A direct reaction to a specific pheromone. The stallion's response to the smell of the oestral (a mare in season or on heat) mare's vulva is one of these. In this case it is not often

clear if this involves the recognition of the oestral female herself, or is a fixed response to the pheromone, irrespective of the female (the latter does not even involve recognition of a female). This has been tested in rams and bulls and stallions by smearing oestral females' urine, containing the sex pheromone, onto castrated males, or non-oestral females. The male then mounts them and attempts copulation although previously he showed no interest (Hafez and Wierkowski 1961). Trained stallions will mount a not in oestrus mare or even a cow (Schaefer 1962). This is one reason why the collection of semen for artificial insemination (AI) is so easy in these domestic hoofed mammals, the male can be so easily taught to mount a model baited with oestral hormones.

2. The transfer of information which may not be acted on in an immediate way. This involves identification of one animal by another, either as a particular sex, age class, or as a particular individual, or all three. This is the aspect of olfactory communication which is perhaps most interesting and most widely used in horses. It is here that we must consider every smell that the animal produces as having some message that can be picked up by another animal and convey all sorts of information.

Early experience and learning of the odours and their meaning during development is important for the correct recognition and reaction to odours. It effects things like the recognition and relationship with the mother; also the selection of mates in many species and undoubtedly in horses too.

Scents can be deposited in a special place, such as stallions urinating where others have urinated or making faeces piles (stallions make droppings in one place normally and these piles of faeces receive much smelling attention from the same stallion, mares and young stock). This can be called scent 'marking', it is a similar marking to dogs urinating on lamp posts. In some species such marking is used to define a 'territory' or defended area. In horses, which on the whole are not territorial, it tends rather to leave a message of 'I have been here and will be back.' Stallions also urinate over the urine or faeces of mares of their own group and occasionally other mares too. The resulting message to another horse is 'This is a particular non-oestral mare and stallion X is with her.' Scents can also be deposited on particular parts of the body. Horses do not have elaborate ways of doing this unlike, for example, the ring tailed lemur who urinates on its hands and then rubs its large strippy tail through its hands. Thereafter it walks around with its tail in the air dispensing the 'cologne'. However, horses do deposit smells over their body by, for example, rolling. In free group living horses, 80 per cent of the rolling will be where another horse has rolled before. This is why rolling rings (provided for horses to roll in after exercise) work so well. Horses choose carefully where to roll by smelling first and thus rolling where others have rolled. The reason for this is presumably to cover the body in the 'group' smell, although there may also be some more subtle messages.

In some species it has also been demonstrated that scent marking is related to the position in the 'dominance hierarchy'. Dominant animals scent mark more often and thus have larger scent glands and produce more pheromones. As we shall see (*Chapter* 6), this rather simple idea of a 'dominance hierarchy' can be a misleading way of describing the social organisation of groups of horses. However, certainly stallions with mares and particularly during the breeding season, do 'mark' more than castrates or young stallions. In fact, in normal stallions kept with other horses, this marking after a period of absence will take precedence over greeting the other horses. Thus the horse as soon as he is released will walk around sniffing the ground and urinating wherever one of the others have urinated. The horse may in this way urinate 5 to 8 times within a 5 minute period, each time producing no more than a mug full of urine and after this is completed he will then rush up to the others and greet them with mutual smelling, squealing, front leg lifting, sometimes licking and nuzzling other parts of the body, or leaping and kicking, the latter as a display usually into the air.

Let us now look at the ways in which pheromones are used in horses and the messages so transferred.

GROUP RECOGNITION

A smell or pheromone can be distributed to all members, by, for example, eating the same types of food which will tend to produce the same types of smells on the breath and in the urine and faeces, but also by mutual rubbing and grooming and rolling in the same place. Common lying sites will also help to produce a group odour. The group odour may be particularly important in horses who have very strong and long lasting social groupings, both mares and stallions not easily accepting strangers into the group.

RECOGNITION OF THE HOME AREA

This is in part the result of learning the scents of the things around in the home areas and those produced by others around too. It does not matter if it is the smell of car exhausts or of, say, tamarisk; if it is associated with the home area it will be followed from a distance. This gives rise to the possible recognition of a 'foot print substance' which does not allow recognition of the individual when being trailed, but recognition of the animals as members of the same group. Using paths and coming across scent marked areas such as defaecation sites also helps with this group recognition.

PHEROMONES TO AGGREGATE HORSES

There are some pheromones which help to bring animals together. The most well known of these pheromones are those that lead ants to sources of food. It is not known if there are similar pheromones in mammals and indeed since horses' food, for example, grass, is readily available and usually well dispersed, this is unlikely to be important. On the other hand pheromones to bring animals together when alarmed (sweat may be important here) or to bring mother to young may be important in horses. Since horses are such good visual communicators it is unlikely that separate specific pheromones for this exist. However, sexual pheromones and pheromones produced by mother and young are important for aggregating animals and we discuss them in this chapter.

Aggregation when alarmed is also helped by group pheromones.

The colonisation of new habitats in feral or wild horses often brings many groups together, particularly where there is food available. This is true too of zebras. A good example being the enormous herds of zebra (thousands of individuals which are collections of family groups) on the Serengeti plains in Tanzania at certain times of the year. This may in part be the result of odours produced which cause others to assemble.

PHEROMONES TO DISPERSE HORSES

By dispersing horses, pheromones can help to maintain the optimum individual spacing.

The most obvious dispersal mechanism by pheromones are those marking home areas. Strange horses coming into the area are warned by the pheromones from urine, faeces, rolling sites and so on of the presence of others. Although wild and feral horses live in home areas, these are usually large and not all defended. However, the horses who inhabit the densely populated Sable Island off the coast of America do defend their home area against others and do appear to adopt a territorial type of strategy and here the scent marking becomes even more obvious (Rubenstein 1981). Domestic horses confined into paddocks tend also to become more possessive of area, less tolerant of strangers and scent mark very frequently. In any case the deposition of smells in droppings, in urine and by rubbing on posts does inform others about the dispersion of conspecifics (members of the same species). The importance of rubbing posts or even places that have often been touched must not be underestimated. Notice how often a horse will smell the top of a gate on a bridle-path, or any object that is likely to have been frequently touched or rubbed by horses, familiar or strange.

Some mice show *anti-aggregation* behaviour to pheromones. For example, when alarmed, sight of another mouse urinating, sight and smell of blood causes fleeing. There are many old wives' tales concerning how horses hate the smell of blood. I do not know if this is more so than for other species, but either way blood is a potential carrier of olfactory messages, and may well cause dispersion.

PHEROMONES TO REDUCE POPULATION GROWTH

Mice also produce pheromones which prevent or *reduce mating* and live births when population densities rise too high. Such a mechanism will take many years to unravel if it exists in the horse.

Female guinea pigs, when unreceptive to the male, spray him with urine which stops his pursuit. Mares who are not in oestrus but pestered by the stallion will urinate frequently, accompanied often by attacking the stallion, and this does appear to reduce his pointless pursuit. However, oestral mares will urinate more often too, to encourage his pursuit!

PHEROMONES AND AGGRESSION

In some species, lemurs for example, pheromones are released as an aggressive act so that two fighting individuals have 'stink' fights. It has also been suggested that territorial marking is performed as an aggressive act to intimidate the intruder. Stallions urinating after smelling faeces (which occurs during male skirmishes) might be considered in this category too. In general, however, horses do not appear to have specific aggressive pheromones, but rather their smell messages are geared to help recognising individuals, or members of specific groups, sex or age classes. The prolonged strong bonds between individuals that are characteristic of horse societies necessitate such individual recognition.

PHEROMONES AND SEX

Smell messages for sex are universally recognised as important, particularly in horses. More than half the literature on pheromones is concerned with sexual pheromones! Their function appears to be to synchronise behaviour so that successful mating can take place and in this way they often act as aphrodisiacs. We will consider the male and female separately to trace out the importance of pheromones in sexual behaviour.

The pituitary gland (*Figure 2.12*) plays a leading role in the organisation of sexual behaviour in both males and females. Sensory messages (smell ones and others) are fed into the pituitary after being analysed and organised by other parts of the brain. The pituitary then sends hormones off to stimulate the sex organs, these in turn cause a feedback to the controlling pituitary.

When the female is in season or on heat, pheromones are secreted in the urine which attract the stallion; these are often so strong that we can easily detect them too. Females often however begin to behave sexually before they are in heat by showing an interest in a stallion, seeking him out and staying near him. Perhaps this represents a heightened sensitivity to his smell at this time, we do not know. Once in oestrus courting (*Chapter 5*) will begin, and this involves a detailed and protracted series of events. Here smell signals are clearly important for both individuals. Both mare and stallion spend time smelling and touching each other all over, as well as sniffing urine and faeces.

Courtship of the mare enhances her excitement and stimulates secretions from the vagina which not only carries pheromones, indicating to the stallion her readiness to stand for mounting, but also speeds the transport of the sperm to the uterus.

In-hand breeding does not allow normal courtships and build-up of excitement of the mare and thus she often has to be hobbled and restrained in several ways.

Lack of courtship may affect the stallion's libido. This may well be one of the prime reasons for the very low conception rates in in-hand breeding studs (Rossdale 1968), very much lower than that which wild populations of other mammals can normally tolerate and still remain extant; even though wild populations (at least of horses), often have a lower nutritional level.

STALLION SEXUAL BEHAVIOUR

Stallions normally keep a check on the reproductive status of mares by smelling their vulva and urine and this is often accompanied by flehmen (*Figure 3.1*). In this way the stallion is able to receive pheromonal messages of oestrus and perhaps of approaching oestrus in the mare's urine. This excites the stallion who approaches and engages in much licking and tactile stimulation of the mare. Presumably the close presence, sweat and pheromones and the erect penis of the stallion all stimulate the mare and the courtship continues until with the aid of the vaginal pheromone, the stallion is permitted and excited enough to mount and copulate.

Contact between the two is retained after copulation and the

Figure 3.1
A gelding 'flehmen', or lip curl, after smelling garlic – not urine

whole performance will begin again after an interval of a few minutes or hours. The original stimulus that activates the stallion again may be the sudden sight of the female, or her smell which he catches on the wind. It is a curious thing to watch; first both of them peacefully grazing, possibly at a distance of 46 m or so, suddenly the stallion will lift his head, whinny, and rush towards the mare to begin the courtship again, as if he had suddenly been reminded of her by something.

It is possible that saliva may also contain pheromones that are important in courtship. The mare and stallion will smell and touch noses and then the stallion will lick and nuzzle the mare. Pig saliva has a pheromone which has been isolated and identified and can now be bought in aerosol cans. A squirt of this around the sow in oestrus is enough to make her take up the copulatory posture. In horses a pheromone is not the only stimulus. It requires the presence of the mare or stallion, involving a whole range of stimuli which gives rise to the various responses. In much the same way as is found in human sex, Wierkowski (1959) showed that visual stimuli seemed rather more important in horse sexuality than odours.

FLEHMEN

The peculiar action of flehmen is well known in horses where it is particularly well developed. I became interested in it some years ago and conducted a series of experiments to see what particular substances initiated this response. It is widely believed that it is only males who perform this action and that it is particularly related to sex and finding oestral females. We found (*Figure 3.2*)

	Stallions	Geldings	Mares	Total	Percentage
Taste	43	52	72	167	63·4%
Smell	38	37	21	96	36·6%
Total	81	89	93	263	
Number of horses	10	18	15	43	
Average/ horse	8·1	4·9	6·2	6·11	
Percentage of total response	42·1%	25·6%	32·2%		

Figure 3.2
The number of flehmen responses to different substances given by different sexes. Substances tested for (1) taste and (2) smell responses were:

Oestral mares urine   Garlic in solution
Geldings urine   Ammonia
Stallions urine   Vinegar
Salt solution   Alcohol
Sugar solution   Distilled water
Lemon juice

The test was repeated with 2 hour intervals on each horse. Total numbers of tests: 1,092.
Mares did not flehmen to lemon, vinegar or water. Response was given to all other substances for both sexes

that flehmen was not confined to stallions or to one substance; strong and unfamiliar smells and tastes also caused mares, geldings and stallions to flehmen, although stallions did it the most.

Stallions show more flehmen to mares' urine (as might be expected) – but mares show more flehmen to stallions' urine – indicating mutual interest.

It is interesting to see the range of substances which caused the response – even to distilled water on occasions with mares! The *taste* of the substance was more likely to cause flehmen than just the smell in both mares and stallions.

PARENTAL RECOGNITION

Another area where recognition is important and to some extent pheromonal, is mutual recognition of the mare and foal. Early recognition of the foal may well be based on the foal smelling of the mare since it has just passed out through her vagina. Initially the smells are strong around new born animals, associated with colostrum, milk and the faeces. Even for humans the smell of new born babies is unmistakable. We can also identify the smell of new born calves or foals.

Gradually the foal develops its own individual smell, while still retaining that which identifies it with its age class. It is unlikely that a stallion recognises his foal by its smell – but as soon as it has obtained the group smell it is definitely recognised as a group member by the stallion.

Communication by smell is considered the most primitive method of communication but that is not to say that in the higher mammals it does not become particularly sophisticated.

The advantages of bringing into service as communicative organs glands in the skin, already being used for other purposes, is clear, but to date we have very little understanding of the detailed workings of the pheromonal system in horses, like most other species. The possible exception is the mouse which has been found to have eleven different pheromones which are capable of many messages. It is possible that we may yet find similar complexity of pheromonal 'language' in horses (and ourselves!) as research progresses. We have seen however just how important pheromones and chemical communication is in horses, but at present the evidence for much of this is still anecdotal.

Taste Communication

Taste and smell are very closely connected. Horses of course use taste to discriminate between good and bad things to eat, but do not seem to do as well as cattle in 'taste aversion' tests. They are nevertheless very fussy feeders, and we see this is with good reason (*Chapter 6*).

As far as we know taste is used in communication when two animals groom (*Figure 3.3*) and lick each other. It is also probably important in courtship when both mare and stallion will lick and chew each other. It may help the mother recognise her foal

Figure 3.3
Two colts grooming each other. Touching and tasting while grooming is an important way of cementing bonds between individuals

Figure 3.4
A colt rushes back from galloping around with his peers to rub himself around his mother. Touch is important here too

immediately after birth which is the only time when she gives it a thorough lick all over. In other words it seems as if taste is used in the recognition of *individual* animals.

Taste is also involved when smelling different substances and then touching and sometimes licking them; for example, when a horse smells another's faeces or even takes some urine into its mouth.

How important taste is, independent of smell, we do not yet know.

Touch Communication

Communication between individuals by touch is important to horses, again at specific times such as during courtship when it plays a very important part in exciting both mare and stallion to the necessary point for successful mating. It is also important in the relationship between mother and foal, frequently one will see a foal approach mother and just lightly touch her (*Figure 3.4*) often with his nose or whiskers before again moving off. The foal may also walk in front of her, rubbing himself lightly against her body or lick her. This serves to stop her walking off or lying down so that the foal can suckle and appears also to reassure him.

This ritual is often performed, when mother and foal have been separated, as a preliminary reintroduction to each other before the foal starts suckling.

Some species, for example, pigs and dogs and particularly some humans (although less in the Anglo-Saxon culture) are called 'contact species', which means that they spend much time actually in contact with other members of their group, touching them and cuddling together. Horses, however, are not contact species but just because they do not spend much time touching each other, the importance of touch in the development of relationships between individuals should not be underestimated.

In experiments I conducted, we measured the amount of time that mares and foals touched each other and compared this to cows and calves of a similar age. We found that cows and calves touched each other for 3 per cent of the time they were observed, whereas horses for only 1 per cent, even though foals suckled more frequently than calves.

In stabled animals then, if we want well adapted, relaxed horses they must be able to touch each other. It is quite easy to design housing where this can be done.

Touch is of course used to a great extent in inter-specific communication between people and horses. People introduce themselves to horses by touching them and stroking them, although as Barbara Woodhouse argues (and I think she is right), the best way of introducing yourself to a horse is in the same way as a horse would to another, blow up their noses and then begin to stroke them and pat them.

Many people spend a great deal of time grooming horses. In many cases this is not necessary for the horse's health, the main effect of this grooming is that it gives the animal and the person time together to develop a relationship. Whether it is important to always have the horse clean is arguable, but it is important that they have time being handled and an opportunity to develop relationships with people – what better time to do this than during grooming? (The only problem is that not always is the groom the rider!)

The most important use of touch for communication between horse and person is during riding. The sensitivity of the horse to touch can be appreciated when riding a trained dressage or reining horse where not only very slight leg or hand pressures will result in many different responses, but incredibly small weight changes. These horses have been taught to respond to these messages. Although horses differ individually in their ability to learn this, some can become extraordinarily good at it, which shows what the horse is capable of.

An understanding of this sensitivity can lead to better relationships between horse and handler or rider.

Auditory Communication

NON-VOCAL SIGNALS

There are many auditory signals that horses can make. They can make them mechanically, by banging their box with their front leg for example, or by kicking the box with their hind leg. They can also make noises with buckets, with straw and noises while eating, sneezing and snorting. The latter two are made with the respiratory tract, but not vocally since they are not produced by the 'larynx' or voice box.

Although such noises may be produced initially for reasons quite unrelated to communication, for example, in the case of sneezing as a result of an irritation in the nose, or an unpleasant smell, nevertheless they may become of importance for communication thereafter. A few examples follow:

Sneezing Sneezing is the noise made when a horse blows through his nose to clear it of irritants, such as a piece of hay or straw, or strong and unpleasant smells. Presumably it communicates to another horse, firstly, that there is a horse there, and secondly that that horse is moving around eating and so on, rather than dozing or sleeping.

I have noticed that my own horses tend to sneeze in batches. One animal sneezing will start another off. This occurs not only in the stable but also outdoors, for example, when out on group rides. It often occurs at a change of activity or direction on the ride and usually is started by a lively horse who is wanting to go faster, or shy, or generally lark about. Others may well join in and so it continues. A batch of sneezing of this sort seems to indicate that the horses are not quite as relaxed as they might appear and prepared to make an excuse to start leaping about.

Sneezing may also occur after a gallop or canter. At this time, the respiratory tract may well need clearing, but again it seems to occur rather more frequently than need be to do this.

I have not carefully recorded sneezing in horses and this will need doing before a well founded argument can be formulated that sneezing is used in communication; but there are indications that it may be used to convey the presence of another horse, or to help convey 'mood' from one animal to another (such as in rows of stables where the horses are visually isolated).

Snorting. This is when the horse sees or smells something particularly interesting which may be potentially dangerous. It is a low blow through the nose which apart from attracting other horses to look in that direction, also functions to clear the

Figure 3.5
A high postural tonus demonstrated by a mare in season when, after galloping around, she stops and snorts

respiratory tract ready for action like running fast or smelling more carefully. It is usually associated with excited horses, horses that have been recently released from a stable, or have had a sudden fright. Its message is '. . . be aware, there is something over there that is frightening and interesting; be ready to run.' It is always either accompanied or followed by a high postural tonus (a high head and tail carriage) (*Figure 3.5*) often with an exaggerated and elevated trot. This indicates that the horse is ready for action – to run.

Sighing.   Sighing in horses occurs in more or less the same situations as it does in humans; that is at a change in activity often related to 'boredom'. The horse will often sigh when he is being saddled up and about to be taken out and ridden. I am uncertain if sighing really has the same meaning as in humans, an 'Oh dear, not again what a drag' type of meaning, but it does seem as though it might do! After a period of schooling the horse will often sigh, or when about to be moved off to repeat a movement again. He may also sigh at the *end* of a period of pain or hard work. We need to study it carefully before we really know what it means and what, if any, effect it has on other horses. It certainly has an effect on human beings who tend to interpret it in the same way as they would a sigh from another human being and thus it affects the way they behave to the horse.

Coughing.   Coughing is of course normally related to a respiratory irritation or infection, but there are also horses that cough when, as far as we can tell, there is no irritation or infection at that particular time. It is tempting to consider that some will cough because they have learnt that by coughing they will be returned to the stable, or not have to work too hard. But again we really do not know if this is true.

The above are some examples of non-vocal sounds made which may have communicative importance in the horse. There are many others of course, noises of chewing, walking around in the box, banging things and so on. Some species, particularly those living in semi-bush environments, like pigs and eland (an African antelope), keep in touch with other members of the group by

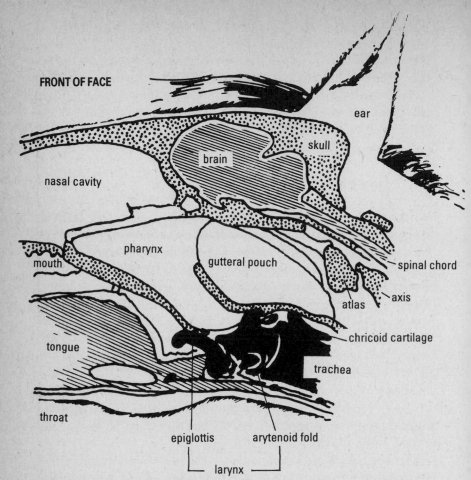

FRONT OF FACE

ear

skull

brain

nasal cavity

pharynx

gutteral pouch

spinal chord

mouth

atlas

axis

chricoid cartilage

tongue

trachea

throat

epiglottis   arytenoid fold

larynx

Figure 3.6
A section through the head of a horse to show the larynx or voice box
and its relationship to the various resonating chambers such as the
pharynx, nasal cavity, mouth and possibly the unique *gutteral pouch*. The
epiglottis controls the air stream by directing it through the mouth, or
through the pharynx and nose if the mouth is shut

making a noise moving around, breaking twigs, crashing and
banging about. Indeed, eland even have knees that click so that
others can hear where they are. Horses, since they evolved in a
more open habitat and are very good at visual communication as
we shall see (*Chapter 4*), are relatively silent in this respect, more

so than cows who one can usually hear on a dark night burping, ruminating and moving around.

However, when horses are kept visually isolated from other horses they do tend to make more noise with whatever they have – straw, food buckets, walls and so on. This may be exaggerated and further developed in order to keep in touch with others, much like the prisoner in a solitary prison cell, knocking on the wall to try and get in touch with a neighbour.

VOCAL SIGNALS

Unlike practically any other signal produced, it is very difficult to see that vocal communication has any other function except for communication. Although horses may prick their ears for other reasons than for communication (that is, to pick up noises better), why should they neigh for any other reason than to transmit a message?

Although Negus (1963) suggests that the larynx or voice box evolved in certain ways depending on the type of life style of the animal and that its prime function initially may have been to allow for such activities as swallowing and breathing simultaneously (rather important in an animal that eats 16 hours a day!). Nevertheless, the evolution of the larynx to the level of sophistication we find in many mammals appears to be directly related to its function for communication.

The larynx works by having a stream of air passing through the vocal membranes which then vibrate making a noise. The amount of air passing through them is of obvious importance in controlling what sound is produced, but perhaps more important are the effects of the various resonating chambers which are the pharynx (the back of the mouth and throat), the mouth and the nasal cavity (*Figure 3.6*). These affect the character or 'timbre' of the sound, as well as how loud it is. If the mouth is open, for example, there is a different sound than if the mouth is closed. A neigh which is given with the mouth open sounds different from a nicker which is given with the mouth closed, and this is not only because the neigh is louder than the nicker, it is also because the mouth is a close ended chamber in the latter and an open ended tube in the former. This means that different overtones are pronounced or suppressed, and this is what gives rise to the 'timbre' of a call. It is possible to make 'sonograms' (sound pictures) of the different calls of the horse and these indicate change. Of course different individuals have different sound pictures too, for example criminals are often identified using voice traces.

The shapes of the various resonating cavities can be altered as a result of the contraction of different muscles and this, together with the movement of the tongue, allows for speech in man. Controlling this is, of course, an intricate network of nerves to and from the brain so that the mouth and tongue can be moved in certain ways; controlling that in turn is the brain and, in man, a particular speech centre situated in the left hemisphere called 'Broca's area'.

Species such as the cat and dog have been studied in some detail to see if they lack the muscles or the nerves serving them, but it seems that this is not the case, yet it is apparently true that chimps at least (who are the most likely to be able to learn to talk in the way we can) are not able to. The Kelloggs (1933) brought up a chimp in their home with a child of their own and spent many hours every day trying to teach it to pronounce words in a similar way to themselves. They succeeded after several years in getting it to pronounce only about two words and those with considerable difficulty. Thus, it is probably correct to say that the *equipment* for human speech is there in many species but that the brain to control the workings of the equipment to produce spoken language is not. This, I hasten to add, does *not* mean that horses do not have a language, it simply means that in theory there seems to be little mechanical reason why they should not produce a type of spoken language that we would recognise and understand, but they do not have a brain equipped to cope with organising and running this type of a system. What happens in the area of the horse's brain that in humans houses the speech centre nobody seems to know.

Wherever someone has written on horses' auditory 'language' they have always described particular calls which have very particular meanings and indeed some people can be quite good at telling what the horse is saying by its call. Some years ago I did a detailed study on the calls of horses and other species, to see if

Situation	Nicker	Neigh	Roar	Squeal	Sneeze-snort	Snort
Confident greeting	+	+	+			
Greeting of equals	+	+	+			
Defensive threat	+	+		+		+
Aggressive threat	+	+		+		
Fear						+
Close contact retaining	+					
Tactile stimulation			+	+	+	
Isolation	+	+	+			
Startle						+
Pain						+
Fear						+
Frustration	+	+	+	+	+	
Anticipation: a) pleasant	+	+	+	+		
Anticipation: b) unpleasant		+		+		+
Disturbance (unidentified)	+	+	+	+	+	+

Figure 3.7
The situations in which the various vocalisations of the horse occur. All the calls occur in a variety of situations

what was believed as the result of anecdotes was or was not true (Kiley 1972). I found in fact all sorts of things which I think are much *more* interesting than the rather boring story of the horse having calls with specific meanings like a very poor, simple form of human language.

I discovered (*Figure 3.7*) that horses used the same call in a whole variety of situations and that it was other cues in the environment that gave the calls a specific meaning as interpreted by human listeners. It also became clear that all the calls were structurally related to one another (*Figure 3.8*). This was clear after the analysis and measurement of 15 different parameters in each of 200 calls.

Not only this, but each individual had an individually recognisable call and that every time a call was given by the same

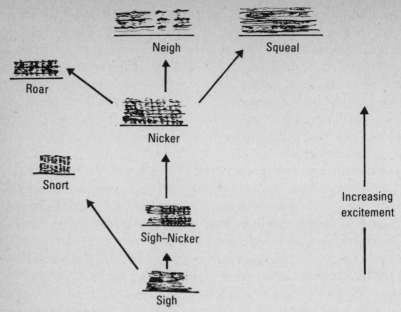

Figure 3.8
The various calls are structurally related. Originally the calls probably arose from something like a sigh or a cough where the air stream was stopped and then released, causing a slight noise. This developed into a noise with a more particular message – the snort, which means 'beware there is something strange around'.

The sigh–nicker is the link between the non-vocal sigh and the vocal nicker. With increasing excitement, whatever the type of situation, the nicker then turns to the neigh, or (less commonly and confined more to sex) the roar or squeal. The calls of the horse are all interrelated. They are *not* like a simple form of human language as they do not normally have a specific meaning

individual it was slightly different from the last one of that type. This may be just intonation of the same message but makes for complication in analysis, and possibly meanings.

What does all this mean? It means that horse calls *are not at all like human language*; there are *not* specific messages attached to specific calls. There are one or two exceptions to this, for example, the roar of a stallion is slightly more common in sexual situations than in other situations. So what do the calls mean?

Well, they act, it appears, to tell the receiver something about the general state of arousal of the horse (his general mood); whether he is excited or sleepy. The specific message related to telling the receiver 'I am feeling sexy' or 'I am feeling lonely' is interpreted by the receiver from other cues in the environment. If you do not believe this and think you can tell what the horse means from individual calls, just try and do this by listening to tape recordings with no visual clues. You will be surprised to find how difficult this is.

Now the interesting question is 'Why have calls in horses *not* developed to the point where specific calls have special messages?' It would seem that this is bound to happen since an animal is likely to give the same (or a similar call) every time it reaches the same level of excitement and that is likely to be in the same situations. Thus, the call would gradually be selected for a specific situation and develop a special message relating to that situation. For example, when the horse is lonely it is excited to a degree and would produce a neigh. This particular neigh, during the course of evolution gradually becomes associated with *that* situation and develops a specific message and structure which means 'I am lonely' and is different from a call produced when the horse is, for example, feeling sexy. This appears to be the way human language has arisen, so why not in the horse, or other mammals for that matter?

The answer to this question is still obscure, but it may be, in some strange way, that in the horse the development of specific calls for specific situations might be more limiting in terms of how much information can be put across – so do not think that horse communication is just a poor imitation of human communication, it appears to be a whole different ball game. Inevitably, since a horse is not a slightly stupid person (or for that matter a person a slightly stupid horse!), we both have our important differences in what we are good and bad at – and different ways of doing things. One of these is communicating.

4 Visual Communication

The story of Clever Hans is quite well known but bears repeating in the context of a chapter on visual communication.

Clever Hans was a horse who was able to count, to do simple arithmetical exercises and was apparently a genius as horses go. During the nineteenth century he was brought before a group of academicians at The Hague in Holland who found that there was no 'trick' in the sense that the horse could solve a simple mathematical problem even when his trainer was not present. Clever Hans tapped out the answer with a front leg. However, when the audience was hidden from the horse by a screen, he was no longer able to do this. What he was doing was responding to subliminal cues (very slight muscular tension changes) that the audience showed when he had reached the correct number; they would slightly relax or tense up. The horse had learnt to do this himself, he had not been taught as his trainer did not even understand how he was doing it. In addition, the slight muscular cues are so slight that other humans (who as a species are not good at this type of visual communication could not sense them.) Recently the 'Clever Hans effect' has come into the limelight again as some researchers believe that talking chimps are responding to subliminal cues.

The point of this story is that it illustrates how good the horse is at picking up visual clues. This indicates that the horse has probably an elaborate and intricate visual communication system; probably much more sophisticated than our own. Human beings have specialised in verbal communication leaving other methods less well developed and less sophisticated.

How then does the horse communicate using vision? Many of the obvious visual signals are very well known, such as when a horse flattens his ears and extends his head forwards (often with the nose wrinkled) he is likely to bite you. Some are less well known and I believe there are many we have not yet recorded. The interest in studying visual communication in horses is in trying to understand not only what the messages are and how they are sent to another horse, but also how they originated and evolved to have the meanings they apparently have. For example, why does the horse normally put his ears back when he is going to bite, why does he not put them forward? I will answer some of these questions, but more detailed information can be found in relevant scientific papers listed in the bibliography.

Posture and postural forms

We will begin by considering posture and postural changes in the horse. Because horses are sophisticated visual communicators, they have developed postural responses to a greater degree than many other hoofed mammals, for example cattle. Thus they have exaggerated high postures where the head and tail are raised and even the gait can become higher with a longer phase of suspension. In some cases we have selectively bred for horses which will readily show this high postural tonus, the Arab and the Tennessee Walking Horse are examples. However given the right situation, any horse will strut around with a high postural tonus.

At the other end of the scale, the horse can have a lower postural tonus where the head and tail droop and in between there are all degrees of raising and lowering. Interestingly the head and tail *usually* go up or down together. There are one or two exceptions; for example, when defaecating the tail may be up and the head down.

When then does the horse have a high and when a low postural tonus, and why? The postural tonus of the horse is not necessarily associated with a particular situation, but rather with a general level of excitement, thus the more excited he becomes, whether it is a sexual, aggressive, or a fearful type of situation, the higher the postural tonus will become. The postural tonus also varies as the horse increases his pace from a walk to a trot and canter. At the gallop, however, streamlining is important so the head and

A   B   C

PACES + NON-SOCIAL
■ sick; pain; tired
■ stand, sleep
orientate
walk
urinate
approach/avoidance
frustration

trot
tactile stimulation
gallop
canter
investigate
non-social play/leap etc.

Figure 4.1
The postural changes of the horse and the situations that give rise to
them. (*Left*) the different paces and non–social situations; (*right*) the
social situations. The black line refers to the types of postures (*above*)
illustrated that occur in that situation.

Postures vary from the squatting of the yearling who is being smelt
by a stallion, A, to the very exaggerated tonus on the right of the excited
stallion F. We can see that the walk, for example, can be performed with
different relatively low postures C or D. Such postures are also assumed
in defensive threat

D   E   F

SOCIAL

fear/submissive

defensive threat

touch

greeting

aggressive approach

sexual approach ♂ + ♀

courtship ♂ + ♀

isolation

oestrus

threaten

fight

social play

tail lower and the body flattens out. Similarly, a lowered postural tonus is associated with sleep, ill-health and sometimes with extreme fear, which in many species leads to behaviour very like sleep, immobility and postural collapse (*Figure 4.1*).

Why should this be the case? As things become of interest around the horse, it becomes alert and in particular ready for movement. The horse is a movement specialist – his defence, and solution, to many problems is to run. Preparing for movement involves contraction of all the muscles lifting the body off the ground. These are known as 'anti-gravity' muscles and enable the horse to leap forward at the slightest sign. The contraction of these muscles results, too, in a high postural tonus shown by the high head and tail carriage at this time.

The message transferred to other horses on seeing a horse with a high postural tonus is 'Hello, there is something interesting about, he is alert and has a high head and tail!' The receiver of the message will then become more alert and look around for the source of interest. Or the message may be 'All is sleepy and relaxed hereabouts', to a lowered postural tonus. Thus, again, the messages transferred are of a general meaning, rather than specific to a situation. There may be other cues in the environment, such as sexual pheromones which say 'This is an exciting, sexy situation', translating the specific message.

The sign of a good stable and good horsemanship surely is to see the horses relaxed and quiet but not too tired to move, too ill or too frightened.

Apart from postural tonus, another sign of excitement and tension can be in facial expression, particularly the position of the mouth and nose. There are ten sets of muscles (*Figure 4.2*) which serve to move the nose, lips and mouth. As a result, this part of the face is capable of many expressions (*Figures 4.3, 4.4, 4.5, and 4.6*), although we may find them difficult to follow. One fairly obvious expression is the tight lipped position with tight mouth (particularly in young horses). The distinctive character here is the protruding top lip. This occurs usually in association with a high postural tonus and eyes that are wide open and moving. Because of this the eye may show the whites. It occurs when the horse is tense.

Other important responses which give rise to 'displays' (activi-

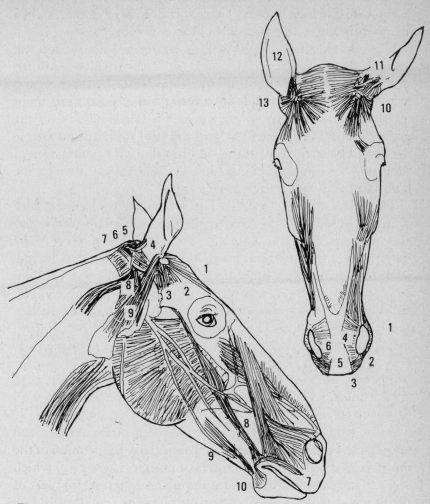

Figure 4.2
The muscles that move the ears and the nostrils. There are thirteen pairs
for each ear; and ten pairs that move the nostrils, lips and mouth. The
numbers indicate the enormous possibilities for facial expression in the
horse

Figure 4.3
Changes in the expression of the eyes, nose, mouth and chin of an Anglo-Arab mare. (*Left-hand page*) A, relaxed, drowsy. Note the half closed eye, relaxed nostril chin and mouth. B, slight interest in something around is shown by her slightly widened eye. C, this is followed by a slight tightening of the chin and, if the stimulus proves of further interest, to D, contraction of the muscles around the nostrils and front of the nose. (*Right-hand page*) E, with a further interest in the stimulus (whatever it is) the head is turned in its direction; the eyes remain wide, the ears are pricked and the chin and mouth tightened. F, the nostrils open slightly and the front of the nose, the upper lip is tightly contracted. G, finally the head is raised further, the eyes opened even wider, the nostrils flared and the upper lip gives an impression of being prehensile, it is so contracted

Figure 4.4
Lip-licking before being fed. A, relaxed mouth and nose accompanied by salivation. The slightly closed eye almost suggests the anticipation of delicious dinners! B, Notice the loose lower lip, relaxed nostrils but slightly contracted top lip

Figure 4.5
Sneezing, showing the extent of the sideways movement of the nose

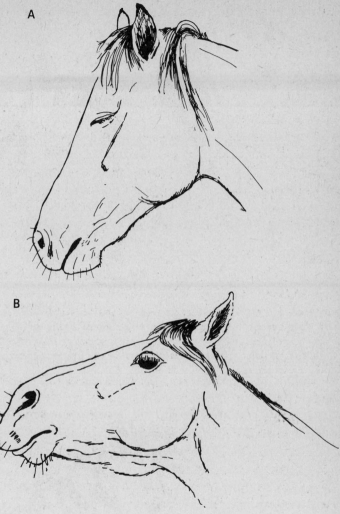

Figure 4.6
A horse is given a taste of something unusual and possibly interesting.
The mouth and chin are contracted as the horse savours the flavour, A,
and then, B, the head is raised slightly with the top lip contracted,
preliminary to flehmen

ties performed particularly for communication) are orientation, irritation and protection.

Orientation

Here, the horse (or any other species) brings its sense organs to bear on a stimulus that is interesting and needs further investigation; since most of the horse's sense organs are situated in the head, it is the head which is rotated in the appropriate direction, the eyes then focussing on the object. Because of the position of the eyes at the side of the head and also because they are all brown and black the horse's eye movements are difficult for humans to follow. It is difficult to see where a horse is actually looking other than when he shows the whites of his eyes. We do not know if a horse can see where another horse is looking and obtain information from this, but it is probable.

After the head and eye movements the horse's ears will orientate on the object, being pricked forward. In horses, the ears are positioned at the top of the head and the absence of horns makes them particularly conspicuous. As a result they are used to a great extent for transferring messages, particularly those regarding where the attention of the animals lies, but also for other messages. Unlike the eye movements, the horse's ear movements are easy for humans to follow. By watching a horse's ears one can learn a great deal about how the horse is feeling and where his attention is directed. If the stimulus is not sufficiently interesting for the horse to turn his head (*Figure 4.7*) then the ears may simply be directed towards it; for example to the rear when attending to the rider, or to something coming up behind (*Figure 4.8*). In aware and healthy horses the ears move much and they act as a scanner of the environment for interesting, potentially nice or nasty things. There are thirteen sets of muscles which move them so they are capable of very accurate independent movement.

The most interesting ear position in horses is the pronounced flattening which is an exaggerated 'ritualised' posture performed particularly for communication. This however owes its origin to protection, not orientation.

By turning his head, the horse's nose and mouth are brought

Figure 4.7

Ear pricking. The pure bred Arab mare, A, has pricked ears and flared nostrils. The stallion, B, has relaxed and slightly pricked ears, but note the mare behind him is not so relaxed as is indicated by her ears and expanded nostrils. Her ears are rotated backwards so that she can pick up any cues from her rider, and anything behind her. Her mouth and nostrils are also tense. The stallion, C, relaxes but his right ear indicates that he is keeping tabs on the people fussing around him on the right, while his left ear is rotated back to keep in touch with the person who is throwing a blanket over him. This shows *unilateral ear movement* closer to the interesting object and the nose may be advanced to smell it (*Figure 4.9*). This results in an extended position of the head which conveys to others that there is an interesting smell at that point. Sometimes the object will actually be licked and again such a movement will have communicative significance.

In many species these 'head extended' postures have become associated with a conflict between approaching (because there is something interesting) and running away (because it is frightening) and are used to convey such a message to others – that the animal is not confident. In this way such postures have become associated with submissive animals.

Figure 4.8
An Irish cob standing, A, relaxed with both ears slightly rotated backwards. Note the *ear withdrawal*. He hears something frightening behind and, B, withdraws his tail as a protective response and rotates both ears slightly more to the rear

Figure 4.9
Here we see the prehensile upper lip as a mare, A, reaches for some food. Her nostrils are contracted longitudinally so as to lengthen the upper lip and her chin is contracted with the effort. An equivalent attitude to pursing the lips in humans. The same expression, B, from the front

Irritation

Many displays (movements performed particularly for communication) have their origins in movements performed in order to remove some irritation from the body surface. Preening movements of birds in courtship are one of these, as are many scratching activities. The reasons why such movements become 'displays' are slightly complicated but relate to the animal being motivated to perform two conflicting things, such as approaching a female to breed, but at the same time not daring to because of the possibility of being attacked. At such times it is thought that a third activity, which is not normally a very important one, such as scratching or preening, takes place instead. Thus a courting male Mallard duck will stop to preen its feathers right in the middle of courtship.

Because such activities tend to occur at similar times, for example, in courtship, then over the millions of generations they have become incorporated into the courtship itself and have a particular communicative significance. Such activities are called 'displacement activities' because they are apparently 'displaced' or appear irrelevant at that time and place. Activities to remove irritations from the body surface, such as head shaking and tossing and tail wagging, can be in this category. Thus, the horse will wag its tail to rid its body of surface flies, but also in social situations, in order to prevent further approach by other animals, or effectively to indicate slight tension, annoyance and frustration (*Figure 4.10*). Ridden horses also tail wag at such times – although there are no flies to cause it (*Figure 4.11*). This is recognised in dressage tests of course, the horse being marked down for tail swishing – a sign of 'resistance'.

Tail swishing or head tossing can develop into a habit. This means that although the original reason (for example, an uncomfortable bit or an irritation at the use of the rider's leg) for its performance is removed, the horse does not stop performing it, because it has become a habit. Horses are prone to develop these 'habits' and they can be a major problem (*Chapter 9*).

Tail movements, head movements, stamping with front and back legs are all movements that horses use among each other to convey messages, usually indicating slight annoyance, but their origin is in movements to rid the body surface of irritants. If we understand the meaning of these movements it can help us in handling and riding our horses.

The skin flicking that horses are able to do is particularly interesting behaviour about which we know very little. It may be that horses use skin flicking between each other to convey messages as well as to get rid of flies – but we don't know.

Protection

The responses related to protection are quite important in communication, often being used to protect the major sense

SOCIAL
Greeting: equal, inferior,
superior

Individual distance violated

Aggression: threat, between bouts of fighting,
   intention to kick,
   withdrawal of superior
   during attacking bouts

Sexual frustration
   pre-copulation, non-receptive female (mare)
                     non-reactive male (mare)
   male unable to achieve intromission
   male when female non-receptive.

Situations in which contact with conspecifics is sought or retained
   Isolation from young, mother or social partner
   Suckling young (mother) particularly during weaning
   Between play bouts

NON SOCIAL
free horse

Skin irritation

Non-social situations Thwarting
   Obstacle preventing obtaining goal
   Suckling young (insufficient milk flow)
   Incompatible signs involving movement
   Forced change of direction or pace
   Restricted movement or pace

Something sought after
   Food searching
   Tactile stimulation (relief from irritation sought)
   Auditory or visual cues of food presence (reminded of something sought
   after)

Anticipation
   food, or to be let out

Transitional types of situations
   after alarm, after stretch; between investigating something;
   between movement bouts; conflict between approach and avoid

Figure 4.10
The situations in which tail swishing occurs in the free horse. It occurs
in both social and non-social situations

Horse	Bill	Solo	Puzzle	Drum	Play	Amb
Age	5	5	5	5	3	14
Type	keen	slow	slow	sch	slow	kee
Violent forward aid	5	4	5		skip	4
Change direction	2	4	5 hd sh			
Change Pace	4	2				
Conflicting aids (hands & legs)	7	4	2	4		3
Control experiment loose reins & no legs	None	None	None	None	None	No

hd sh = head shake
sch   = schooled

organs. For example the origin of frowning has been suggested to be the result of a lowering of the eyebrows to protect the eyes when approaching an adversary. Now we use it in slightly different circumstances. It has become 'ritualised', but nevertheless its origin remains in protection.

The most obvious and exaggerated protective response in horses is ear flattening (*Figure 4.12*). This is a ritualised movement, one of the few in horses. Here the ears are placed back and rotated onto the side of head. In this way they are better protected from any blows towards the face. This ear flattening has become associated with aggressive and defensive situations and become exaggerated particularly for communication and hence is now used as a signal meaning 'Get out of the way; go away' (*Figure 4.13*).

Another protective response is withdrawing of the tail, typical in horses frightened from the rear, or being attacked. Here the movement is originally protective; cold or frightened horses

'd	Mouse	Bak	Shir	Sheeba
	6	10	7	23
1	slow	sch	sch	slow
up	4	2	3	5
	5			
	3	5	4	3
	1	4	8	5
ne	None	None	None	None

Figure 4.11
The number of tail swishes performed by eleven horses in response to various conditioned stimuli (aids). This illustrates that tail swishing occurred as a result of (1) a violent aid; (2) a change of pace; (3) a change of direction; and particularly, (4) as a result of conflicting aids (go and stop at the same time). When the horses were allowed to go freely, there was no tail swishing. It occurs therefore as a result of slight frustration, or irritation

stand hunched up with their tail pressed between their legs (*Figure 4.14*). Because it is done by a frightened horse, it becomes associated with a message 'I am frightened'. The next stage is for the behaviour to become exaggerated, particularly to convey this message and slightly more subtle ones such as indicating non-confidence or appeasement.

Other movements

There are a couple of other obvious movements that horses make which do not fall into the categories discussed above. There is 'snapping' (*Figure 4.15*) a movement made particularly by foals and young horses, usually to their superiors, and in particular to adult males. Snapping indicates fear or non-aggression and is an action of stretching the neck forward, withdrawing the corners of the mouth and frequently opening and shutting the mouth. Recent evidence is given by Wells, Goldsmith-Rothschild (1979)

Figure 4.12
A horse with intense ear withdrawal almost ear flattening, a withdrawn tail and contracted haunches as a result of being frightened from the rear. The tensions in the nostril and chin and the high head position indicate that this is not aggressive

Figure 4.13
The previous figure contrasts with this. Here the mare flattens her ears, contracts the corners of her mouth to expose her teeth, and extends her head forward towards an approaching horse as a threat. If the intruder does not withdraw, he will be attacked and bitten in all likelihood!

Figure 4.14
A mare being groomed where she is ticklish, demonstrating how the ear, nose and postural positions are put together to form the whole display. The ears are pricked and the head turned, A, to smell the girl, demonstrating attention and orientation. B, the ears are slightly withdrawn, the head raised slightly, and the nostrils extended with the upper lip contracted; indicating slight irritation. Further development of this, C, with the addition of tail swishing and the left hind leg preparing to kick forward, indicating protection and skin irritation reflexes. D, further ear withdrawal, nostril and lip contraction, head raising, tail swishing and a forward kick. Intense displeasure, annoyance and more intense movements related to skin irritation and protection (ear withdrawal and kicking)

which suggests that colts snap more than fillies and more than half of the snappings performed were in response to an attack.

Observations on my own experimental herd confirm this. Snapping appears then to be appeasement behaviour, to stop or inhibit an attack. The only trouble is that it does not seem to work well! My own stallion will happily attack a filly or colt who is snapping and, instead of running, the youngster will continue

Figure 4.15
A stallion (*right*) and a yearling colt smell each other. The colt is 'snapping' (opening the mouth and withdrawing the mouth corners to indicate fear, non-aggression, submission)

to snap sometimes putting himself at considerable risk by so doing.

Another display which may have visual significance is flehmen as previously discussed. No obvious response to lip curl from any other horses has been reported by anyone, but as we know from the introduction to this chapter that does not necessarily mean that no message has been sent.

Communication with people

Because horses are very good at visual communication, they are able to tell the emotional state of many humans. For example they will sense if a person is nervous or if they are relaxed and confident and many more subtle indications.

Because emotional states are 'catching' or 'imitative' (in the sense that when in the company of happy people it is easier to become at least temporarily happy rather than remain gloomy), horses with their delicate sensitivities to moods may 'catch' a mood from a human. Thus, a slightly nervous human may make a horse slightly nervous and wary. This scares the human more, who reacts by jumping about, tightening all his muscles if riding and may even cry out. The result is that the horse becomes more nervous and so the vicious circle continues.

Behavioural problems of horses which may become of great importance frequently are the result of lack of communication between horse and human. The handler must be aware that the horse is receiving and interpreting much information from the handler concerning his mood and his next likely action. If the handler can do likewise, or at least give serious consideration as to how the horse may be feeling, there is a greater possibility of overcoming the problem.

The communicative system of a horse is complex and different from ours and they are very much better at, for example, visual and olfactory communication than we are. Unfortunately it is only too true that the majority of problems with horses are due to a lack of communicative skill of the people working with them. The horses will read us, but what do we want them to read and can we read them? All we can do is try, but we have far to go in learning their language although they seem adept at learning ours.

Thus it is extremely important to think of the way one moves, what one does, how one holds oneself, even what one says when working with horses, particularly young ones.

When ridden the horse will learn to respond to certain 'aids' or stimuli such as leg pressures, weight distribution, hand pressures and the position of all these and more. Different types of riding require different levels of sophistication and skill. However, there are two important points here that all who handle or ride horses must realise.

Firstly, that horses can be taught what you want them to do and what you do not, and they can learn by many different methods. For example, Moyra Williams (1960) once trained a horse to go hunting and to jump around an arena with no bridle – the horse was taught to respond to neck pressures.

Secondly, at the highest level of any type of riding the communication is two-way. It is not simply a question of making a command and having it obeyed, it is a question of the rider learning to be almost as sensitive as the horse. If achieved, the rider can respond to the slight muscular changes and movements of the horse which indicate when is the time to ask for a movement which will result in a response from the horse. Failure to understand this two-way process leads at best to obedient but mediocre performances in any form of riding or handling horses and how much less interesting it is.

The fundamental reason why some of us ride is to obtain that feeling of intercommunication with the horse which once felt is addictive. Unfortunately the emphasis today in riding is so heavily on competition that many people never feel or work towards this intercommunication and do not understand how essential horse to person communication is in any aspect of riding or horse management and training.

Extra-Sensory Perception

Much has been written on extra-sensory perception (ESP) in horses. Henry Blake (1975) in his charming books on horses, which are full of delightful and useful observations, has demonstrated his conviction that horses can be telepathic. Unfortunately his tests are not scientifically convincing. The only convincing work (and even that many scientists would not agree with) is some work that has been done in Russia (Ostrander 1980) using both dogs and humans. There, much emphasis has been placed on trying to:

1. Demonstrate whether or not such things do occur and can be measured.
2. If they do, can they be taught and who can learn to do it? The motivation in the Russian experiments is linked to national defence purposes. If messages could be sent and received from captains of submarines with no way of them being intercepted or interpreted, this is obviously useful.

As a scientist I am at this time not prepared to say that telepathy does *not* exist although there is no convincing evidence that it does. In all the cases where it has been reported in horses or between people and horses there are other explanations possible. One of the most obvious is that the horse is feeling changes. It is tempting when one is riding a very well schooled horse, or a horse that one knows very well indeed, to think that the horse is receiving telepathic messages. However, it may just be slight movements of the rider which are interpreted by the horse and acted upon.

I also think that if telepathy, of whatever kind, does exist that both people and animals can be taught to use it and I would predict that over the next two or three decades this may well become a much more important field of research. Educational programmes may be developed to teach people and animals, although telepathy may end up not being what we think of it today, but be of a more subliminal character.

It is not unreasonable to consider that horses may have senses that we cannot perceive because we ourselves do not have them. For example, bats use ultrasound and migrating birds use a galaxy of cues that we cannot perceive of and what about the famous bees that von Fisch (1967) found were using polarised light? So let us not dismiss other communication methods that may exist in horses. If they do have some elaborate communication system this might help to explain why they have such large convoluted cerebral hemispheres (*Chapter 2*).

This chapter is a brief summary of the types of responses that are important for visual communication in horse behaviour. It is not intended as a complete record of every message a horse is capable of sending, or all that we know about (and goodness knows how many more there are that we do not know about).

I hope what has been discussed will help people look more closely at their horses, understand them better and think about how communication works – the first step to understanding.

As visual, olfactory, taste, touch and auditory communication can be put together to *create* the message the horse wants to send, so these (postural, protective and irritative) pieces of the jigsaw can be put together to *transfer* the messages.

When all these senses and all these reflexes are brought together in one particular activity, for example, in courtship and sexual behaviour (*Figures 4.16, 4.17 and 4.18*), we see a complete 'display'. The actions of the horse, or horses, involved will be familiar to many readers and, hopefully, this chapter will illuminate for such people *what* these actions are and *why* they are displayed.

Figure 4.16
An oestral mare with a gelding, A to I, showing the relative importance of the different senses in communication. (*This page and opposite and following two pages.*)

A, The mare (*right*) raises her tail and urinates a little (visual and olfactory cues). The gelding approaches and smells her and the urine (adding taste cues). Note the position of the mare's ears indicating where her attention is directed; and her high postural tonus indicating her state of excitement.

B, He smells her tail and follows her (olfactory and visual cues).

C, She urinates and flashes her vulva, he smells again (olfactory and visual cues).

D, As she flashes her vulva again, her attention is obviously directed behind her. He, as he is a gelding, loses interest and watches something more interesting in the bushes!

E, The mare takes on a position of 'lordosis' (sexual readiness) elevating the vulva and giving visual cues. He ignores this and begins to graze; the ultimate brush off!

F, She walks off, but still with her attention on him (indicated by her right ear and eye).

H

G & H, Much to her chagrin, he does not even follow.

I

I, May be there is another male somewhere else? Raised postural tonus, ears pricked, nose and mouth tense (attention and readiness for movement)

Figure 4.17
Courtship and sex and the displays, A to I, involved. (*This page and opposite and following two pages.*) This sequence (and variations of it) from B to H may be repeated several times before the mare will stand for copulation.

A, Visual, touch and smell cues are used in the greeting between a stallion (*left*) and a mare. Note the stallion's contracted mouth and nose muscles, expanded nostrils and the mare's slightly tense nostrils. The inside ear of each horse is directed backwards towards the other's rear.

B, The stallion then licks the front leg of the mare, using touch and smell, giving and receiving smell and touch messages. The mare turns her head away, and swishes her tail, visual cues indicating she is not prepared to stand for copulation.

C

His penis erects. C, after squealing she walks away with an upright excited posture, he follows with a roar (auditory cue) and a fore leg lift (visual cue), his penis erect (further visual cue), and possibly olfactory.

D

She stands again, D, while he licks and smells her front leg (he may touch lick and smell any part of her body, but it is usually in front of the withers). She reacts in the same way, tail swishing (excitement and slight frustration) turning her head away but directing her ears towards him.

E

She shakes her head, E, and then squeals again before moving off. Both are by this time excited, and vocalisations are frequent. He roars again, and kicks out with a hind leg. Notice the tighter lips and nose of the mare.

F

She trots off, F, kicking out with both hind legs. He is used to interpreting signals of intention to kick and moves over to the side to avoid being kicked, while still following her closely. Throwing the tail up may well distribute the pheromones from the vulva more effectively.

G

G, he reacts by attempting to smell her vulva, and to touch and lick it, but she continues to trot off.

H

She stops, H, now more ready to be mounted and he smells and touches her vulva.

I

I, The mare takes up the copulatory posture with a contracted belly, legs apart and the weight pushing against the stallion. The stallion mounts and achieves intromission. Young stallions, in particular, may mount frequently before achieving intromission

		Vision				
		Posture	Facial expression	Touch	Smell	Taste	Hearing
A	♂	++	++	++	++	+	+
	♀	+	++	++	++	+	+
B	♂	+	+	+	+		
	♀	+		+	+		+
C	♂	++	++		+		++
	♀	+	++		+		++
D	♂	+	+	++	++	+	+
	♀	+	+	++	++	+	+
E	♂	++	++		+		++
	♀	+	+		+		++
F	♂	++	+	+	++		+
	♀	++	++	+	+		+
G	♂	++	++	++	++	++	
	♀	+	+	++	+		+
H	♂	+	+	++	++	++	
	♀	++	+	++	++		+
I	♂	++		++	+		+
	♀	++		++	+		+

♀ = mare   ♂ = stallion

Figure 4.18
An assessment of the relative importance of the different sensory modalities in Figure 4.17

5 Sex, Maternity and the Foal

Sexual behaviour in horses, when they are allowed to court and breed naturally, is quite a long and complicated business as we have seen. (*Chapter 4.*) In this chapter we will discuss other aspects of reproduction and the birth of the foal.

Oestrus

The period when a mare is receptive to a stallion's sexual advances and will stand for mating is described as 'oestrus', or as it is more commonly known, 'in season'. Oestrus is controlled by sex hormones which are in turn controlled by the brain (*Figure 5.1*), in particular the pituitary (*Chapter 2*).

The description of the sex hormones and their relationship to behaviour is given in any good text book, but there are two or three points which are particularly interesting about oestrus in mares as opposed to other species.

In the first place oestrus is controlled by day length, as is the case in sheep. However mares come into season with lengthening days (sheep come into season with shortening days). Each year, mares experience 'anoestrus', a period of time when they do not come into season at all. Anoestrus occurs as days become shorter. This means that the mare can naturally conceive, in the northern hemisphere, in the spring and summer (April to September) but not in the late autumn and winter. This is logical since the mare has an eleven month pregnancy. The foal will then be born at a time when there is likely to be good weather

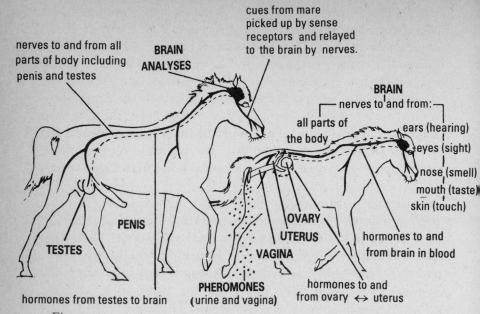

Figure 5.1

The role of the fore brain (the thinking part) in co-ordinating the behaviour and physiology of courtship and mating. All the information from the senses and *feelings* generated by hormones is assessed and analysed by the fore brain which then acts on it. Although there is an innate (or instinctive) tendency to act in certain ways, it depends on the fore brain's assessment including such things as past experiences or the individual mare or stallion and how he or she behaves as to whether the two excite each other and achieve successful copulation

and enough nutritious food to meet the demands of the mare who has to feed herself and her offspring.

Because the foal is a *follower*, unlike the calf, he follows his mother everywhere. If the weather is cold the mare may be grazing in an exposed place, therefore the foal is exposed to low temperatures and winds and is greatly at risk. Anyone who has bred autumn foals outdoors knows what a pitiable sight this can be; a small, cold, shivering foal standing resolutely by his unconcerned mother, who may be grazing in the rain when there is plenty of shelter nearby. A calf, because he does not follow his mother around, will be snuggled into the shelter with his calf friends. So, in order for the foal to survive with the particular evolutionary strategy the horse has adopted, it has to be born when the weather is reasonably good. Thus, it must be a seasonal breeder. By contrast, the cow does not need to be because its calf has a different behaviour. Nowadays, particularly, the racing world and also, misguidedly, the rest of the competitive horse world, are interested in having horses foal earlier in the year than is biologically desirable. They wish the horses to foal as near the first of January as possible. To do this physiologists have developed a veritable battery of drugs to bring mares into season in the winter (Dawson 1984).

Perhaps it is time to ask ourselves is this really necessary or indeed desirable? Why does the registration date for horses have to be set by man's calendar and not that of the horse? Surely the first of April, or even the first of May, could begin the horse year and then we could breed *with* the adaption strategies of the horse instead of constantly working *against* them, and thereby encountering more and more problems. The major objection to this rescheduling of the racing calendar is that there would be fewer money making spin offs for drug companies and some veterinarians who therefore violently oppose any proposal for change.

Breed or Type	Duration of Œstrus (days)		Locality	Author
	Range	Mean		
Draught	4–21	7	U.S.A.	Aitken (1926)
	1–14	5	U.S.A.	Andrews & McKenzie (1941)
Korean and other	4–14	9	Japan	Satoh & Hoshi (1932)
	1–15	6	Japan	Nishikawa (1959)
Light	1–37	6	U.S.A.	Andrews & McKenzie (1941)
Thoroughbreds	3–15	7	England	Hammond (1934)
	4–7	5	U.S.S.R.	Krat (1933)
Welsh and Shetland	3–30	7	England	Hammond (1938)

Figure 5.2
The length of oestrus or 'season' in the mare. Note the variation. (From Hafez *et al* 1962.)

A further interesting feature of oestrus is that the mare has a very long period of oestrus, up to 10 days (*Figure 5.2*) as opposed to the 12 to 24 hours for cattle. Why should this be? This is a difficult question, but one answer may be that courtship is particularly important in horses, that the prolonged courting and resulting mutual excitement is very important for successful conception. We know that for cows and indeed women, courting results in excitement and uterine contractions and secretions which help to speed the sperm up the vagina to fertilise the egg. Although this has not been measured in horses, it is likely to be similar. The development of a secure bond of mutual attraction and recognition probably relaxes and excites the mare and again aids conception. Prolonged courtship and oestrus will ensure this.

Another factor to consider is that the development of a deep bond between the mare and stallion is facilitated by the long oestrus and courting period. This bond keeps the stallion near so that he is in the group when the foal is born and can help directly, or indirectly, with its survival thereafter.

Just in case some readers are still doubtful about the importance of natural courtship to help conception in the horse let me mention the six maiden mares who have been presented and covered by my stallion (who always runs with the mares from before oestrus until they have missed the next oestrus). None of them have stood for the stallion until day 3 of their oestrus. The courtship has been very prolonged and much of the time the naive maidens have had to be wooed and caressed by the stallion before they would stand. Judging from their behaviour this was a direct result of fear.

I have many times witnessed maiden mares being roughly and quickly covered, in-hand, by mature large stallions who have become conditioned to running out of the stable and jumping on a mare with practically no courtship. Such management must biologically be a very bad idea and indeed it is reflected in the very low conception rates in thoroughbred studs (Rossdale 1968), even with all the modern drugs and manipulative aids used today.

Such practice can also be considered ethically wrong. Frequently, maiden mares covered in this way, often hobbled, sometimes twitched and forced to stand show every sign of trauma thereafter. They shiver and sweat and show a reluctance to return to the area or the experience. In short, it can be considered a type of 'rape'. Some mature mares, because of their experiences as maidens also react fearfully to being covered again and there are a host of problems associated with infertility in mares which are being met by the veterinarians with a battery of drugs and manipulations. This has reached a point where natural service is almost unheard of. Perhaps breeders should pause to think if in-hand breeding (and its almost essential accompaniment of drugs and manipulations) is either necessary or in the long run helping us to breed better horses. We are, of course, not selecting against infertility in this way, which means our horses will become less and less 'naturally' fertile.

There are indeed risks to the stallion in running him with mares. On the other hand if the horse has run with his mother until naturally weaned, then with his family group, he has had experience of mares and of courting mares. Similarly, the mares are familiar with colts and young stallions and the act of breeding is not their first encounter with an entire male. In this way the stallion becomes adept at courting and avoiding injury. Not only does the stallion interpret intention to kick and other signals from the mare – but because he keeps his distance until she is sufficiently interested in copulation, she kicks less.

Unfortunately, if one runs a stallion today with mares at stud, the chances are that many of the mares will have been sent because they are difficult to breed from, often because they have a 'hang up' about sex as a result of thoughtless in-hand covering.

If in-hand breeding (which does not allow for natural courtship) is neither ethical nor appropriate how can we manage matters when one stallion is required to cover many mares? It is true that when running with mares the stallion can cover fewer, because he uses up energy courting, bonding and covering them frequently. When a mare is in full oestrus and receptive the stallion may cover her 8 to 15 times in a day; and many of those will be initiated *by the mare* who may become extremely excited, approaching the stallion and rubbing her quarters against him in an effort to arouse him. The obvious solution to this is Artificial Insemination (AI). Stallions rapidly learn to mount a dummy and their semen can easily be collected and stored. There is no evidence that the injection of semen in the vagina of the mare is a particularly traumatic or frightening experience, provided of course she is used to being handled. Rather than going through with the painful and frightening process of in-hand breeding the solution is AI. It is easy and cheap as well as having the added advantage of reducing the risk of venereal infections which have recently become of much concern in the horse breeding world.

Let us consider, however, if it is a good thing for the equine species – and for people – in the long run if one horse covers very many others? We have the situation in cattle now where the selected cattle perform better under the present agricultural conditions of relatively cheap and available drugs and fodder. How would these same cattle perform in a world, which we may well be moving towards, of relative scarcity of such things? Indeed, we have lost many of the minority breeds of cattle, and similarly, are on the way to losing some of the well adapted tough pony breeds, the Exmoor for example, as more and more people breed the 'Horse of the moment' which will win in the competitions of the day but may actually not even be able to reproduce itself without the aid of drugs. If few stallions are used and approved of to cover the mares of the day, the entire population becomes more related. This means that characteristics which we may need in the future, such as toughness and ability to survive on nutritionally poor diets, may be lost to the gene pool.

The horse establishment should be more cautious of the condemnation of people breeding horses with different objectives to their own, for example gypsies. It may be by the turn of the century that it is they, rather than the establishment, who will have the most appropriate horses.

Pregnancy

The gestation period of horses is eleven months, two months longer than other similar sized species. Why should this be? This is a question to which I do not really have an answer. It may be that the foal is more precocious at birth and it immediately has to get up and run and keep up with the herd and therefore needs the extra months in the womb to mature enough to do this. But such a requirement is also true of many antelopes, such as the gnu which only has a nine month gestation period.

One thing that is clear, however, is that pregnant mares continue to live like the rest of the group and with the rest of the group. This is not true of many ruminants though who do not stay in the tight family group, but pregnant females will form their own group; the males another, and the young another.

Mares may (in an area which provides a good level of nutrition throughout the year) spend almost their entire lives pregnant. Again, one should realise that horses have adapted throughout many millions of years to their environment and that this is the particular strategy the species evolved. Because the horse has survived, it is therefore very successful. Thus, it is not bad husbandry to breed from mares every year provided they are kept in a reasonably natural way and preferably have free access to their family and group, including the stallion. However, because of the psychological strains of isolation, restriction and often excessive feeding, breeding every year from confined mares may well shorten their lives and reduce their breeding performance.

One aspect of horse management which has not been grossly interfered with by humans is the care of pregnant mares and mares and foals. For some reason there seems to have been a tacit agreement between breeders that to interfere with such things would lead to problems.

Thus, it is pregnant mares and mares with young foals which are the only horses normally able (to a degree at least) to live out the type of life that they have evolved to live in a more or less suitable environment. They are usually at pasture or in groups, they can make their own time budgets, they can wander where they like within their fields and take their own behavioural decisions about shelter, warmth and so on. They do it very well and there is rarely any problem.

In feral horse society, the pregnant mares tend to associate primarily with their families and with each other. This is for obvious reasons; as pregnancy advances the mare feels heavier and is less likely to rush about and she also eats more. Thus, they

	Proximity (nearest neighbour & next nearest neighbour) %	Affiliative behaviour %	Aggressive behaviour %
Mares			
Kin	15	73	26
Non-kin	3	3	12
Stallions			
Kin	13	10	21
Non-kin	4	4	16
Yearlings			
Kin	19	19	11
Non-kin	4	16	9
Foals			
Kin	22	25	6
Non-kin	3	4	8

Figure 5.3
The preference for neighbours being either family members or not, for the different sexes and age groups in the feral Camargue horse. The distribution of affiliative behaviour (grooming and friendly contact) and aggressive behaviour (head threat and kick threat) is also given.

We can see in all groups a preference for association with family members (kin). There is more affiliative behaviour to family members in all groups, although this is less obvious for yearlings. There is also more aggressive behaviour directed towards family members in all groups (except foals). (Adapted from Wells *et al* 1979.)

have similar physiological demands which can be fulfilled in the same places so they tend to be together (*Figure 5.3*).

Pregnant mares, like pregnant women, should not be treated with enormous delicacy. Like women, it is important for them to continue a normal life, although this obviously should not be too strenuous. However, with discretion, until a month or so before foaling mares can be ridden, worked in harness and on the land. This keeps them fitter and occupied and does them nothing but good, although obviously a thoughtful and considerate approach is necessary. A well run, economically viable stud should work their pregnant mares with discretion at least until their eighth or ninth month.

Foaling

There are many books describing how to spot approaching foaling, and foaling itself. We will briefly mention the signs and emphasise the changes. The approach of foaling will be spotted by the waxing of the teats, a slight swelling of the vulva region and swelling of the udder several days before foaling.

Behavioural indexes of approaching foaling have been published by various sources, describing signs in detail, but in my own studies of horses we have found that several of them are not accurate. Mares will vary greatly in how they behave. In the wild, they do not tend to withdraw from the herd as is so often said, but rather they tend to get left behind as the herd moves on. In paddocked horses which cannot move on they may withdraw – but we have never seen this in the 15 foalings where we scored the mares' behaviour.

A mare may continue to graze and behave normally right up to and even during labour. The best indicator of closely approaching labour is that the mare begins to look around at her flank. Some mares also nicker quietly (cows produce a soft purring sound at this time). The mares also seem restless, changing what they are doing more frequently.

BIRTH

Labour is usually relatively quick in horses, and has been described in detail many times (Rossdale 1983). *The best thing to do is to leave well alone.* The worst enemy of reproducing mammals are over anxious people fussing around and sometimes not able to resist prodding and poking. Horses usually give birth at night or in the early morning and it seems as though they may have an ability to stop or delay birth if disturbed. This would be a particularly useful mechanism in a species which is preyed upon and whose main defence is flight because, if danger threatens, labour can then be delayed until it is past. There are other species, such as the gnu, who appears to be able to interrupt labour in a similar way (Estes 1966).

Maternal Behaviour

A normal mare will be pre-programmed by her hormones and physiological changes in her body to pay attention and care for her new foal. Exactly how maternal behaviour is actually triggered off and how it is controlled is not entirely known, but at birth and shortly after there are large changes in the balance of hormones which are monitored by the pituitary of the brain and result in maternal behaviour and caring for the new young.

The foal is usually born as the mare stands up and it may dangle out of the mare head first for a short while, before the quarters are expelled and it falls to the ground. The umbilicus is still attached. It is important not to cut the umbilicus at this stage (Rossdale 1983) since by doing so the foal may be deprived of a quantity of the mare's blood which serves many functions, including improving its immunity to infection.

Once the foal is expelled the mare will then, when sufficiently recovered, turn around, smell and touch the foal and begin to lick it. She may also make short nickers at this time.

The first task of the mare is to dry off the foal and begin to recognise it. She does this by licking it. Some mares are more thorough than others. It is only at this time and in courtship that a horse licks another in any prolonged way (unlike cows, for example, who throughout their lives groom each other by licking).

After a normal birth licking has two functions: firstly, it dries off the foal and apparently stimulates the blood supply to the skin, and secondly, by so doing the mare tastes and smells the foal. Although initially the foal may smell predominantly of the mare herself since it is covered with secretions from the mare's own birth canal, gradually this fades and its own individual smell is superimposed. Frequent smelling and touching of the foal by the mother is noticeable at this time.

It is important not to rush in and start rubbing the foal or to interfere in other ways at this stage, or the process of *imprinting* may be disrupted. Imprinting is a type of rapid irreversible learning. The mare learns which is her foal and foal learns who is his mother.

Figure 5.4
The first drink. The mare stands and turns her head to smell and touch the foal who staggers around learning to walk, and looking for the teat

Suckling is important here as the mare is rewarded by the relief of the pressure in her udder and the foal receives a drink (*Figure 5.4*). Thus, suckling is the *positive reinforcement* (*Chapter 9*) of this type of learning. Most instances of maternal rejection are due to problems with imprinting called *mal-imprinting*.

It is very important to realise that most mares who reject their foals do so because of over- or mis-management. If they are allowed to give birth and suckle the foal undisturbed it is very unusual that anything goes wrong. For this reason I always consider that it is much better for the mare to foal outside where there is some shelter and where she will be less disturbed by people. Provided horses are given enough options and allowed to take their own behavioural decisions concerning what, where and when they do things and how they keep warm, then there is, normally, no need to worry about foals. However the trend towards horses of all types giving birth earlier in the year may mean that they are foaling in very bad and very cold weather in which case the foal may be at risk. Therefore supplying extra shelter or even bringing them inside may be necessary.

After a few minutes, or even up to half an hour, the foal will attempt to get up. It will begin by shaking its head and then moving itself. Several attempts to get up will be made and in so doing the foal will collapse. This, again, is the natural order of things and the foal has evolved mechanisms to cope with this. What it has *not* evolved to cope with is landing on a hard cement floor, so there must be a deep bed. However, deep beds may also be slippery and it is important to ensure that the foal can obtain a foothold in order to raise itself. In some experiments with cattle (Kiley-Worthington and De La Plain 1983) the time to first standing of calves was significantly delayed in those animals which calved inside on bedded floors, as the calves found it much more difficult to obtain a foothold than outside at grass. This is important because it is necessary for the calf or foal to obtain his first drink as soon as possible. The reason for this is that the *immunoglobulins* (large molecules that contain the necessary substances for the foal to obtain immunity to various infections) are in the first milk, and also they can only be absorbed by the foal close to birth.

As mentioned above, it is important that the foal suckles as soon as possible but on the other hand it is not so urgent that people should rush in and place the foal on the teat which may cause behavioural problems ultimately for both foal and mare. The disadvantages of these behavioural problems may far outweigh the advantages from the extra immunoglobulins.

The mare is often said to 'push the foal when on his feet to the teat area' and assist in the finding of the teats. Some mares do seem to be doing this. However, what mares always do is to turn the head to smell the foal as it approaches her and moves along her body. The greatest aid she gives the foal is to stand still while it attempts to find the teats. This may take a considerable time, particularly if the foal is not very strong (up to 45 minutes from first standing). The mare will also contract her belly (*Figure 5.5*) even though it looks as if she is wincing, but in fact all normal

Figure 5.5
Contraction of the mare's abdomen or belly when the foal suckles. A normal response which apparently functions to make the udder and teats more obvious

mares do this every time they suckle their foals until weaning. The function is obscure, but it may be to do with milk let down, or contraction of the uterus. This action makes the udder and teats more obvious to the searching foal.

Milk let down is controlled by a hormone called oxytocin. The presence of the foal and the manipulation of the teats sends a message to the pituitary of the mare's brain which releases oxytocin and stimulates the production of prolactin. Prolactin is probably most important for milk formation; oxytocin leads to the ejection of the milk from the mammary gland by causing the muscles to contract in the udder. The presence of the foal is important (*Figure 5.6*) because if things are not going right (such as the foal not being recognised) the mare is very nervous or disturbed and worried, then these hormones will not be released. It is possible to condition (*Chapter 9*) the release of oxytocin. Animals including humans, will learn to associate a particular stimulus with an action. For example, the noise of buckets will be associated by a cow with milking; the cry of a baby by a human mother with suckling. When this signal is received the milk is

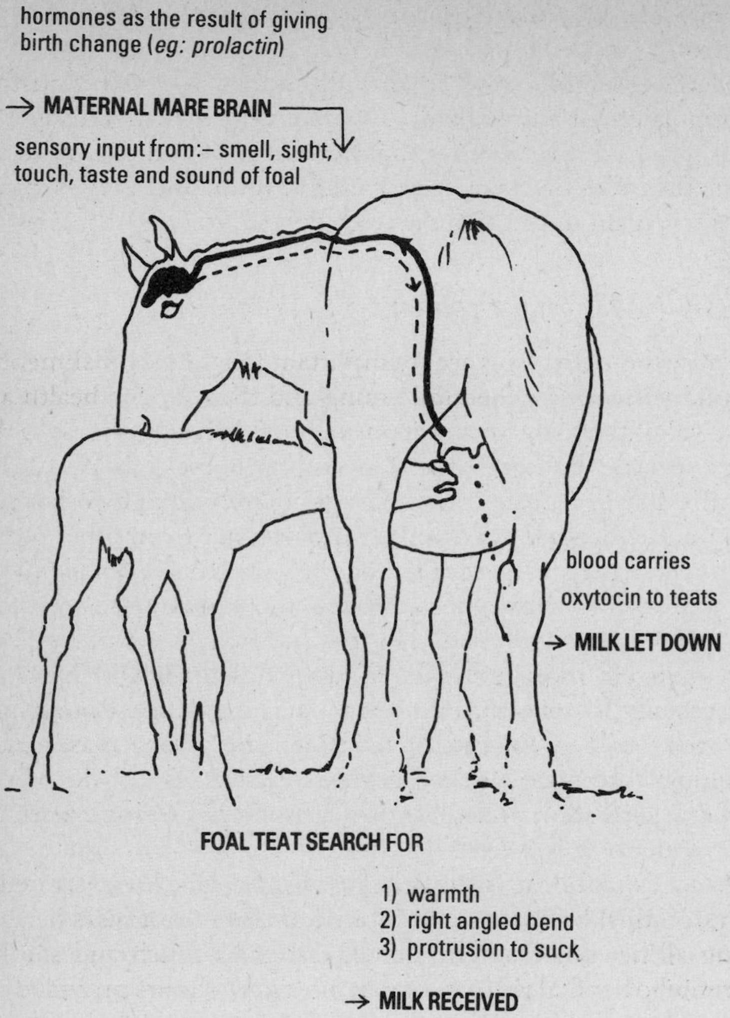

hormones as the result of giving
birth change (*eg: prolactin*)

→ **MATERNAL MARE BRAIN**

sensory input from:– smell, sight,
touch, taste and sound of foal

blood carries
oxytocin to teats

→ **MILK LET DOWN**

FOAL TEAT SEARCH FOR

1) warmth
2) right angled bend
3) protrusion to suck

→ **MILK RECEIVED**

Figure 5.6
The importance of psychological factors and the presence of the foal in
the initiation and continuation of maternal behaviour. Although after
birth the mare is normally psychologically prepared to behave
maternally, this is dependent on the establishment of a relationship
between foal and mother as a result of cues from the foal which act on
the mare to release her milk. Rejection as a result of physiological
malfunction in mares is rare. Foal rejection is usually the result of
human interference as a result of a lack of understanding of how
maternal behaviour works

released, whether the mother wants it to or not. This is a Type 1 conditioned response (*Chapter 9*) and is not under conscious control.

Mares resemble sows in that the udder and teats must be manipulated for a time before the milk is let down. This is why foals go up to their mother, put their nose in and play with the teats, then take their nose out and look about and a few seconds later try again until the milk is let down.

Possible Maternal Problems

Because these first days are so important for the establishment of a bond between mother and young and thus for the health and survival of the foals, mares are usually slightly aggressive at this stage in order to keep others, including horses, away. Out at pasture and in a group every normal mare will defend her foal and the area around her from any interference from other horses or potential predators, such as dogs or sometimes even people. If the mare is a socially adjusted horse, there is no need to worry that other mares will 'steal' her foal and bully her away as even the youngest most 'submissive' animal will defend her foal, successfully. Even in a confined area the established 'dominance' hierarchy will be changed as a result. This is one reason why thinking in terms of 'roles' may be a better way of describing social organisation. The role of the mother is to look after the foal, and she will defend this right.

As far as we know (although there has been little experimental work on this) by analogy with cattle, a mare recognises her foal using all her senses; sight, smell, taste and touch and she has learnt who her foal is in a matter of one to two hours provided she is not disturbed by visitors.

It is quite possible for a mare to recognise her foal as her own, but not allow it to suckle. This is *not* maternal rejection and there are usually other reasons for this. One of the most common is that she has tender teats which have never been touched before and she is very sensitive. It only requires her to kick once or twice for the very young foal to be put off suckling, at least for a time and this often makes the problem worse as milk production increases after birth, further extending the teats and making the whole area even more tender. If you have ever had a baby and had sore teats you will understand only too well how the mare feels. Thus, it is *not* a question of taking the foal away because she is kicking it when attempting to suckle, but rather one of soothing and gentling her, if necessary milking her out yourself and then manipulating the foal onto the teat yourself, but only as a last resort. The foal will rapidly learn not to go near the quarters if he has been kicked once and may show a reluctance until he has had a successful drink, in which case it may be necessary to help the foal suckle and soothe the mare for the first several days.

Manipulating the foal onto the teat can be a tricky business as the mare is probably sore and inclined to kick when she feels anything touching her belly. However, with patience and determination it can be done. A useful trick is to have the foal's quarters in front of your knees and then lean forward and gently place his mouth around the teat and hold it there, while squirting milk into his mouth. This allows you to have complete control over the foal and to avoid him running off when the mare swishes her tail, the first sign of an intention to kick. It does not prevent the mare kicking however and if gentling and caressing her to win her confidence does not work, shifting her attention to eating a feed or being scratched or rubbed hard on the neck by your assistant may. Failing this, picking up the front leg on the same side may be enough to allow you to relieve the pressure of milk in the udder by milking out a little.

If all else fails (but it rarely does with a skilled operator), then you may have to twitch the mare until she has fed the foal. The moral here is make sure that your mare is easy and used to being handled all over, including the teats, udder and under the belly. Also make sure before she foals that she has confidence in you and that you are not frightened of her. It is useful to know how to milk a little too as fumbling efforts on a sore teat are not likely to be relished by the mare. The teats should have reasonably hard skin so that they do not become sore easily. Gentle rubbing and touching of the whole udder can begin six weeks or so before foaling and, as human mothers do, application of methylated spirit to harden the skin is useful. Do take care however not to express any of the milk as this will break the waxy seal and open the teat for infection to enter.

Approximately 90 per cent of rejections of the foal by the mare are the result of mismanagement, usually inappropriate interference during the crucial first few days of the relationship between mare and foal either at the present foaling or a past foaling, so it is vitally important to understand that interference must be avoided as much as possible. It is rare that a mare will give up behaving maternally even if her foal dies as she is physiologically programmed to so behave after the birth of her foal, in just the same way as human mothers do. The presence of the foal itself is important to keep this physiological and behavioural state going. If foals are to be fostered on to different mares, then it must be done as close to birth as possible. The reasons for this are:

1. She then has more chance of imprinting on the foal and accepting it as hers.
2. She will be more likely to be maternal than if this is left until later.

However, it is possible to foster another foal onto a mother who has lost her foal up to three weeks after birth, provided there is not a long gap after losing her own foal and being given another.

There is, of course, always the occasional mare where the correct maternal behaviour is not triggered off because of a malfunction in the physiology, usually related to the release of various hormones, but this is very unusual. It is also possible that socially maladjusted mares who have rarely, if ever, had the opportunity of mixing freely with other horses will have problems and may be aggressive towards, or frightened of, the foal. The experience of having been reared by a mother in most species affects how she behaves when she becomes a mother; so mares who have been bottle reared may have problems, although if socially adjusted in other ways this is avoidable.

Mares, particularly maidens, occasionally will ignore their foals. This is usually the result of their lack of contact with other horses. Such mares may well be more firmly attached to humans and in such cases it is useful to help the mare by going in with her and leading her over to the foal, even scattering a little food along the back of the foal to interest her in it.

A mare who ignores the foal immediately after birth, or is

clumsy or sick may not remove all of the birth membrane. This can become stuck over the foal's nose and prevent breathing. This is, however, a freak circumstance and is rare.

The afterbirth will be expelled from between a few minutes to some hours after the birth. Unlike many species, horses do not eat the afterbirth. The reason for this is also obscure, since eating the afterbirth can reduce the traces of the birth and hence clues for predators. It is also suggested that the afterbirth serves as a source of trace elements for the mother who has excreted them previously. Presumably in horses, the herd moves away from the place of birth so quickly that eating the afterbirth might delay the mare's movement and hence be a disadvantage. Mares will show an intense interest in the birth fluids, only for a very short period after birth when the foal is coated in them. However other mares do show some interest in the smells and tastes around birth, frequently smelling around where the foal was born and displaying flehmen.

The experience of motherhood effects how a mare behaves at foaling and after, as in other species – including women. The intricasies of motherhood must be learnt and, on the whole, mares, like humans, become better at it with experience. It may therefore be necessary to soothe and calm a maiden mare particularly if she is a nervous agitated creature.

A mare that is aggressive to human beings after foaling is often a blessing to herself as she will discourage interference and manipulation. It can however be difficult to get near a mare in order to make some essential manipulation, for example, freeing the foal from being tangled in a rope or stuck under the manger, but with proper stable management or better still having the animals at pasture, these accidents do not arise.

Thus, the first two to three days of life of the foal are very important for the establishment of a good relationship between mare and foal and since the foal is an opportunist as we will see, it is the behaviour of the *mare* that has to be nurtured and allowed to develop naturally if the foal is to be well raised with no problems.

There is a depressing increase in mare 'rejections' these days, particularly in thoroughbred studs. The reason for this is usually increasing manipulation and interference at a very sensitive time. The raising of mares in stables, isolated from free association with other horses for most of their lives also contributes to this problem. It is quite detrimental to rush in to wash the mare, or administer any medicaments (unless absolutely *essential* for her health) or interfere in any way. Foalings are always better watched behind one way glass or through a video recorder so that the mare is not disturbed.

The Foal

As we saw earlier the first task the foal has is to get to its feet. This can be a long and rather rough process where it gets up and collapses again and again; persistence is essential. Having got to its feet the foal then has to learn the appropriate co-ordination for walking. The foal is innately pre-programmed to walk, of course, just like human infants, but it still has to learn how. The difference is that the foal learns in about one hour from birth whereas a human infant, born at a much less advanced stage of development, takes a year or so!

Having organised the walk more or less the foal will wobble over to mother. It seems at this stage that it is attracted to her warmth, possibly by her smell. The foal will then smell and touch her and gradually begin to run his nose underneath. Work with lambs (Bareham 1972) showed that in searching for the teat it is warmth, right angles, bends and the texture that is sought after. This explains why many foals and calves seem to get stuck behind the mothers elbow in their teat searching. However, after a time, if they receive no reward then they will gradually try another place. The process is often painful to watch as it seems to take so long, but eventually the foal may clumsily grasp a teat in its mouth, only to lose it again. The foal has to learn where the teat is and the intricacies of suckling. To start with it is clumsy and bad at it, obtaining little if any milk, but in these first few hours the capacity for rapid learning is amazing.

If the mare does not allow the foal to suckle, for various reasons, then the foal may well be conditioned not even to try; it is not worth getting kicked to obtain a drink. In such cases the foal will often become 'fixated' on some other object in the stable, such as a protruding plank or a dangling piece of string and will play with this for long periods.

IMPRINTING ON THE MOTHER

The foal, like most young mammals, is initially an opportunist and will suckle from any mother who will allow him to. He becomes 'imprinted' on the mother as a result of staying near her and suckling from her. The foal appears to follow and stay close to large moving objects and if the mother is not there may well choose any other large moving object such as a tractor, a human or anything else. The foal will also (before the individual recognition of the mother is established) run to and follow any other mare. This is why it is important that the mother keeps other horses away at this time. However, it is only a matter of hours before the foal has learnt which is his mother and from whom he can drink without being kicked off. At this stage the recognition of the foal by the mother is more important than *vice versa* for the survival of the foal. This is why it is possible to raise young animals including foals on bottles: because they are opportunists, at least for the first few days. After this it will become more and more difficult to get the foal to take a teat. This can usually be achieved, however, with persistence, provided the foal is hungry enough.

The Mare and Foal

The mare and foal will stay very close to each other all the time for the first few days. Generally within about 10 m of each other (*Figure 5.7*). Some of the time will be spent touching and smelling each other and in this way the mutual recognition is firmly and irreversibly established. As we have already discussed the foal is a 'follower'. That is, he follows his mother everywhere and does not associate with other foals for much of the time. The result of this strategy is that the mother and foal have a particularly strong bond and this is, of course, as we have seen, the basis of the strong prolonged family ties in horse society. This is not the same in many other species. Some species of deer, for example, are 'hiders' in that the young lie away from their mother in some concealed place and their mothers will congregate to graze and occasionally return to feed them. As the fawns grow older they may come out of hiding and follow the herd, or form crêches where they stay lying and sleeping with their peers.

Calves fall in between these two extremes. Here distance between the mother and the calf is generally much greater than for a mare and her foal and the calf spends more time near his peers than near his mother and this behaviour increases as the calf grows older. The effect of this is that cattle society is differently organised and the bonds between peers are almost as strong as the bonds between mothers and offspring. In practical terms this means that keeping cattle in groups of similar ages is to a large

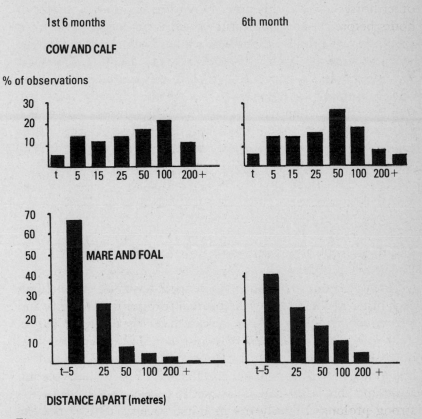

Figure 5.7
The difference in the distance that cows and their calves and mares and their foals are apart. The mare and foal stay much closer together for more of the time even when the foal is six months old than do cows and calves. Total number of observations 6,000

extent the way cattle would associate in the wild or feral state and
is successful. On the other hand, this is not the case with horses.
Peer groups are rarely formed for anything except short bouts of
playing, even after the foals are weaned. The prefered associates
remain the animal's relatives not his peers.

SUCKLING

Linked with this close association between mother and foal goes
frequent suckling in foals. If we compare the number of suckling
bouts and their length with that for cattle (*Figure 5.8*) we find that
foals suckle more frequently than calves for the first month. The

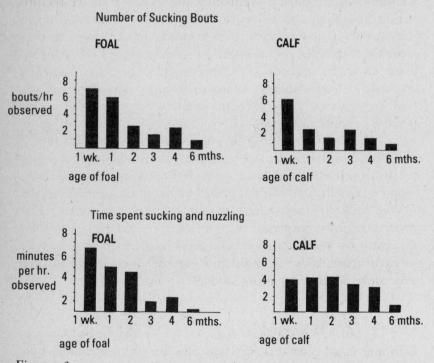

Figure 5.8
The number of sucking bouts and the time spent sucking in foals and
calves from birth to six months old. Note that foals suck much more
frequently than calves up until they are two months old. They also
spend more time suckling for the first months, but then less than the
calves who show little change in the amount of time they spend
suckling for the first six months of their life

need for frequent suckling would ensure that the mother and foal stay within easy reach of each other. The small size of the stomach of the horse may mean too, that frequent suckling is necessary for health and growth.

Another reason for the frequent suckling bouts may be to reinforce the mother-offspring bond, ensuring their close association and the survival of the foal. If the mares are to be parted from their foals for riding, work or for other reasons, it is necessary initially not to part them for longer than the normal period between suckling bouts so that this does not cause any upset of the normal feeding intervals of the foal.

On my own property we cannot afford to have our mares standing around during pregnancy and lactation so we recommence working our mares for very short periods (first 10 minutes away from the foal, then gradually lengthening to 1 hour by 2 months, and 2 hours by 4 months and so on) from about two to three weeks after birth as long as both mare and foal are healthy. The advantage of this procedure is that the mare and foal, from an early age, become used to being apart for short periods of time and do not worry about it. The foals are initially left with other foals and mothers, either in the pasture, or at least at the beginning in a safe stable or yard, but not isolated. By nine weeks from birth they can be safely left out at pasture with their relatives and the rest of their family while the mare is taken out for work and neither worry, or even neigh to each other. This procedure must however be developed gradually. It is very traumatic for both if, after several months of unrestrained access to each other, they are suddenly parted which is the normal procedure adopted by most studs.

IS WEANING NECESSARY OR DESIRABLE?

Weaning is, of course, a standard practice on most studs. Like many standard practices, whether or not is it either sensible or necessary is very rarely considered. When horses with behavioural problems are presented to me it is frequently possible to trace the establishment of the problem back to the period around weaning. Because of this I have been considering weaning and possible alternatives for some years now.

Strong attachments   It is reasonable to suppose that the prolonged very close association between mare and foal results in a strong attachment between them. Indeed, this is borne out by studies done on wild and feral horses (Tyler 1972, Wells and Goldsmidth-Rothchilde 1979, Waring 1983). Here it is found that the mother/daughter association is close and often continues throughout life, so that the basis of the social group is small family groups based on mother/daughter bonds. The sons are likely to stay with their mothers if there is no pressure from a stallion who will otherwise kick the colts out around puberty. Thus, given a chance, the mother/son relationship will be as strong as the mother/daughter. I have one mare who has four foals, each of which has grown up with her unweaned and the gelding (her eldest now aged eight) has apparently a similar attachment to her as her daughters do.

Since we know this, separating the mother and foal, isolating the foal or even putting it in a group of animals of its own age (which might be reasonably appropriate for cattle) might be expected to lead to behavioural problems of one sort or another. For example, foals may often develop stereotypes (crib-biting, wind-sucking, pacing and weaving) if isolated at weaning. They may also be bad-tempered, or in other ways less pleasant to manage, developing neuroses about particular stable procedures, (for example, having their stomachs or legs cleaned) which, if not carefully treated, may develop into phobias.

Effects of isolation.   The traumatic effects of isolation on later behaviour and its development in social mammals has been widely demonstrated ever since Harlow's (1959) historic experiments with infant monkeys. There is no reason to suggest that the horse is any exception to this rule. Thus, often the foal at weaning suffers a double trauma:

1. He is isolated from his mother with whom he has a particularly close relationship.
2. He is isolated from other members of his own, or even other species.

One of the reasons given for isolating foals at weaning is to socialise the animal to humans, by analogy to dogs where pups have been shown to socialise best with people if weaned and isolated from their siblings and mother at eight weeks (Scott and Marston 1950). The difference is, however, that usually the horse is *not* living in close association with the human (as is the case of the pups). If given sufficient attention at this stage, it is possible that this strategy could enhance trainability as a result of the foal being well socialised to people (although such a strategy would probably work better if the socialising process were begun much earlier). More often than not, however, the foal is deprived of both maternal *and* human contact for the majority of the time after weaning.

As a result, when foals are weaned and isolated from their mothers they become far less tractable and much more over-reactive and nervous, thus more difficult to handle than when they are kept with their mothers. I suggest that the best way of socialising the foal to benefit the next stage of its training, therefore, is:

1. Either to wean him and substitute a great deal of human contact (at least ten hours a day). Unfortunately most of us do not have the time for this; therefore, it is recommended that . . .

2. A foal be left with his mother where he can be handled and the early training done with her. Under these conditions he will be more relaxed and easier to handle and thus less likely to develop neuroses than when isolated.

The close relationship between mares and their foals leads to another important factor and that is that foals appear to learn a great deal from their mothers. For example, what to eat and where, general behaviour towards people, other species and so on. I have found that young animals raised at all times with their mothers and having had an opportunity to watch the mare being ridden, schooled and so on, have been extremely easy to train. They all showed a significant reduction in the training time required before first being ridden which is an indication of their quietness and quickness to learn compared to related but weaned youngsters (*Figure 5.8*). This may, in part, be due to familiarity with the routines as a result of watching their mothers. It is, of course, important to have a nice-mannered mother in this case, but it is not often that one wants to breed from mares that are not.

Thus, I would suggest that proper, responsible management, geared towards raising behaviourally well-balanced, well-mannered and quick learning youngsters, should *not* practice weaning. The foal is naturally weaned at between nine months and a year by the mother and her nutritional requirements to cope with longer lactation can normally be easily organised. The foal will also benefit from receiving small amounts of mother's milk, more than he would from the compensatory concentrate foods that are often fed to weaned foals.

No weaning of the foals will result in family groups composed of mares and different offspring of different ages. This is the type of horse group structure that is normally found when horses have the option of arranging their own social lives. This also benefits the two- to four-year-old since they are disciplined by their elders. A young horse only once takes the kind of liberties with his family group that he often takes with his contemporaries or, if isolated in groups of youngsters, with visiting humans. Many is the time I have been in fear of my life as a bunch of rearing, cavorting, kicking and bucking two- or three-year-old horses come roaring up to me in a field. Such behaviour if performed when they are with their elders is quickly sorted out with a sharp bite or kick. Next time they are more cautious and certainly generalise this caution to strange horses and human beings.

One objection to keeping horses in family groups is that management becomes more difficult in terms of, for example, feeding or other individual attention that the different group members require. Compared with farm livestock, however, even on large studs, the amount of individual attention each animal gets is very high. If one adds up the number of man hours of labour used for raising a horse without any training it works out very much higher than, for example, a cow. So what is all this labour doing if it is not handling the horses and giving them individual attention? I'm afraid the answer is that it is sweeping the yard or 'tidying up'. Now in many people's books, the welfare of the horse should come before the tidiness of the stud, unless we have got our priorities very wrong. Frequently it is a question of re-dispersing labour time.

There are many strategies that can be used to help with

individual feed requirements; for example, creep feeding, individual feed boxes or even catching and handling the youngsters for a short period each day while they eat their food – often the best investment of time and money for easy training later on.

Of course, there are exceptions to this rule, very old mares who have lost condition, or mares with behavioural defects that one does not want passed on, would be in this category. But at the same time, if weaning is practised, the responsibility of the weaner to the mare and foal must be recognised and a considerable amount of time put aside to substitute for mother's contact with the foal.

Frequently mare owners say to me 'Oh! I so dread weaning, I feel so hard hearted and cruel.' The answer is, 'Why do it then?' Just bear in mind, if you *do* do it, that indeed you *are* being hard-hearted and if cruelty is defined as causing distress and suffering, yes, you are also being cruel. And this cruelty may well result in permanent scars in the form of behavioural problems for the foal later on.

Another commonly held misconception is that mares cannot be used when lactating or with foal at foot. If the mare is suddenly isolated from the foal for the first time when the foal is three or four months old and used, then, indeed, she will behave badly and her concentration will be seen to lapse. However, if separation is made gradually, as discussed earlier, all will be well. Like all sensible horse management, it is a matter of combining commonsense and gradual training procedures.

The usual objection to this whole argument is 'Well, I have never had any trouble.' The fact of the matter is that *you* may not have noticed any trouble, but you may have sold potential trouble on. There is trouble, because horses continue to have behavioural problems, many of which can be traced back to around the weaning period. On the other hand, how much easier and nicer the horse might have been if you had not weaned it.

Do not believe that not weaning will guarantee a beautifully behaved animal; of course, it will not. Handling, training, all his other experiences throughout life are going to affect how the foal behaves, but sudden weaning is, I believe, an unnecessary practice which is an important factor in causing or precipitating behavioural problems, as it comes at a time of rapid physical and mental development when the young animal is particularly prone to emotional change.

The fact that so many horses manage to weather this particular management practice showing few permanent scars only points to the extreme adaptability of the horse.

SOLVING BEHAVIOURAL PROBLEMS

Foals like any young animals are at risk from disease. There are various diseases of foals, some of which have behavioural consequences, such as 'barking'. Here, however, we are considering behavioural problems with no obvious origin in the physical health of the foal. We have already mentioned that the foal may become fixated onto a protrusion or object in the stable if confined inside and unable to suckle. This need not develop further if the foal is suckled and the relationship with its mother re-established. If the mother dies, or is incapable of suckling the foal, then it may be necessary (but I would stress only as a last ditch measure) to find a foster mother or raise the foal on a bottle. In this case the first task is to get the foal to take the bottle. If he is more than a few days old, this will be difficult, since he has become imprinted on his mother as the only source of milk and it will be necessary to wait until he is very hungry indeed and then infinite patience will need to be exercised.

Bottle rearing.   Young mammals will take a bottle eventually if they learn to within three weeks of birth and if they are sufficiently hungry and great patience is exercised. It is quite pointless becoming frustrated or agitated, as the foal then also becomes agitated and is *less* likely to drink.

The first thing is to ensure that the foal obtains the taste of the milk by placing a few drops on the tongue. If the teat is hard and relatively small, like a mare's the foal is more likely to take it. Sometimes it helps to tuck the bottle and teat under a warm pliant article such as a cushion which the foal must then push under. Make sure the foal has to hold his head up in a similar way to when drinking from the mare.

If the foal persists in not sucking, then take a firm hold of him and place and keep the teat in his mouth while squeezing the bottle to release some milk and simultaneously moving the teat on the foal's tongue. After several swallows, the foal will usually start sucking – but he must be hungry. If all else fails a pediatric nurse who has skill in getting sleepy babies to suck may well manage to get the foal to take a bottle. Practise with calves and lambs or pups and babies is invaluable – it is a knack that has to be acquired.

Two points must be borne in mind when bottle rearing foals:

1. Foals have very small stomachs and normally suckle frequently during the day and take relatively little at each suckling. Thus very frequent small feeds are the most effective and successful. Special formulae are now manufactured for foals which, in the absence of mare's milk, can be used. However, if possible, taking some milk from another mare will benefit the foal more. Mares' milk is very high in sugars, and relatively low in fats and although cow's milk is not a good substitute it can be made adequate with skimming and the addition of glucose. It is vital that the foal obtains callostrum (the first milk).

2. The foal is a very social animal and normally has a very close relationship with his mother. Thus to isolate him in a stable for the majority of the time, or even to keep him with other orphan foals is to deprive him of essential relationships. It is best to allow him to stay with an older horse or, failing that, some other companion such as a goat or a dog, or even a human being with nothing much else to do – or bring him into the house!

Fostering.   It is possible to foster foals onto mares that have lost their foals and indeed there is now an agency in Britain specialising in putting one in touch with the other. It is also possible, but rather difficult, to foster a second foal onto a mare who already has one. This requires a complex series of actions soon after birth. It should only be attempted by competent people who know exactly how to do it.

The fostering of foals onto mares who have lost their foals involves careful management as well and a lot depends on how soon after birth the mare lost her offspring and how quickly she can be introduced to the new foal. Since mares recognise their foals using all senses, confusing her on several of these is important. The draping of her own foal's skin over the foal to be fostered so that he smells of it is one old way. However, blindfolding her (to reduce visual clues), using strong masking smells, or preventing her smelling (by temporarily anaesthetising the olfactory tract) are useful and sometimes necessary methods.

One of the main reasons why fostering foals is preferable to bottle rearing is because successful bottle rearing requires great skill and much time to ensure there are no behavioural problems thereafter. Potential problems arise because the foal will become 'imprinted' onto people and may never be treated by them with the level of roughness and discipline he would have in the horse group. The result is that the foal's horseplay may be directed to people and can of course injure them. Thus, occasionally strong discipline is essential but without frightening the youngster so that he becomes neurotic. Since the foal is already severely deprived and often does not have anything like sufficient social contact compared to his mother-reared peers, this means walking a tightrope between not frightening the foal and being a disciplining social partner. An over indulgent upbringing may not appear to be wrong until the young horse come in for training, or becomes sexually mature when he may direct all his sexual behaviour towards people!

A friend of mine once raised a giraffe on the bottle, and his exuberant greeting when he was two weeks old and 2.5m tall was a little difficult to cope with.

Another behavioural problem that occurs only later in horses is turning 'sour' or bad tempered. This is seen in mother-reared horses too and is the result of being handled, fed tit bits and generally fussed over, but never disciplined, by people. Thus, when people do start to ask the horse to do something, he decides not to and finds he is punished. This is a new experience and because the horse has no fear and has learnt no respect, he then attacks the person. This can be overcome by proper handling and sober treatment, even when well established in mature horses, but it is much easier not to let the foundations be established in the first place.

Summary

Courtship is prolonged and elaborate in horses and probably very important for conception.

It is important to recognise that mares usually will be the best judges of how to look after their foals and any disturbance either at foaling or the period after, when mutual imprinting so vital for the further survival of the foal is being established, is very undesirable and can lead to further problems. Rarely do mares reject their foals for physiological reasons, it is usually the result of mismanagement and can be avoided by following the reasoning given in this chapter. The foal is precocious and learns very rapidly indeed in the first few weeks of his life and it is possible to use some of this capacity to learn by teaching him appropriate behaviour very young, but after the imprinting period. This will help with his behavioural development in later life.

The relationship between mother and foal is particularly strong and well developed and should not be abused by a weaning process which is unnecessary and traumatic, if later behavioural problems are to be avoided.

The horse is a very adaptable species and it is quite remarkable how they often manage to be socially adaptable, charming companions despite backgrounds which should have turned them into raving maniacs! Nevertheless there are many horses with behavioural problems which could have been avoided. Many stemming from the time of weaning.

6 Horse Society

The question we shall address in this chapter is, how do horses and ponies organise their societies? This includes wild, feral (which includes the majority of the free range horses today) and domestic horses.

Why be social?

Horses are, of course, gregarious and social animals, but why? The answer must be that being social increases their survival value. How does this work? The answer to this question is more difficult. Two answers are usually advanced. In the first place there may be an advantage in terms of the distribution of food. Secondly, there may be an advantage in that it reduces the risk from predators.

FOOD DISTRIBUTION

Birds and primates, in particular, may be fussy eaters and their food may be found in isolated patches. In this case being in a group may help the individual to find the food, since more individuals are searching. On the other hand, there will be controls on how large the group can be, since if it is too large, the food may be finished before an individual arrives at it.

For horses however, the distribution of food is unlikely to be very important in inducing social behaviour because it is spread over a very large area and is equally available (or scarce) for all; rarely is there any need for competition over food for the horse in a natural environment. On the other hand because of the wide distribution of food, there is little disadvantage to horses being social, except perhaps where the food is very scarce and patchy, such as when covered by snow. Under these types of severe food shortage conditions, we find that horse herds do split up.

PREDATOR DEFENCE

There are pros and cons here too. For example, it is an advantage to the individual in a group for spotting, say, an approaching lion – several pairs of eyes and ears are better that one. At the same time a group of animals is easier for the predator to find than a single animal and, therefore, groups often attract more predators. On the other hand, the chances of the individual being taken out of the group are smaller as the group grows. So effectively, there is a trade off and groups will be as large as is likely to maximise the chances of the survival of the individual. This will depend on environmental circumstances and may change from time to time.

There is usually no reason for the survival of the individual horse to be jeopardised by living in a group on the grounds of food availability. Thus, it seems as if the main reason that horses are social is because it is to their individual advantage in terms of survival against predators. It may also help with finding a mate (although solitary and semi-solitary species, like the roe deer or dik dik of Africa, seem to manage in this respect).

Behaviour that has arisen to ensure the animal's survival is genetically programmed and is therefore unlikely to change rapidly although it may be ruffled around the edges. Horses are genetically programmed (like humans) to be social animals because it is advantageous to their survival and the breeding of the individual although they can adapt to live under many different social conditions as a result of their experiences during their lifetime.

In order to decide what the basic innate social organisation of the horse is, it is necessary to study herds of wild or feral horses. Unfortunately we do not have any truly wild horses left except possibly some of the Mongolian ponies, but there are many populations all over the world of feral horses and ponies and during the last decade these have been the subject of much study. As a result, we now have a good idea of how horses organise their societies, where their strongest bonds and loyalties lie and so on.

The Family

MARES

The most consistent factor from all these studies is that the bonds between family groups, based on the mare, are very strong and long lasting. The bond between mare and foal is particularly strong even when compared to other hoofed mammals. The foal will be naturally weaned by the mother at around nine months, or just before she gives birth to the next foal. However, if there is not much to eat, she may continue to suckle the yearling after having given birth to a new foal. Natural weaning is a slow and gradual process as we have already seen and the yearling will continue to remain closer to the mother than to any other horse until it is a two- and sometimes three-year-old. Thereafter, the young horse, if given the opportunity, will continue to show that his mother is high on the list of his preferred associates and this association, particularly between mother and daughter, will continue through their lives. (Wells and Goldsmidth-Rothchilde 1979; and Kiley-Worthington in preparation).

If the foal is a colt (and indeed sometimes a filly too) when it becomes pubertal at around 18 months it may be chased out of the breeding group by the stallion. The young males may then move off to form their own bachelor group, sometimes with some fillies.

Other strong preferences are sometimes shown by mares for other mares. In this case it is usually animals that are peers and have played and associated together when young and growing up, that are preferred as companions. However, these bonds tend to be less strong than those between the generations.

From my own research on domestic horses, over a ten-year period, we found that elder sisters (or brothers) and younger sisters (or brothers) tend to associate together more than would be expected (*Figure 6.1*) and this confirms what others have found in the study of feral horses. The family groups, consisting of a mare and her offspring, forms the stable social nucleus of horse society.

Figure 6.1.
Horseplay. A two-year-old colt and a yearling play wrestling and nipping games. Note the retracted nostrils and tense mouth of the two-year-old as the yearling tries to nip him.

THE STALLION

Horses are one of the species where only one male stays with a group of females and young. The stallion is very aggressive towards other mature males that may come near the mares and youngsters, particularly during the breeding season, although out of the breeding season, adult males and other breeding herds may come near or even mix in with the herd.

In the early 1960s when studying the Camargue horses I was offered a gelding to use as my transport. It very nearly cost me my life as I was ignorant at the time of the ways of stallions. One day I approached a stallion, whilst mounted on my gelding. The stallion rushed at my horse, feet flailing and teeth exposed as I, naively, tried to take notes! I had finally to give up the romantic notion of studying horse behaviour from horseback, having had a camera smashed and one set of precious notes trampled. This illustrates how sacrosanct the stallion considers an area around his herd against intrusion from other males, even castrated ones.

Normally geldings, colts and visiting stallions will withdraw from such an attack provided they are able to by having sufficient room. Often the result is that the stallion and mares and youngsters are in one part of the field, while the geldings and post-pubertal males and even one or two fillies are in another part.

There is no doubt that stallions can remain with family groups long enough for their own daughters to mature. Does the stallion then breed with his own pubertal daughters, or kick them out of the herd? Inbreeding is not always a bad thing biologically speaking.

For example, in many of the bee and social ant colonies all the individuals are related and they are very successful species. The answer to 'inbreeding – good or bad?' is, we don't know. But in my own experimental herd we have found that the stallion is very intolerant of young colts *and* young fillies between 1-year-old to 2½-years-old. After this age, he attacks them and chases them out of the group. Is this a mechanism to prevent incest? Does the stallion recognise them as his own daughters? Or is it just this one crazy stallion that does it? Nobody knows yet.

Herds

If food resources permit, many family groups may come together and form quite large herds at certain times of the year. Hence the zebras on the Serengeti in Tanzania come together in herds stretching as far as the eye can see. Yet, under duress, they will all split up into their small family groups.

From time to time in horse groups resident stallions may be threatened by a young male from a bachelor group and they will have a 'sparring match', fighting with their teeth and front legs. If the stallion is beaten, which will only be when he is getting too old or sick, then the young horse will remain and breed with the group.

Does the stallion gallop about the group herding the mares, protecting them and generally being the archetypal chauvinist? My studies in the Camargue and on domestic horses and several other studies on feral horses have shown that the stallion has often to play second fiddle and follow on after the mares who set the pace. (*Figure 6.2.*) The exception is when there is the threat of another male approaching the mares. Then the resident stallion will attempt to herd the mares away with great determination by galloping around them with his ears laid flat back, his chin extended and his head moving up, down and around on the neck, giving the impression of a snake.

As we have mentioned, unlike many other species of large territorial herbivores, the stallion is resident with the mares for years and forms strong bonds with them. This was brought home to me when I took my stallion and a number of mares he lived with to a show. Although he is normally perfectly behaved and relaxed and can be ridden out with his own and strange mares, in season or not, without any trouble I was unprepared for the fuss he would make when his mares went off to different classes and he was surrounded by other strange horses. What made him behave so atrociously in a ridden horse class was not his mares going away, which is mildly upsetting but something he was very used to, but them going off with *other* horses without him being able to do anything about it!

If an animal is social, then there must be mechanisms for keeping the group together, of cementing the bonds between

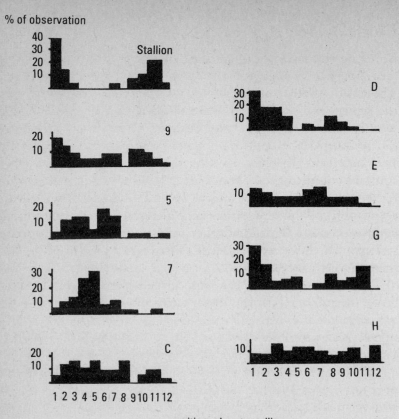

Figure 6.2
Leadership in the Camargue horse. The percentage of time that different mares and the stallion were in different positions when travelling in single file. The stallions tended to be either towards the front or towards the rear. The mare H showed little preference, but the mare 7 travelled usually in 4th or 5th place. Each horse is different and there is no straightforward pattern. (Adapted from Wells *et al* 1979.)

individuals and communicating between them. Having described (*Chapter 3*) how horses communicate, now we will look at the roles of the individuals and how social organisation works on their level.

Dominance and Affiliation

Thinking about social organisation of groups of animals the first idea that springs to mind is of 'dominance' or 'pecking order'. The idea that there was one animal who was 'boss' and controlled the group and that every other animal had its place in the 'dominance hierarchy' arose from some work in Germany (Schjelderup-Ebbe 1913) on chickens and was then used to try and understand certain primate societies. Such species have constant competition for food which is dispersed in patches and for which they have to search. In order to cut down direct aggression and fights, a 'dominance hierarchy' where one animal defers without a fight to another might well be an appropriate strategy. On the other hand such a social set up pre-supposes that there is constant competition for a restricted resource. The idea of 'dominance hierarchy' was then applied to every other species under the sun as it is a nice simple idea and is now bandied about and used as an explanation for much behaviour by too many people who misunderstand the concept, thinking there is little else to how animal societies are organised.

Very frequently horse owners will tell me, when talking about their horse, all about the 'dominance hierarchy' in their group of horses; much less often can they tell me about the 'affiliative' relationships (who likes whom most) between their animals.

Social Cohesion

In a species such as a large grazing herbivore where there is no inter-individual competition for food and rarely for other resources for most of the time, it is very unlikely that the dominance hierarchy, which has apparently evolved to reduce conflict between individuals, would be the prime mover in organising society as there is seldom any conflict. Should we not rather consider that the behaviour which will be primarily important is that geared to keep the group together? This must be *affiliative behaviour*.

As a result of thinking about this, I decided to measure affiliative behaviour and any behaviour which could be construed as aggressive, or behaviour relating to dominance as

Performed	Aggression	Affiliation	Total performance	Total socially involved (performed + received)
Adult mares (7)	92	147	239	464
Yearlings (fillies) (2)	59	192	251	485
Geldings (2)	56	66	122	193
Foal (colt) (1)	29	239	268	454
Stallion (1)	134	335	469	640
Total	370	979	1349	1236

Receive			Total received	Receiver or Performer? Ratio to P to R
Adult mares	140	85	225	1·06 Receiver
Yearlings	198	36	234	1·07 Receiver
Geldings	41	30	71	1·71 Performer
Foal	167	19	186	1·44 Performer
Stallion	141	30	171	2·74 Performer
Total	687	200	887	

Figure 6.3

The total interactions between horses in a group of thirteen, both at pasture and in a yard. The horses were recorded for 288 hours. There are less aggressive encounters (and in this category we place all behaviour that might be related to assessing 'dominance' such as withdrawals, determined aggressive approach, slight ear withdrawal and so on) than affiliative behaviour. This indicates that *cohesive or friendly behaviour may be far more important in social organisation than most people think.*

If we look at the figures for the total number of interactions performed, we find that the stallion performed most of all types of interactions, the foal next and the geldings least. However, the yearlings received most encounters, and they were mostly aggressive. The mares received next most and the geldings the least.

We can then ask if certain animals or groups of animals tend to be primarily performers and others receivers. We can represent this as a ratio. All the groups perform more than they receive (this is because it was not always clear who the behaviours were directed at), but it is the geldings and the stallion who show a disproportionate ratio in favour of performing. We have individual records on all these behaviours and many more which are neither obviously aggressive or affiliative and can take this analysis much further. Even this far it does show that the relationship between age and sex groups is much more complicated than was previously thought (Figures are the numbers of that behaviour per horse.)

observed in cattle and horses at grass and in yards. We found that there was more affiliative behaviour in both species than aggressive behaviour (*Figure 6.3*).

Thus, although affiliative behaviour in horses has not received much attention to date (because it is more difficult to see perhaps), nevertheless, it is very important. In fact, I would suggest affiliative behaviour is the most important thing in causing groups to stay together.

However, when the situation is changed, when there is, for example, a conflict over a source of food or space, or some other resource, then indeed we see more aggressive behaviour and behaviour related to dominance than affiliation. In such groups it is possible to work out a 'dominance hierarchy' (Houpt and Keiper 1980).

But we must not forget that what we are looking at is the result of a particular and different set of conditions from those that the horse encounters every day. Confinement and isolation do increase aggression (Kiley-Worthington 1977) and an increase in aggression may well lead to a more obvious and better developed dominance hierarchy, but do not let us conclude from this that a 'dominance hierarchy' is very important in normal horse society.

Horses do show strong preferences for other individual horses – as anyone who has looked after horses knows – and they also show dislikes. Our data shows this.

Personality Profiles

To take it one step further and try to find out how horses relate to each other and to people we spent 288 hours recording every type of interaction of every horse of a group of thirteen with every other that we could (*Figure 6.4*). From this we found that there were other important aspects of personality, such as how much the individual was involved in social contact. Another factor is that some animals receive more messages than others. We have called them 'receivers' and yet others perform more actions than they receive; they are 'performers'. By scoring all these indexes for the herd of thirteen horses we have been able to build up simple personality 'profiles' (*Figure 6.5*), of the horses in company of others.

Withdraw, Kick,* tail swish,* bum turn,* bite,* head shake,° head nod,
° watch,° head extend,* ears back, nose wrinkle,† nicker,† neigh,† squeal,
° leg strike,* ears prick,† lick head or neck,† suckle,† lick back or loins,
† smell, °other, † groom other horse, snort,° ignore,° approach,† champ.
  More than one can of course be performed at once. (Thirteen horses in
the group, recorded for 288 hours, a total number of interactions recorded
8,177)

* – aggressive
† – affiliative
° – other interactions not yet analysed

Figure 6.4
List of the behaviours scored in observations on interactions between
thirteen horses

There were many points of interest arising from this work in
relation to horse communication as well as social organisation.
For example, foals and other young animals tended not to be
very socially involved and did not display to other animals very
much, but they did tend to be the centre of attention from others,
not only their mothers.

These observations will, I hope, be a start in the study of
individual personality in the horse and I am sure we can become
much more sophisticated at this than we are at present.

As far as understanding horses and training them goes it is
vitally important to realise that successful training, handling and
riding comes through *co-operation* – not being 'dominant' to the
horse. It is also vital to understand that the stallion is not by
nature 'dominant'. In fact as we have seen in the group, he has
very little control over the others except when there are strange
stallions about. He follows along and often seems to be trying to
integrate himself with the group, but is rejected by the mature
horses and has to make do with hovering around the edge and
playing with the foals. (*Figure 6.6.*)

Practically no horses are naturally aggressive but they can be
made that way if training is based on 'overcoming' the horse to
show who is dominant rather than on a proper understanding of
how their rather more complex and relaxed organisation works.
Of prime importance are individual preferences between horses

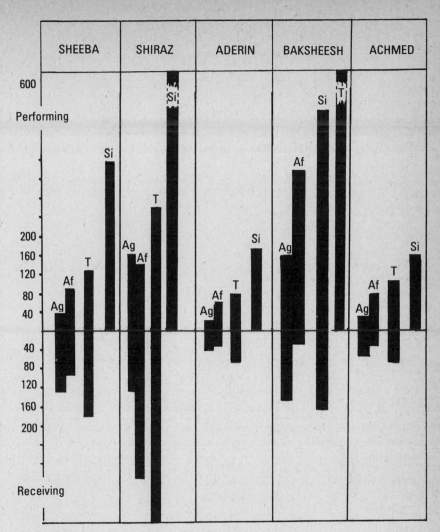

Figure 6.5

Personality 'profiles' of three mares, Sheeba, Shiraz and Aderin; a stallion, Baksheesh; and a gelding (son of Aderin), Achmed. Note how different the three mares are and how some horses are predominantly receivers (for example, Shiraz) and some performers (Baksheesh) and yet others not very socially involved at all (Aderin and Achmed)

Ag = aggressive actions
Af = affiliative actions
T = total performed or received
Si = total social involvement score (all performed and received)

Figure 6.6
Normal well balanced socialised stallions do not hurt foals. (*Top*) a wild Camargue stallion rests after playing with one of his sons. (*Bottom*) an Anglo–Arab stallion plays with his yearling colts

and this can be extended to humans. Make sure therefore that you are *liked*, not *dominant!*

The 'showing off' in horses that Lucy Rees (1983) observed as being a 'dominance display' is not that; it is merely *joie de vivre*, like children rushing around screaming when let out of school. Horses happen to do it by raising their heads and tails and galloping or strutting about; it is our interpretation that is wrong. There is little bluff in real conflicts between two competing stallions or mares and very few gentlemanly niceties; they are out to hurt each other and sometimes they do. That is not to say that two stallions cannot relate well and in a relaxed way to each other at other times.

I have kept Arab and Thoroughbred adult breeding stallions together out at grass and with geldings with no problems. There may well be competition for mares however if they are also placed with the group. It must also be remembered that most breeding stallions these days are not normally socially adapted horses. They have often been raised in semi-isolation from other horses since weaning – as we have seen (*Chapter 5*) often a traumatic process – and, in addition, they are kept throughout their lives with no facilities for any normal contact with other horses. Such horses can and often do become 'psychopaths'. The tragedy is that many horse owners really believe that these horses are by nature aggressive and difficult animals that will kill foals and other horses that come near them! If that were the case in the wild, how would horses ever perpetuate themselves? Of course such behaviour is usually the result of mismanagement and lack of understanding of horse behaviour.

Preferences

Although horses predominantly associate in family groups when allowed to, and these are long lasting and stable relationships, nevertheless, there is contact between individuals outside family groups, and horses do form relationships with non-relatives.

In fact most domestic horses only have the opportunity to develop such relationships. Most horse keepers are aware that their horses 'like' some of the others, and dislike others; in fact they have preferences of association. One way this can be

Figure 6.7
The relationship between individuals in the experimental herd based on the interactions between individuals: *affiliative* (likes) and **aggressive** (dislikes). Only the numbers of aggressive or affiliative actions between pairs that are significantly higher than the average are shown. For example Crystal aggresses Aisha 36 times, Omeya 40 times, Willow 107 times and Stardust 59 times. All of these are much higher than the average which for Crystal is 348/13 = 26·7. Crystal also shows more affiliation for Baksheesh than expected (25, compared with an expected figure of 7·8).

(All the figures set in **bold** = aggressive behaviour; in *italic* = affiliative behaviour.)

PERFORMER		Total	Cryst	Sh
Adult mares	Crystal	**348** *102*	■	
	Sheeba	**380** *89*	**33**	■
	Aderin	**54** *37*		
	Shiraz	**397** *121*	**33** *20*	
2 yr old fillies	Shereen	**183** *123*		
	Aisha	**140** *161*		
Geldings	Jim	**71** *62*		
	Achmed	**146** *71*		
Lactating mare	Omeya	**140** *319*		
Colt foal	Omani	**34** *239*		
Stallion	Baksheesh	**258** *335*		
Adult mares (new)	Willow	**33** *31*		
	Stardust	**29** *11*		
	Grand Total	**2,213** *1,802*		

assessed is by finding out who one horse's nearest neighbours are over prolonged periods of time (for example this was done for mares and foals, *Figure 5.7*).

Another way is by measuring all the interactions between members of a group. This I did with our horses (*Figure 6.7*) over a 288 hour period of observation. It shows well that the horses have very obvious 'likes', and indeed, 'dislikes' (shown by aggressive behaviour) towards other individuals. We can see that there is no doubt but that the newcomers, Willow and Stardust, are disliked by four other horses and no horse shows a significant amount of affiliative behaviour towards them. Thus, they are not well integrated into the group. They show no great effort,

...ri	Shira	Shere	Aisha	Jim	Achme	Omeya	Omani	Baksh	Will	Stard
RECEIVER										
			36			40		25	107	59
		37 *33*	47				36		69	61
	■					241 *62*		24		32
		■	34 *59*				35 *55*		43	
		53	■				37		57	34
				■						
		32			■		34			
	81 *182*					■	57	61		
		55	42			105	■			
	69	44	37			130		■		
									■	
										■

apparently, to integrate since they do not act in a very friendly manner to the others (Willow 31, Stardust 11 total of 'friendly' efforts).

Of the rest of the group, many of whom are related (*Figure 6.8*) and all had lived together for two years at least, there are varying dislikes and likes. For example, the old mare Sheeba (mother of Shiraz and Shereen) only shows a significant liking for her two-year-old daughter, Shereen, and even this is tempered by a significant amount of aggression towards her! She dislikes Crystal, Aisha (the other filly) and the colt foal Omani, as well as the two new mares. By contrast Shiraz, her five-year-old daughter, has an ambiguous relationship with the mares Crystal

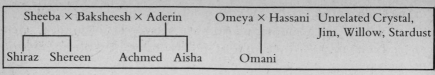

Figure 6.8
Familial relationships within the group

and Omeya, showing more affiliative and aggressive actions towards them, but she just plain likes the stallion, Baksheesh, her father. The stallion likes the old mare Sheeba, their daughter Shiraz and Omeya, but not the others, although Crystal likes him a lot! The two geldings keep a low profile, although Achmed (Aisha's brother and son of Aderin) does show friendliness towards his sister, but dislikes the colt foal Omani, and so on. . . .

The ambiguous relationships are not uncommon; for example, there are five relationships when the individual is both more aggressive and more affiliative towards another; very like human families. There is also a tendency for the likings to be mutual, 7 out of the 19 significant ones are. In other words, if you are nice, other horses will be nice to you. Retaliation does not necessarily follow nastiness though.

What does all this mean? Primarily, that the relationships between horses are just as complex as between people, and to describe them in simple terms, such as 'dominance hierarchy' is inadequate and pointless. I have known this group for twelve years now and some have grown up, had their foals and their foals had foals now. I have handled, looked after, trained, ridden, driven and competed on them, as well as studied them professionally and I suppose I know them as well as anyone knows a group of horses. Yet I still cannot describe a 'dominance hierarchy'. There is indeed an aggressive hierarchy. But what does this tell us about how each relates to every other? The more information one has, the more clear it becomes that these relationships are complex, intricate and subtle.

Growing up a Horse

The young horse remains with his family group until he is about a two-year-old (or 2½ if fillies), but even then such youngsters are still deeply involved with their mothers (for example, Shereen and Aisha with Sheeba and Aderin respectively. *Figure 6.7*). They are then usually forced out of the group by the stallion. He may accept some of the fillies and let them stay, but the others must leave.

As we have seen horses do not naturally associate in groups of one age although cattle do. Even the bachelor groups have old and young males in them as far as we know. But we know little about these as in all the feral populations that have been studied so far, the extra males are castrated or removed. The bonds between generations are normally stronger than those within generations.

On large studs groups of yearlings, two- and three-year-olds, are often kept in separate year groups with no adult company. Such groups of young animals are unruly, undisciplined and unpredictable. Such practice works well with cattle however since they normally have very strong bonds *within* generations. By contrast, if horses are kept with their normal family group, equine discipline will be instilled and the animals will learn with whom and when they can play; they will learn to be cautious, but not particularly scared when approaching other horses (*Figure 6.9*) or another species, such as people.

Young horses also learn much from their mothers as a result of the close relationship they have with them. Thus, if the mother is friendly and relaxed with people, the youngster will see and imitate this behaviour towards people which will make training easier and quicker.

We compared the time required by the same trainers, using the same methods, to train two groups of horses up to the time for first mounting. The two groups were:
1. The unweaned foals raised in the family groups.
2. The weaned youngsters living away from their mothers from eight months old.

The weaned horses required a greater training time before first mounting, and this was significant (*Figure 6.10*). Of course these data are only preliminary, and we need a larger sample size, however it suggests that weaning and group living can effect other aspects of behaviour, such as learning and relating to human beings.

Figure 6.9
A three-year-old mare (*right*) greeted by a stallion. The young mare is cautious and although wishing to nose-to-nose smell him, extends her head to keep the rest of her body away in case she needs to rush off

One of the objections to the keeping of horses in groups instead of singly stabled is that it is more difficult to feed them individually; and because of this individuals may not receive enough attention. After six years of testing and modifying, I find our group system very easy to manage and each animal can have his own ration if they are tied at feeding time. With such a system, an added advantage is that there is far less manual work, the extra time available can then be spent by the groom on extra handling, and relating to the horses.

In this way we have found that top-class Arab racing horses and long distance, dressage and display horses can be raised to be easily managed and socially balanced, relaxed horses that can be taken anywhere and will always fit in. I remember one Arab flat race meeting I attended and insisted on putting our two competitive horses in one stable. The look of horror on the faces of the stable manager and other competitors turned to one of consternation when they found that one was a mare and the other a stallion; we won the race the next day though!

Mare	Stallion	Foals	Hrs handled 1st summer	Hrs lunged etc	Total hrs to 1st mount
Not weaned		1) Achmed	5	3	8
Aderin 12·2 hh	Backshesh Anglo-	2) Amy	sold at 10 mths	—	—
Welsh mountain	Arab 15·2 hh	3) Alia	3	4	7
		4) Aisha	2	5	7
Sheeba	,,	5) Shiraz	5	4	9
(15·2 hh)	,,	6) Marleesh	2	4	6
Cob	,,	7) Shereen	1	6	7
Melanie	,,	8) Bakini	3	5	8
15·2 hh	,,	9) Masad	2	4	sold
Thoroughbred	,,				
				mean = 7·4 hrs to 1st mount	
Weaned at 8 months Mary 16 hh Cob	,,	1) Snip	4	16	20
Lilith 15 hh Lippizzan Cob	,,	2) Lashley	4	15	19
				mean = 19·5 hrs to 1st mount	

The means are significantly different: $p < 0.01$ (t test)

Figure 6.10
The difference in the training time required to achieve first mounting compared for 11 related horses, some weaned some not. Less than half the time is required if the horses are left with their mothers and not weaned

Summary

The main points of this chapter are:

Horses are gregarious animals who normally associate in family groups with one stallion and several mares and their foals, yearlings and two- to three-year-olds.

The relationships between horses are deep and long lasting and they show obvious preferences and dislikes of individuals. Only in abnormal, confined and restricted conditions, or when there is severe competition for a scarce resource, is a 'dominance hierarchy' evident or important. In wild or pastured horses, this is very rare. Horses usually show as much, if not more, affiliative or cohesive behaviour as behaviour that can be related to 'dominance', aggression or social dispersal.

They also have individual personalities which as riders we may know, but now we are beginning to be able to measure and outline how and where they are different.

Young horses stay with their parents up until around two- to $2\frac{1}{2}$-years-old and bonds between generations are very strong and long lasting. During their growing up they are disciplined and taught basic equine social etiquette by their elders. There are indications that raising young horses in their normal family groups makes them easier to train and perhaps more relaxed.

It is possible that an understanding of horses normal social organisation can help us redesign environments better suited to the horse's psychological needs.

7 Feeding Behaviour and Digestion

Until very recently, nutritionists who have studied how to feed our domestic animals, have almost totally ignored the behavioural variables that will affect what is eaten and how much of it. They have done tests (and indeed still do) on animals in what are called 'metabolic crates' and found that they grow at a certain rate if fed a certain product, and then tell the farmer how he must feed his livestock. Often such information is quite irrelevant on the farm because it does not take into account the behavioural variables; for example, the amount and what is eaten depends on whether the animal is alone or not, who he is with and his own age, sex and so on. It also depends on what is on offer, his own past experience, including what he may have learnt from his mother or other social partners. It is a very complicated subject and horse nutritionists and manufacturers of horse foods are just as guilty as any other livestock producer in not taking into account all these behavioural variables. The fact is we do not know exactly how such variables are inter-related in any animal, let alone the horse.

The task in this chapter is then, to point out what the variables are and how they can affect feeding.

One of the areas that has been the subject of research recently is how to feed horses for particular tasks – particularly racing. Many of the diets recommended by nutritional advisers and feed merchants emphasise the importance of compounded diets and feeding of extra supplements. The advertisements can convince the naive that the feeding of these particular 'equi . . .' products will almost guarantee that the race or show will be won. Perhaps

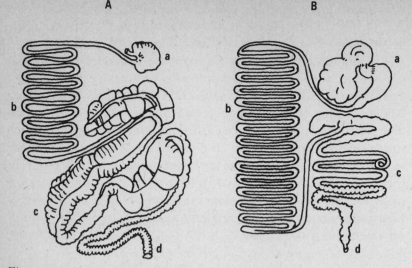

Figure 7.1
Comparison of the digestive tract of A, a pony (body length 164 cm)
and B, a sheep (body length 110 cm). The ponies digestive tract differs
in having a smaller stomach having a shorter small intestine, and having
a very enlarged caecum and colon (the large intestine). This is where
most of the digestion takes place. (Adapted from Sisson 1977.)

because of the emphasis on competition horse-keepers appear to
be particularly gullible to such hard sell techniques. The result is
they almost *dare* not feed these marvel supplements and additives
in case the horse might be disadvantaged.

Although the physiology of the horse's digestion and growth
is partly understood, it still requires a great deal more research.
For example, whether or not electrolytes are essential for top
performance in racing and long distance events. It is probable
that there are as many problems of health, both physical and
mental, in the horse that arise from overfeeding, or feeding of
unbalanced diets which are supplement rich, as from
underfeeding.

The anatomy of digestion

It is well known that the anatomy of the horse's digestive tract is
designed to allow it to digest and extract nutrients from food that

is high in fibre and relatively low in nutrients, such as proteins and carbohydrates. There are some unique characteristics of the horse's digestion (*Figure 7.1*) which allow it to do this.

The horse's teeth are the first of these characteristics in that they are adapted to allow grinding of plants so that the cellulose cell walls of the plants can be crushed. To do this the horse has to have many flat teeth, and therefore a long face to house them in. The teeth become very worn as they are used a great deal, much more than those of humans for example, so the evolutionary answer to usage is to keep the teeth growing slightly throughout the horse's life. Some herbivores have a different solution – the elephant, for example, develops new sets of teeth at the back of its mouth which are then gradually pushed forward by another set throughout the elephants life.

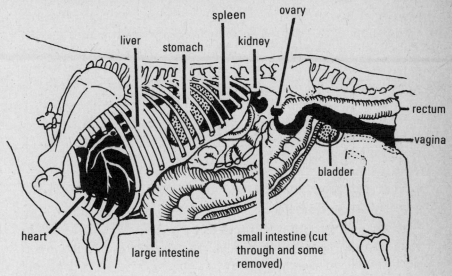

Figure 7.2
The topography of the gut of a mare showing the positions of the various organs. Note in particular that the heart is more or less the same size as the stomach. The lungs, which cover all the area under the ribs, have been removed. The enormous intestines take up almost the entire abdomen.
L = liver; SP = spleen; ST = stomach; K = kidney; O = ovary; B = bladder; V = vagina; R = rectum; LI = large intestine; SI = small intestine (cut through and some removed). (Adapted from Sisson 1977.)

Grinding food can only be achieved by a sideways movement of the horse's jaw. This, therefore, is the main jaw action and needs large muscles to do it. After grinding, food is swallowed and travels down the oesophagus to the stomach. The remarkable thing about the stomach of the horse (quite different from a cow for example) is that it is very small. In fact it is only just bigger than the horse's heart! This is very surprising in a herbivore who usually has to have an enormous stomach (or, in the case of a cow, several), to store the vast quantity of food they have to take in. How does the horse manage to digest this enormous quantity of bulky food? It does it mainly in the very long large intestine behind the stomach (*Figure 7.2*).

Another unique characteristic is the first part of the horse's digestive tract. Its construction means the horse cannot vomit, so material that has been swallowed accumulates in the stomach and because of a system of one way valves, cannot be released back up the throat. It must therefore pass all the way through the long digestive tract to the anus. If the horse has eaten anything harmful, therefore, it cannot be sicked back up. Why have this risky mechanism? At the moment there does not seem to be a good answer to this question; presumably there is a disadvantage in allowing material to be regurgitated or vomited but what this is has yet to be explained satisfactorily. In any event, for the horse such a disadvantage must outweigh the advantage.

Not being able to vomit, there are other ways in which the horse ensures protection from taking in unsuitable substances and these are behavioural. If the animal learns quickly what to eat and what not to eat and is very fussy about what he eats, then there is less risk of eating the wrong food.

Selection and Nutritional Wisdom

Food selection is very complicated and, to date, we are only beginning to scratch the surface as far as understanding it is concerned.

Nutritional wisdom is the notion that the animal has some way of knowing either when something is poisonous, or when there is a dietary surfeit or deficiency. He will then act appropriately to correct the problem, by avoiding or seeking out the substance.

This nutritional wisdom normally works rather well in horses kept at pasture and presented with the types of food and textures normally encountered in the wild. This behaviour works less well and breaks down when processed concentrates are given to the horse. There is too the learning effect here. The young horse is always cautious in eating if the food is a new substance or plant or even a tit bit; the horse will (wisely, since getting it wrong may mean he does not get another chance) take initially very small portions and only after repeated exposure to the substance will he tuck in. Once, however, the horse has learnt that the substance is good and does no harm, he will eat almost without a thought. This is dangerous as once the horse has learnt that the food in the food bin is delicious and does no harm, he can often be fed (and will gulp down) materials that *will* do him no good at all. Here, the results of conditioning have overcome the horse's natural caution. This may be an explanation of the rather unexpected results which convinced Houpt (1979) that horses were bad at learning what *not* to eat.

Another way horses apparently learn to select their diet is by imitation. The close association of mare and foal allows the foal to learn much of what to eat from its mother. This can result in horses, raised in certain environments where there are poisonous plants, not being poisoned although new horses to the area may be. With highly poisonous material it is difficult to learn what not to eat except by imitating others because if you get it wrong with one trial, you die!

Apart from selecting material that is good for them, horses will, of course, select food material which they like the texture and taste of. All grazing mammals are highly selective and all of them have slightly different criteria with which they select their food.

There are very many factors that can affect selection. For example, the digestible quality of the available fodder, taste, physical form and learning. These facters may confound innate preferences and may or may not be related to the nutrient value of what they select. The stage of growth, spcific parts of the plant, as well as the species are important in selection. Archer (1973) found that horses ate a much larger variety of plants, particularly many of the broad leafed plants, than was previously expected.

To some extent the selection of plants depends on the age and sex of the animal; for example, foals are inefficient grazers and they tend to pick off the tops of flowering grasses. This means that their diet contains more of the carbohydrates and proteins stored in the seeds, so at particular time of the year or when the grass is mature and high in fibre, they obtain a more nutritive diet than adult horses, which graze predominantly at the base of the sward. However, when the grass is young and growing this is not the case.

The sex of an animal can affect its grazing pattern. This has been reported in the scientific literature for both horses and sheep. Certainly the stallion, whose grazing is interrupted during the mating season, has not only his time spent grazing affected, but also *what* he eats, although this has not yet been studied.

Selection is, to some extent, dependent on the variety and type of flora available. When there is not very much else to eat, horses will eat unpalatable species of plant, or even sometimes poisonous plants. It is therefore important to see that there are no poisonous plants in a paddock, particularly if it is going to be heavily grazed. The presence of a disliked species of plant can also affect where animals graze. Areas around these species will be left. There are also individual differences between horses in selection. We all know horses that will not eat certain things and others that will. Some of this variation is the result of all these factors above – but some just because they have individual aversions.

It was originally thought that the main factor controlling selection was digestibility, that all animals would choose the most digestible plants and parts of the plant from the sward (Blaxter 1967). However, we now know that this is not the case and that some animals and species will actually prefer and choose the less digestible herbage depending on all these other factors we have mentioned. It is a balance between *all* these factors which results in what the horse chooses to eat.

There are, however, some differences between species on this score mainly because of the anatomy and physiology of the digestive tract. Horses are able to cope with a large amount of fibre in their diet. In fact, with their long intestines, they are naturally adapted to digest fibre and to keep eating bulky food. It is as well to remember this whatever expectations people have of their horses.

One of the main reasons for many behavioural problems in the horse is the interference with what the horse is adapted to eat, what he is given, and how much time he needs to eat, compared with the time he has available.

On planted 'ley' pastures that are composed of only very few highly productive and nutritious grasses and perhaps clover, horses as well as other livestock will frequently be seen grazing in the hedgerows and in the corners which have not been ploughed and reseeded. This, it appears, is the result of a 'monotony factor'. Here the animals are seeking out different tastes and textures or perhaps even less digestible material than their normal menu. This is rather like someone craving old dry bread when fed exclusively on roast beef.

How long do horses spend eating?

Because the stomach of the horse is small, it stores little food, unlike the four stomachs of the cow where large amounts of food are stored for digestion later. The result of this is that the horse must spend much time grazing, or eating food if it is to obtain enough. The time horses spend grazing or eating is therefore considerable. It has been estimated (Caison *et al* 1983) at 16 hours a day and my own studies confirm this. By contrast, cattle spend from eight to ten hours a day eating and about eight hours ruminating, the function of which is to grind up the regurgitated material to facilitate digestion.

The horse does all this grinding when he eats, so eating is relatively slow and then the material passes down through the stomach and there is a constant flow through first the small intestine where digestive juices work on the material and then through the large intestine where further breaking down of the material and absorption of nutrients occurs. Compared to cattle the horse eats slowly and for longer periods of time. Cattle eat relatively fast and then can retire to places of safety and at their leisure ruminate the food. This can be tested simply by giving a similar sized pony and cow an equal amount of hay, the cow will have finished when the pony is about half way through.

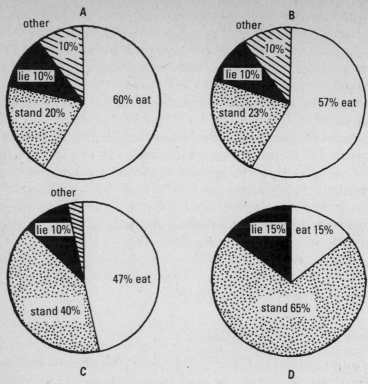

Figure 7.3
How do horses spend their time?
A: The average time budgets for Camargue horses throughout the year. (After Duncan 1980.)
B: Time budgets for a group of eight horses in a yard with *ad libitum* hay and straw
C: The time budgets for three horses in individual stables fed *ad libitum* hay and straw and able to see and touch each other
D: Time budgets for horses in stables where they cannot touch each other and only see each other over stable doors; they were fed restricted fibre (about 3 kg/day, horses of 15·2–16 hh)

One would expect that the time spent grazing would be dependent on the availability of food, thus a horse with masses of palatable grass around would spend less time grazing than one on a rather bare sward. To a degree this is true, but it appears that both in cattle and horses, the time spent grazing does not depend on the availability of pasture half as much as one would expect. In cattle, the time can be increased by about three hours on very bare pasture and reduced by an hour or so on plentiful pasture. We do not yet have many figures for horses, but it appears to be a similar story; a horse will increase his grazing time by about 2 to 3 hours on a bare paddock and reduce it a little on a plentiful one, but there is a maximum and a minimum time that horses will spend grazing and this is not dependent on other factors; it seems to be internally programmed.

In terms of management this means that if horses are put out in a pasture full of palatable herbage, they will not stop grazing when they have had enough, but will continue until they have spent about 14 hours grazing. The result of this, as many of us know, is that they grow far too fat and are at risk from diseases involving the balance of protein in the body, such as laminitis. Similarly, if the horse is in a paddock that is rather bare, he will *not* burn the midnight oil to try to scrape a living; he will stop searching for food and stop eating after about 18 hours, go hungry and grow thinner (*Figure 7.3*).

How much does a horse eat?

The curious thing is that the total intake of food consumed by a horse at pasture has never been measured although there are quite sophisticated and easy techniques of doing this available. Manuals published by the British Horse Society, for example, have tables of what horses 'should get' depending on work, but again no information of how much they *will* actually eat. Some opinion believes that a horse will eat much more then does a cow of similar weight. In my view this is incorrect, and until we have some good scientific results on this it is safer to assume that horses eat about the same amount per kilogram live weight. A rough estimate of the total weight of fibrous material that a horse of about 500 kg (15·2 hh middleweight) will eat is around 13·5 kg over 24 hours with free access. This works out, for most practical purposes, at around 75 per cent of a small rectangular bale of hay or straw. This varies from horse to horse and also with its physiological demands. If the horse is lactating, pregnant or using a great deal of energy, it may eat more, but we do not really know how much more. We have no reliable information on how much horses eat when at grass.

8 Grazing and Grassland Management

We do know that horses are more 'wasteful' of their pasture than cattle and that it is easier to mismanage a horse grazed pasture and gradually reduce the amount of grazing available. The reason for this is not because horses eat more, but because they have different defaecation patterns from cattle. As we have already seen (*Chapter 3*) horse droppings are an important source of chemical messages (pheromones). They are frequently smelt by all ages and sexes and are deposited in particular places. Cattle, by contrast tend to scatter their muck over the field. Mares will smell others' droppings and then defaecate themselves; stallions, by contrast, will smell their own muck or that of another stallion and then move forward and defaecate. The result of this is that mares and geldings have areas of the field which are latrines and these tend to spread; stallions have piles in restricted areas of the field, often outside the latrine area used by the mares.

Thereafter the horses will not eat around the faeces. The biological reason for this is probably to reduce the risk of reinfection from parasites. Most intestinal parasites do not migrate far from the faeces and so this works well in a free range environment. Not eating around the faeces and the constant deposition of nutrients from them, leads to quicker growth and eventually to a different floral composition in the latrine areas than in the rest of the field. In the New Forest for example, thistles and ragwort became much more common in the latrines (Edwards and Wallis 1982) and different grasses became established.

Oldberg and Francis Smith (1977) found that it was the actual presence of the faeces that the horses were avoiding. Grass picked from the latrine areas would be readily eaten when it was presented to the horses without the faeces. Collecting faeces from paddocks (which is sometimes advised and practised, although only where there is a lot of cheap labour) will not overcome this development of latrines as all trace of the droppings cannot be removed and the presence of urine is also important.

Because of the mucking behaviour of mares and geldings the latrines grow, and more and more of the grazing area becomes unavailable. The rest of the field, the 'lawns' consequently shrink. As they have more grazing pressure, their floral structure changes and they have typically very short grass. This is where the horses graze most of the time (*Figure 8.1*).

Various strategies have been suggested to overcome this

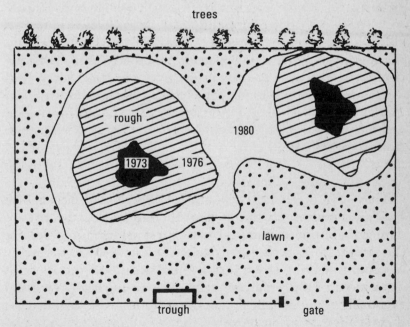

Figure 8.1
The spread of defaecation areas (roughs) in a field exclusively grazed by horses with no grassland management from 1976 to 1980. As the roughs expand, the lawns receive more and more grazing pressure and the carrying capacity declines

development in horse grazed paddocks, largely because the paddocks can support fewer horses year by year. I had experience of this where two paddocks grazed exclusively by horses on our farm boundary carried initially one 16 hh cob per two acres for nine months a year without subsidiary feeding. At the end of five years, the latrine areas had grown large and the growth on the lawns was retarded by trampling and continual grazing. The same area could support only one horse per four acres. Over a four year period we managed it with a mixed species grazing programme and succeeded in increasing its carrying capacity and reducing (if not totally eliminating) the distinction between latrines and lawns. The field, again, carried an equivalent of 2·5 similar sized horses per acre, including some grass cut for hay.

However even after re-seeding, the latrine areas were not completely eliminated. Now it has returned to exclusively horse grazing and the carrying capacity has already dropped after one year.

Various ways of managing grass to avoid the problem and keep the carrying capacity high have been suggested. These involve mixed grazing with cattle or horses, the addition of fertilisers and so on. In keeping with other ideas on integrating horses with agriculture carried out on our farm and stud we have developed a relatively complex but successful grazing management strategy which any stud and many private owners could adopt.

Integrating Horses into Agricultural Systems

In addition to improving grassland management at no extra cost, one of the important things to consider here is the integration of horses into an agricultural system. It is possible that in the next two decades, pressure on land, world-wide food shortages and a growing world population, together with the world recession and a growing shortage of oil, may force controls upon keeping large animals for pleasure who consume large amounts of what are the world's food resources. There is an estimated 1,000,000 horses in America and some 250,000 in Britain and these figures are rising annually. However, if horses were integrated into agriculture and contributed to it by, for example, providing energy then future restrictions on horse keeping may well be reduced and the conscience of the owner's be clearer.

There is no reason why *any* horse should not at least help provide their own food. For example, they can be used to harrow the grass they eat, help with the hay making, cart muck and so on. The added advantage is that you then own an adaptable horse which can be made at least partly fit for competition by working rather than having to be ridden uselessly round and round.

On my stud we have trained pure-bred Arabs, part-breds and Thoroughbreds to do these tasks, and it's fun too! I can never understand why all 'respectable' riding schools and training establishments have a tractor and harrows specifically to harrow the indoor school, while at the same time they often have students doing ridiculous tasks like holding a hose to water the school (sprinklers cost a few pence and no labour). Why are the students not taught to work the animals in harness and harrow the school? This is an ideal job for first working with horses in harness. This way the school is harrowed, and the students learn something useful, and more about handling horses; something many of them lack when they leave conventional training establishments!

Self-sustaining Grassland Management

For the last eleven years we have been developing and practicing a self-sustaining grassland management system for horses and other species. Further details can be found in the publications listed in the Bibliography, but I will outline the system briefly below.

1. Subdivide fields into two or four sections (depending on the size and number of horses to be grazed).
2. Place the horses to graze in one section until you consider they need to move on because of lack of grass. Remember that any horse should not have access to long lush grass in abundance. On the other hand, pregnant mares in the last two months of pregnancy, mares and young foals after the first week of foaling and lactating mares and young growing stock require more than maintenance so they must be rotated rather more rapidly around the fields. Competition horses,

however, will probably be fed concentrates as well as grass and should not have access to too much soft, quick growing grass as they do not require it and will waste it. On the other hand for most racing or competitive horses a high fibre grass is a necessity to supply sufficient fibre to compensate for the low fibre in the rest of their diet.

The majority of riding horses require maintenance only and hunters at grass and many ponies must be kept short if they are to avoid health problems as a result of overeating.

3. Horses should preferably be grazed first with cattle and later, when there is less grass, with sheep. This can quite easily be arranged by any competent manager and adds very little to work, but can add substantially to financial returns.

4. The animals are then moved off the first section of the grass onto the next and the first section is topped (mowed with the mower set at approximately 10 cm above the ground). This can be done by hand with a scythe or sickle, or with a horse drawn mower, or an autoscythe. This results in the removal of the seed heads of grasses and such 'weeds' as thistles, docks and other broad leafed plants to control their spread. It is not necessary to use herbicides which can be dangerous and expensive.

5. The grazed section must then be harrowed with a chain harrow. This can be pulled by one or two horses which helps to make them physically fit. Harrowing should be done during the grazing period. It spreads the faeces and reduces the chances of a latrine area developing. The more times the grass is harrowed, either during or just after grazing, the better. Harrowing also aerates the soil and encourages grass growth.

6. The muck from the muck heap can be spread after the graze. We have had particularly good results spreading it on the incipient lawns and omitting the latrine areas. This helps even out the grazing pressure since all the sward is covered with muck and the horses then have less choice of grazing.

The muck can be forked onto a little flat cart that any handy man can make from a pair of old motor car axles, and taken out to the field by your horse. Forking muck off as the horse walks along is the easiest way to control where the muck goes and then it can be harrowed if the lumps are too large.

By contrast, fertilisers from the bag tend to kill off the clovers in the sword so once you start applying them, you may have to continue since the natural nitrogen fixation is taking place less and less and hence natural growth is reduced. The only disadvantage of the self-sustaining system is that it takes two to three years to establish and convert to being highly productive, but then it will continue to improve if carefully managed.

The added advantage of returning the muck is that there is no loss of nutrients from the system and in this way clovers which fix nitrogen and help with growth are encouraged. The humus content of the sward is increased and this in turn increases the number of earth worms and other invertebrates, bacteria and fungi who make their living by breaking down organic material and liberating the nutrients.

Weed control is important, but this can be done by topping off the flowering heads of persistent weeds that are likely to take over. If this is done over a period of two to three years, forests of nettles, docks, thistles and braken can be turned into open productive pasture without the use of herbicides, reseeding, nitrogen or even lime in some acid pastures. Recent work on low input systems in research institutes in central France and our work at Druimghigha has demonstrated this very effectively.

7. A tight graze will encourage growth so it is important, if possible, to ensure that the animals stay on the field long enough to have a short even sward.

Edwards and Hollis (1982) found in the New Forest that cattle and deer spent 98 per cent of their time grazing ponies' latrine areas, hence reducing the grazing effect of lawns and latrines created by horses, increasing the grass production and the carrying capacity. It is quite well known now that mixed species grazing increases the carrying capacity of grass.

8. This grazed section is then grown-up, preferably for hay. If it is not possible to make hay, then it should be kept without any animals until there is about 12 cm of growth (depending on the terrain, the weather and so on).

9. Hay is made next on the section. This feeds the horses in the winter and you should expect 1,016 kg per acre perhaps more in a good summer after several years management in this way. The cutting of each section, preferably once a year, after allowing growth and flowering of the grasses will again reduce the latrine and lawn effects, increase production and rejuvenate the sward. Although I do not recommend mowing with a horse-drawn mower unless the horse is very reliable and reasonably quiet, the rest of the hay making can certainly be done with your competition horses.

   The making of the hay, turning and rowing-up is one of the most pleasant of summer jobs. If you do it with your horses not only do you get to know them much better, but it has the added bonus of being silent and with no diesel fumes; just the smell of the countryside and the odd snort from your horses and the swish of the hay; a very romantic afternoon's occupation.

   The hay can be brought in loose on your cart, by the horse, if the quantity is small. Or, you can contract it to be baled and then bring in the bales with your horse and flat cart.

10. After haymaking the field is shut up to grow again and thereafter it is grazed again.

Of course not every portion will be hayed every year and each year will be different, the grass will grow at different rates and so on, but on a reasonably good piece of lowland Britain, one 15 hh cob per 0·65 ha can be carried and that includes providing a fair amount of winter hay.

In experiments my colleagues and I conducted in the south-east of England, we carried 3·6 bovine units; per ha (the equivalent of one horse per acre) and that included producing some hay for the horses' winter feed. We used no fertilisers, or chemicals, and mostly horse power.

The great advantage of this system is that it is cheap to maintain, provides some winter feed for the horses and it will go on forever provided these techniques are used. It also involves horse owners with the land and yet they are working with their horses and learning different skills at the same time.

Perhaps the most rewarding thing is that you can sit back and say 'Well, we did it.' It is often much more satisfying than spending lots of money on hiring contractors with tractors and fertilisers. In this way you may develop a renewed and rewarding interest not only in your horse, but in how and where he lives. This may also encourage you to make some effort about your fences, plant some trees and think a little about landscape design. This is something the farming and general public, when considering horse owners, often have a legitimate complaint about. Many is the time I have gone to lectures on grassland management at equitation teaching centres and found that what they preach is very different from what they practise!

9 How Horses Learn

With very few exceptions, behaviour of any mammal is the result of a careful mixture of 'nature', or instinctive behaviour, and 'nurture', or experiences, during the animal's lifetime (learning in other words). In the early days of ethology (the study of animal behaviour) fierce arguments raged concerning exactly what percentage was due to nature and what to nurture. On each side of the debate stands were taken in which professors and students sometimes became so deeply entrenched that they were unable to extricate themselves! The remains of this debate still sizzle. For example, between Skinner's school of experimental psychologists, who believe that all behaviour is learnt and some followers of Lorenz who continue to maintain that most, if not all behaviour, is the result of pre-programming by the genes.

Up to this point I have described the behaviour of the horse that is largely inherent or innate although, as with such things as maternal behaviour and social relationships, this can be modified greatly by learning. In this chapter we will consider in more depth how learning works and particular characteristics of the horse in this respect; what they learn and how to use this knowledge to help with horse training. This is perhaps one of the most important aspects of horse management particularly for the riding and driving of horses.

The majority of horse behavioural problems which are brought to me have their origins in incorrect conditioning (learning). I would therefore stress that it is *vitally* important for owners and trainers to clearly understand simple learning theory so that they can avoid causing problems in the future and horse management and training can then improve.

There are some great trainers and handlers who have not the

remotest idea what a 'conditioned reflex' is, but yet turn out some marvellous performers. These are however the lucky few. But it may even help these people, as well as the less able majority, if the elementary theory of learning is spelt out. Each person can then apply this knowledge in his own way to his own situation. Perhaps the mysteries of horse handling and training are not really in the realms of magic, even the moderately intelligent and keen person will be able to achieve much more than they think in this sphere!

I have tried to use the minimum amount of jargon in this chapter, but some is unavoidable if one is aiming at clarity. The ideas are very simple and it is very important to understand them if you are going to make a success of riding, driving or training your horse.

Pavlovian, or Classical, Conditioning

Conditioning is the process whereby a *stimulus* of some sort becomes associated with a certain *response* with which it was not previously associated. This, in a nutshell, is learning.

There are 'unconditioned reflexes' (unlearnt responses) which occur as a normal bodily response. The knee jerk reflex is one of these and blinking is another. By shining a bright light at the eyes, blinking and its speed can be increased (unconditioned *stimulus* is the light; unconditioned *response* is the blink).

If a bell is paired with the light being switched on, soon the sound of the bell will be enough to initiate the blinking. Now the bell has become the 'conditioned stimulus', and the blinking to the bell the 'conditioned response'.

For an unconditioned stimulus to become conditioned, it is necessary for there to be some *reinforcement* (reward). In the above example the reinforcement is that the eye is not dazzled by the bright light because it blinks when the bell and light goes on. Thus, the reinforcement is avoiding pain to the eye. A reinforcement can be a positive reward, like this, or food. In another famous example Pavlov's dogs were rewarded with food after a bell. In this case the bell had become the 'conditioned stimulus' for salivation (*Figure 9.1*) and the 'conditioned response' was salivation in expectation of the food.

Blinking – example 1.			
Unconditioned Stimulus	----->-----	Unconditioned Response	Reinforcement
a) Bright light		Blink	Reduced pain
b) Bright light & bell		Blink	Reduced pain
Conditioned Stimulus ----->-----		Conditioned Response	Reinforcement
c) Bell		Blink	Reduced pain
Pavlovs dogs – example 2.			
Unconditioned Stimulus	----->-----	Unconditioned Response	Reinforcement (positive)
a) Food		Salivate	food
b) Bell & food		Salivate	
Conditioned Stimulus ----->-----		Conditioned Response	
c) Bell		Salivate	food

Figure 9.1
The classical, or Pavlovian, conditioned response

This type of learning is called 'type 1', 'classical' or 'Pavlovian' and normally involves responses which are *not* under the conscious control of the animals, but rather controlled by the autonomic (reflex) nervous system. However, there is another type of conditioning which is more important in many ways for horse training.

'Instrumental' or 'Operant' conditioning

Here the horse (or any species being conditioned) *does* something voluntarily as a result of the conditioning. Let us take the horse moving away from a whip as an example. This is one of the first things that the animal learns in formal training. In this example (*Figure 9.2*) the reinforcement is a reduction in pain or fear. As a result of having been reinforced when it moved away (that is, the

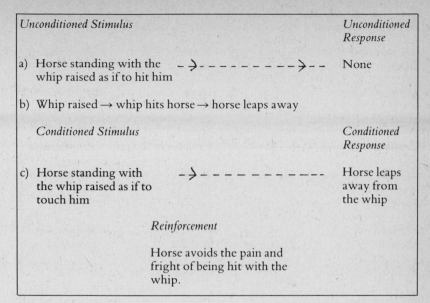

		Unconditioned Response
Unconditioned Stimulus		
a) Horse standing with the whip raised as if to hit him	– ‍›‍ – – – – – – – – ‍›‍ – –	None
b) Whip raised → whip hits horse → horse leaps away		
Conditioned Stimulus		Conditioned Response
c) Horse standing with the whip raised as if to touch him	– ‍›‍ – – – – – – – – – – –	Horse leaps away from the whip
Reinforcement		
Horse avoids the pain and fright of being hit with the whip.		

Figure 9.2
The conversion of an unconditioned stimulus to a conditioned stimulus

pain is reduced) the horse has been *conditioned* to move away from the whip. After the first conditioning of touching with the whip it becomes unnecessary to touch the horse with it again. Raising the whip is sufficient to elicit the horse's response. If the whip is normally held behind the horse, it will move forward away from the whip and hence learn that the whip means move forward. A further stage of learning can be reached by pairing the leg aids of the rider with the whip behind. Here the horse is conditioned to respond to the leg aid by associating them with the already conditioned response to the whip (*Figure 9.3*).

The next stage is that the whip is *not* used. The leg in the horse's side has become a *secondary conditioned stimulus* to elicit the conditioned response of moving forward. However, if the rider does not reduce the leg pressure when the horse moves forward, we can see that there will be no reinforcement or reward for the horse and hence the leg aid will not become conditioned and it will continue to be necessary to use the whip behind to elicit the forward movement of the horse.

Thus, in thoughtful and successful training, the leg aids must

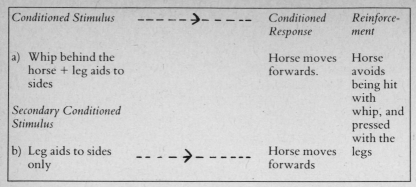

Figure 9.3
How a secondary conditioned stimulus is formed

be initially paired with the whip, provided of course that the whip has already become a 'conditioned stimulus'.

It can be plainly seen that a learning strategy does not have to end here. For example, the legs can be used in different ways to elicit different types of responses. By appropriate conditioning, the horse learns that when the right leg is applied, it must move to the left, or, more sophisticated, when the right leg is used well behind the girth the horse must move its hind quarters to the left; but when the leg is applied further forward, then it indicates to the horse that a more energetic forward movement is required. The reins are also conditioned stimuli which also can elicit a range of responses, provided a gradual learning programme of pairing conditioned with unconditioned stimuli is built up. Then the leg aids and rein aids can be put together in various ways and combinations, and lo and behold the horse has learnt a flying change, or piaffe (a suspended slow trot on the spot with a slightly exaggerated leg elevation). What 'aids' are used in which combinations, to elicit the various responses is to a certain extent a matter of taste and different schools of riding have variations on a theme – each insisting theirs is best!

In much of these learning schedules, once the initial conditioning to go away from the leg and halt with a pull (or feel) on the rein has been established the reinforcement is an avoidance of something slightly unpleasant (that is, the 'aid' being applied more forcefully and perhaps backed up by the whip), but it can also be a positive reinforcement – a reward. This can either be in the form of a tit-bit given when the horse performs the action well, or even just the voice.

More and more elaborate movements, as a result of conditioning sequences, can be learnt. The final result may be the 'airs above the ground' in the classical dressage horse, the circus horse who appears to answer questions, or the Western Reining Horse. More commonly however it is the normal riding or competing horse. Some of these will have 'good manners' and behave appropriately, some will have 'bad manners' and have behavioural problems. Although there may be a tendency for some of the latter to be the result of the genetic make up of the horse a large part of the responsibility for these problems must be borne by the handlers and trainers who have not understood basic learning theory.

This is all there is to learning. However there are several points to remember that we should make here; these are discussed in the rest of this chapter.

We have already discussed what intelligence might be (*Chapter 3*). There is a tendency for people to underestimate what a horse can learn and many writers and trainers consider that horses are really rather stupid. It is rash, and arrogant, to make this claim. Those who take the trouble to learn about their horse's behaviour are normally more impressed by their quickness to learn. Recent investigations of other animals indicate that they can learn far more than we thought; for example, both chimpanzees and pigeons can learn to correctly identify all sorts of objects shown to them on slides. Pigeons can apparently remember over 300 of these (Herstein 1984). If pigeons can do this, how much more can a horse do? No one knows, but a guess is they are probably as good if not better.

Learning to Learn

Before we go any further, it is important to realise that the horse, like a child, must 'learn to learn'. As he gains more experience at performing these conditioned responses, the horse will gradually become quicker at learning and be able to cope with more sophisticated and elaborate stimuli or signals. Of course, not all horses are able or equally fast at this. A skilled rider, however, will be able to estimate the correct approach and speed at which new stimuli for new responses can be presented to any horse.

I have found it helps a great deal to teach young foals to learn and continue their education until they start working on the lunge or under saddle. Young foals learn very fast; they have to in the wild in order to survive, and their behaviour is very plastic – they have not yet formed habits which are difficult to change. Thus they can be taught a variety of 'tricks'. Even if you do not want to teach young horses these sorts of things you can teach them to respond to your voice (come when they are called), to stand still on command and to lead. Gradually, too, you may expose them to strange and potentially frightening environments. This will ensure that your young horse has learnt to learn (to form conditioned stimulus to conditioned response) and by the time he begins his serious training he will develop easily and pleasantly.

I taught my young stallion some tricks, just for fun and also to test whether his learning speed increased. He took several trials to learn to shake hands, fewer to shake his head on command and quickest of all, was the third 'trick' of a similar nature which was to paw the ground. He is now learning to count with his front leg, but does not yet show the genius of Clever Hans.

Now these results are not scientifically proven by so few trials but I did notice that he learnt the new movement faster than the previous one. He has 'learnt to learn'.

Reinforcement

An understanding of reinforcement is crucial for learning. Both positive (reward) and negative (something unpleasant or the avoidance of something unpleasant; it is *not* punishment) reinforcements are used in training horses. The quickest way to condition appropriate behaviour is often a combination of both. For example, when training a horse to go away from the whip the horse may initially do one of many things when the whip touches him (negative reinforcement). He may rear, buck, kick out, run backwards, rush around in circles and so on. Once the horse has done the correct thing (that is walk forwards) it is

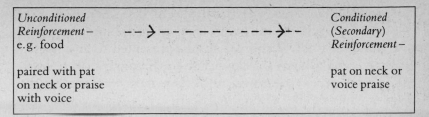

Unconditioned Reinforcement – e.g. food	Conditioned (Secondary) Reinforcement –
paired with pat on neck or praise with voice	pat on neck or voice praise

Figure 9.4
The development of a secondary reinforcement

sensible to reward him (positive reinforcement; for example a tit-bit, or a soothing voice).

Rewards can themselves be conditioned. Although initially rewards will be unconditioned – food being offered and eaten – the offering of food can then be paired with either a pat on the neck or by praise with the voice. In a short while, the pat or the vocal praise will themselves act as a reward, or *secondary reinforcement* (*Figure 9.4*).

Because horses are so co-operative, such able visual communicators and seem to form associations between stimulus and response very rapidly they are extremely easy animals to teach. Because of this the many different trainers use very different methods. This does not reflect so much on our great knowledge of horses and the competence of trainers, as on the amazing ability of horses to learn under what often must be very 'sub-optimal' conditions. However, for the quickest learning, it is best to use a mixture of both positive and negative reinforcement. Punishment is not negative reinforcement. The reason for this is that negative reinforcement comes *before* the response, punishment *after* it. We will discuss the difficult question of punishment later.

CONTINUOUS REINFORCEMENT

When beginning to condition a new activity, it is important to reward it *every* time it occurs. This is called '*continuous reinforcement*'. It has been shown in rats (from where most of our understanding of learning comes) that continuous reinforcement leads to the quickest conditioning, until the response becomes well established (that is about 90 per cent of the conditioned stimuli result in the conditioned response).

PARTIAL REINFORCEMENT

However, thereafter, *partial reinforcement* appears to be more effective in ensuring an energetic and well performed response. Partial reinforcement is when only *some* of the responses are rewarded, usually in a random order so that the horse never knows whether he will be rewarded with a tit-bit or not. The result is that he tries harder to do it – just in case.

Extinction

When the conditioned response no longer occurs to the stimulus it is called *extinction*. It normally happens eventually when the response no longer obtains any reinforcement; whether this is a reward, or a reduction in something unpleasant. Thus, when a horse is finally persuaded to enter a trailer that he is frightened of, he is given a reward (a feed, and patted). If after a number of repeats, there is no reward, the horse may well 'reason' that it is not 'worth' entering the frightening trailer and refuse. When this happens the handler becomes angry, for after all the horse has boxed well before. The handler may then use negative reinforcement (hitting from behind with a whip). The result may be that the horse goes in, but if again he is not rewarded, the next time he may develop many strategies to avoid the whip without going in.

After a few more times (perhaps the horse has, during these attempts been reinforced in his inappropriate behaviour by the handler giving up) the horse may well have been well conditioned *not* to box at all. And all because the handler did not continue to make it worth the horse's while to enter the first few times; that is, positively reinforce him.

Another example of extinction of a response in horse training is when the animal is asked to do a movement too frequently with insufficient reward. Constant kicking of the horse's side by a rider is an example of this, only too often seen and a sign of lack of understanding of horse learning.

The moral is that if you want to maintain an energetic and correct response to a conditioned stimulus, then it is a very good idea to reward. Even with an obvious reward or primary reinforcement such as a lump of sugar, carrot, an apple. Sometimes, but not always, this partial reinforcement not only increases the chances of the response being performed with energy and well, but also reduces the chances of extinction of the response occurring for some reason no one completely understands. Friske (1979) suggests that the ultimate reward for the horse is to stop doing everything, to strip him off and let him relax or even leave him loose or take him back to the stable. Others have also suggested that this is the ultimate reward. I am not convinced that this is, in fact, the case with many horses. For example, those with much energy find stopping much less rewarding than going. It may work on a horse that some would call 'stale', but perhaps we should not work our horses to that point if we want them to learn. A good trainer will know the horse well and be able to work out what that particular horse finds rewarding.

We have already mentioned extinction in relation to partial reinforcement. However, there are several other relevant points here.

The concept of extinction runs counter to the 'practise makes perfect' belief. In other words, too much practise of a response leads not to an improvement of the response, but often to its disintegration and finally extinction. Motivation is important as a well learnt act will not be performed without incentive, or *motivation*. A new act will not be learnt without it either.

Also important in preventing extinction is '*habit strength*'. This idea came from work with sheep. Sheep had been taught to flex their foreleg when a small shock was given to the leg. The position of the shock was then moved to the body. Instead of developing another response nearer the shock, the sheep continued to flex the same foreleg. This substitute reinforcement as such phenomena are called, may account for the puzzling persistence of habits which seem to keep going by inertia.

The horse is a species that has a particular tendency to form persistent habits. One example of this resistance to extinction which was very awkward to deal with concerned a young horse about which I had been consulted. The horse had learnt to kick out backwards to the touch of the whip. In an effort to overcome this, the whip was replaced by the spurs, but the horse continued to kick out when the spurs were applied, because the kicking out had become a well established habit.

Whether this tendency to form habits easily is related to the horse's overall level of reactivity to all sorts of things, we do not know. There is much difference between breeds and individuals in this respect. One thing that is certain is the resistance to extinction that is characteristic of horses. Thus, it is much easier to train a horse correctly from the start than to retrain an animal that has bad 'habits'. When a horse persists in doing something that is not required, although the cause may have been removed, it will not necessarily stop the 'habit'. For example, head throwing as a result of heavy hands and too severe a bit, may persist even though the bit has been changed and riders hands improved (or removed!). The horse is here showing a *resistance to extinction* and the reinforcement of this inappropriate behaviour may simply be to ride the horse. Changing the habit may require other approaches.

Jost (1897) discovered in rats and other species that recent learning tends to fade out more rapidly than older learning. This is, again, something worth thinking about in relation to training. It can immediately be seen that there is a scientific basis for the often preached, but less often practised, idea of giving the horse a good solid foundation in his schooling. If correct early learning and thorough conditioning of manners and movements to appropriate aids (conditioned stimuli) is established in the beginning, then it is always possible to combine simple well learnt instructions to obtain more advanced movements. For example, if the idea of bending the horse's body on a circle to the leg aids is well and correctly taught in early training, then this bend can simply be developed into a shoulder-in using similar leg aids. If the horse has not been well conditioned in the use of the leg aids to control the bend and lateral movements, then the shoulder-in will be a disaster. If it is a disaster the first few times it is tried (which after all is not unlikely even if the foundations of the movement are well learnt), then the horse is quite likely to forget this and revert to the correct bend as a result of his early training the next time it is tried.

This, of course, applies to all types of learning in the horse. I have recently been amazed to find how well this works. During the process of some pilot experiments in horse communication, I trained a young pure-bred Arab colt to walk up some steps, through the kitchen and into the sitting room to play the piano. As a foal the colt found this a relatively simple exercise and did it every day. The colt was then left untrained and almost unhandled until his first birthday, a period of about six months. I then tried the same procedure thinking that this much larger, wilful and nervous (reactive) colt would find the exercise traumatic and frightening. As it turned out he behaved beautifully, despite the difficulty of squeezing his bulk around the arm chairs and past the stove! I can only think that this must largely be the result of the thorough early training he had received.

Punishment

Punishment is distinct from negative reinforcement. This is because negative reinforcement comes *before* the response. Punishment comes *after* it. Even a well established response can be temporarily eliminated by punishment. For example, if rats are rewarded for pressing a bar, then shocked after pressing it, they temporarily cease to press; but will begin again the next day. It therefore appears that punishment does not eliminate the apparent fascination of doing something previously learnt. It is also, of course, possible to punish for an activity that is *not* done (for example, hitting the horse when he will not go over a jump). The result of this is often that the activity is thereafter done with a minimum of exertion; as laboratory researchers have found with rats. The same applies to horses who may with reluctance perform the right response after being punished. For example in jumping the horse may just get over the jump, or, in dressage, perform the movement but without energy, brilliance or 'goodwill'. There are certain schools of riding that base their training more on fear and submission and punishment than rewards. The results are usually obedient performances but without brilliance or flair.

There are, however, a few instances in the training of horses where punishment may be appropriate. For example, the use of spurs after a horse has stopped at a jump is a punishment for stopping; but at the same time it will also act as a negative reinforcer for jumping (the act of jumping eliminates the pain caused by the spurs and thus is re-inforcing). In the same way, if the horse is turned away from the jump and then spur or whip is used, the wrong movement that is, turning away from the jump rather than stopping at it is punished. Thus the horse has been turned away from the jump when not inclined to jump it, that is, the horse has also been *rewarded* for the incorrect response (for *not* jumping).

It would seem that, on the whole, punishment is much less effective at stimulating the response than positive (reward) or negative reinforcement. Certainly the less experienced rider should *never* use it as they may well be rewarding the *incorrect* reponse. Many times the wrong response is thereby rewarded before the punishment is administered – a good recipe for confusing the horse.

The punishment must also be very close in time to the incorrect response otherwise it will not be related to it – and this is often difficult.

Motivation

To do anything, the horse, or any other animal for that matter, must be 'motivated'. The performance of largely innate behaviour is usually considered to be motivated by 'drives', or tendencies to perform that behaviour because by so doing, the animal will improve its chances of survival.

Is learnt behaviour also motivated by increasing the chances of that animal's survival? In the long run this must indeed be the case, otherwise learning would not have evolved. But in more immediate terms, how does this motivation work? Experimental work into learning and motivation in laboratory animals has shown that the level of motivation will vary but that it can, to a degree, be manipulated. For example, by making rats very hungry, their motivation to work to solve a problem (by pressing a bar or whatever is required) for a food reward, was increased.

What of horses however, what motivates them to learn? They, like children or laboratory animals will often be motivated to do certain things for a food reward, particularly an especially sought after reward. Indeed, the motivation can sometimes be increased by hunger or thirst. This can sometimes too be appropriate to use when, for example, a horse refuses to enter a trailer. A period without food or water may encourage him to enter provided he can see the sought after reward inside. This however will not help in school work to obtain co-operation and attention from a horse – quite the reverse.

Another way of increasing the motivation of horses to learn is by having a particularly close relationship with them, so that they are motivated by pleasing you and, therefore, learn conditioned responses quickly. However, here one must be very careful not to abuse the relationship by omitting to praise them when they have done the appropriate movement. Dogs are motivated particularly easily to learn this way. Horses too can be, with the proviso that training them requires more skill, given that they are bigger and stronger and, if they are being ridden, the rider must be quite confident. This is important in order to avoid muddling the horse by confusing the conditioned stimuli. Otherwise, however highly motivated the horse is in wishing for approval, he will not know what is required – and the whole relationship will suffer and will be less useful for increasing the motivation thereafter.

I well remember the first jumping round I ever did either in private or public on my Anglo-Arab stallion. We had never jumped before and I was so surprised by his leaping over the first fence that I praised him profusely – the result was that we went on to do a clear round and to win a cross-country event – with me praising him after every jump! In this case he apparently 'cared' how I responded and presumably then discovered that it was all quite fun anyway. He was *positively reinforced* by my verbal praise.

Generalisation

When a response that has been conditioned to one stimulus occurs to other stimuli it is *generalised*. This is something horses do very frequently and one of the reasons why it is a very bad idea to teach a horse an advanced movement or a trick unless the foundation learning is very well established. My elder sister taught her pony to rear to a conditioned stimulus (a voice command). This was achieved relatively easily but, thereafter, the pony would rear as a result of very different stimuli. Sometimes this was acutely embarrassing to say the least.

Obtaining the correct response

In the acquisition phase of learning, when the response is becoming conditioned, a whole series of different responses may occur to a stimulus; as with our example of conditioning the horse to go forward away from the whip, initially the horse may buck, rear, kick, rush off and so on. The importance of rewarding *only* the appropriate response is obvious, but not always as easy as it sounds.

With more advanced training, where movements that are not often part of the normal behavioural repertoire of the horse are required, this becomes a very teasing problem.

There are two possible approaches here. In the first place it is normally possible to use previous conditioning to lead to the next step. For example, one way of teaching the piaffe is to develop it from stop and go signals given alternatively in quick succession. Thus the four steps for the learning of this movement:

1. The horse learns to go away from the whip, then the leg and to stop on the use of the reins.
2. The horse is then taught trot to halt using these conditioned stimuli (aids) and partial positive reinforcement (tit-bits sometimes, or praise with the voice).
3. The horse is then taught to perfect the trot to half-halt, thus the legs of the rider are used before the halt is complete. This is, again, partially reinforced.
4. Finally, alternate stop-go signals are given in succession, starting several seconds apart and gradually coming closer

together. After the movement has been obtained, even for one stride, it is immediately rewarded and the exercise temporarily ceased.

There is more to it than this of course. In particular, the horse must be able to obtain a high degree of collection in a good outline and the rider can use his own back and weight as extra conditioned stimuli. All of this has been described many times by many authors, but it is another thing actually doing it.

The second way of obtaining a required response is to find a time and place when the horse will naturally do the movement or a similar one. When the horse is doing it, pair the response with the aids you will give and the reinforcement and repeat this several times. Thereafter in a similar situation give the aids and obtain the movement. After some practise, it should be possible to obtain the movement to the conditioned stimuli alone with no need for the situational cues (the right time and place).

For example, if one wishes to start to teach an extension it is not difficult to find a place where the horse will naturally perform this, often in long grass or water or soft sand. The aids are then coupled with the action, this is repeated several times and then the aids tried to induce the action.

Although in theory this is a good way of teaching advanced movements, several practitioners I have talked to about this find that it rarely works well and they usually stick to the first method; developing one movement out of another with appropriate use of conditioned stimuli.

Discrimination learning

Discrimination learning is the opposite of generalisation learning. The animal has to distinguish between two objects or noises in order to obtain the reinforcement. The horse is first trained, for example, that a red button when pressed releases a food reward but a green button does not. Then slightly different shades of red and orange are introduced to test when the horse can discriminate between them. In this way it is possible to find out more about perception in animals. Dixon (1966) tested the ability of horses to distinguish different shapes and patterns. Her work and that of others indicates that horses are capable of discerning remarkably complex patterns, but since they are very large and expensive experimental animals, relatively little discrimination learning has been done with them. It is a useful technique for learning more about how different species perceive the world and offers a fruitful area for research on horses in the future.

Memory

Memory is obviously very important in successful conditioning. To date we have little knowledge on how good horses are at remembering compared to other species. Again, Dixon (1966) found only a 15 per cent memory loss of complex patterns previously learnt after six months, which is relatively good. Some young children do not perform as well on similar tasks.

There is plenty of anecdotal evidence to suggest that horses remember very well. Mother and foal separated at a few months after birth will apparently recognise each other, often after several years. Most of us know how good horses are at remembering a bad experience. An animal that has had a bad and frightening experience, such as being led into a particular trailer even years previously, may well baulk at entering *that* trailer even though he may have loaded well after re-training into other trailers. Horses are also very good at apparently remembering a route after only one exposure to it, but here they may be using other cues such as smell. Recently, when riding in an endurance race, I was amazed how my horse remembered the way after going around once only when I certainly did not. Was he remembering, or had he learnt to follow the piece of plastic on the trees marking the way or was he following a scent trail? We do not know.

Attitudinal importance

It has been found that in humans, dogs and rats the attitude of an individual is important in relation to the speed of learning. For example, when humans are told that they must not withdraw their hand when it is shocked, they manage to overcome the unconditioned response to withdraw the hand.

There are two things that are important here. In the first place there are physiological factors that depend on the number of repetitions, 'linkage strength' of the stimulus and response. Secondly, there are psychological 'qualitative' factors. This means that subjects will show different responses depending on what they are told about the experiment.

It is usually considered that this only applies to humans over five years old. I am not, however, convinced that this is true and that it does not relate to horses. We are all aware that the same horse may respond differently in training sessions from day to day and that he will respond differently to different people training him. Many of us will have seen what we have described as 'personality clashes' between horse and rider or trainer. This is not always the result of incompetence of the rider, as he or she may be experienced and obtain very good results from another unfamiliar horse. Horses certainly have different moods and display different emotions (fear, excitement, aggression and so on). It is more reasonable to consider that the responses will not only be individual, but will also vary with their mood, who is handling them, their past experiences and many other internal and external factors such as the weather, the place and so on. One example is the rather different behaviour of mares when in oestrus. Because of this they are often discriminated against for important competitions. 'Mares Lib' awake!

All of these factors probably affect the 'attitudinal responses' of the horse. However, these responses are likely to be relatively unimportant compared to the conditioning or learning phenomena we have mentioned in this chapter; they are the fine adjustment if you like. It is far more likely that it is the handlers lack of understanding of how learning works and hence his unconscious reinforcement of the wrong response that is to blame. This is usually the case when the horse is unco-operative and difficult even with very experienced people. The chances of the horse really having a screw loose are very small indeed!

Part of the make-up of 'attitude' is how emotional the subject is which does affect learning in horses. Fiske (1979) found that relatively excitable horses, 'warmbloods', learnt a maze less well

Figure 9.5
An Arab yearling galloping around a circle to the left, showing that he does *not* bend to the left. The bending to the inside of a circle is not a natural movement, it is a learnt trick

than those who were more placid. However the emotional, excitable horses also spent more time in the maze because they were cautious and distracted. In other words they were less motivated to perform the task, but this does not mean that they *knew* it less well, perhaps they were just not motivated to do it. This illustrates the difficulty of using conventional learning theory to explain and measure all horse learning capacity.

Fiske also found that in horses speed of learning and remembering a maze was dependent on their learning environment. For example, she showed that horses that scored well when taught a maze at two years old, after a year in a rigid training environment in a school where there were no concessions made to individual horses, scored less well than the ones that had a poor score to start with. This illustrates how important it is to shape the learning schedule to the individual horse's requirements.

The classical school of equitation, particularly the Viennese school maintains that all the movements they teach their horses develop out of natural movements that the horse normally performs in a free untutored state. They thus make a rigid distinction between the movements that they teach (classical equitation) and many movements that the circus teaches (such as a Spanish walk) which they regard as 'tricks' and are therefore scorned.

This is neither fair nor correct. Free, untutored horses do *not* perform a levade, a capriole, a piaffe, a palisade nor a corbette of any worth. Such actions that resemble these in the wild would score only one mark in a dressage test. In fact, horses at liberty will even go around bends at speed with their heads at least bent to the outside (*Figure 9·5*) – not, as is considered 'correct' in the trained horse, with a spinal bend to the inside with their head following the bend. In the wild the horse performs all these movements *and many others* including the Spanish walk, in a very different way to the way he is conditioned to perform them for the benefit of people.

The learning of all these movements is, thus, a highly conditioned process which is built up step-by-step and most horses can learn very complex tasks with careful and appropriate conditioning procedures. In a sense then, all horse training is just the learning of tricks, but that is not to say that it is not highly skilled. One can only admire a highly trained horse whether he is performing in the circus, in the Spanish Riding School, or in western riding; or even the well mannered quiet hack or harness horse. They are an indication of the successful partnership between a knowledgeable and thoughtful person and the quick learning and co-operative horse. What in any case are tricks? Surely my writing of, or you reading, this book can also be considered *a trick*.

There is a great deal not known about learning in general and very little reported work on learning in horses in particular. However we have perhaps covered the most important areas for the person training a horse to bear in mind. It must also be remembered what we have said about the world the horse lives in and how it will naturally behave.

By putting all this together (and when things go wrong sitting down and thinking what you as the trainer did wrong) you will eventually be able to understand a great deal more about your particular horse and thus be able to improve his performance.

I do believe, however, that we have really only scratched the surface of what the horse could learn if we could only present the training schedule correctly and build up to the more complex learning that many consider unique to man. It may be that we find it more difficult to understand the horse, not because he cannot learn but because he is different from us.

Before you call your horse 'stupid' because he does not appear to have learnt, remember two things: firstly, why is the horse bothering to co-operate with you at all? He certainly does not have to; he is bigger, stronger and could even kill you whenever he wants. Secondly, is it not *you* who are stupid and inadequate and the horse who has learnt how not to do what you want him to do for his own reasons?

Much of what has been said in this chapter may sound like commonsense and be intuitively known to the good horse person. Even she, however, may benefit from considering *how* it all happens.

10 Behavioural Problems

It is impossible to discuss all the behavioural problems of horses in this chapter, and this is not the intention.

It is easy to assume, because the horse is not behaving appropriately as you wish him to, that he is 'neurotic', 'mad', 'stupid' or 'has a screw loose'; and that this is anatomical and physiological and that therefore there is nothing that the owner, trainer or veterinarian can do about it except give a drug, use surgery, or suggest the knackers yard.

Unfortunately veterinary education has not kept up with behavioural knowledge and developments and few vets are given any serious training in ethology from competent ethologists. Thus they are not in general qualified or any more knowledgeable to cope with behavioural problems than the owner or trainer. There are now some enlightened vets who realise that it is necessary to have, and to use, specialists for the advancement of different aspects of animal health and who will refer owners of animals with psychological problems to animal psychiatrists.

Animal psychiatrists are the first to admit that their knowledge is incomplete and that they may not always be able to help the animal, but they will always try and by doing this, in just the same way as in the development of human psychiatry, they

Figure 10.1 (OVERLEAF)
Some of the behavioural problems encountered in horses (*left*) related to their environmental causes (*top*). ⊗ indicates a particular demonstrated relationship. ? don't know, × relationship has been shown. This table is based on 800 cases

Behavioural changes:	Pain	Sudden environmental change	Excessive environment stimuli	Crowded, insufficient space	Restriction/tied	Absence key stimuli	Absence bedding	High temperature	Low temperature	Poor ventilation
Increase in aggression	×	×	×	×	×		×	×	×	×
Increase in activity	×	×	×	×	×				×	×
Panic/excessive excitement	×	×	×	×	×					×
Reduction in fertility	×		×	×	×	×		?	?	
Non-recognition œstrus	×		×	×						
Œstrus behaviour causing disturbance	×		×	×	×					
Insufficient libido	×	×	×	×	×	×				
Mother ignoring young	×	⊗	⊗	⊗	×					
Mother aggressing young	⊗	×	⊗	×	×					
Mother preventing suckling	⊗	×	⊗	×	?	?				
Non-recognition of mother by young	×	×	×	⊗	×	?				
Weaving	×	×	×	×	×	×		×	×	×
Crib biting	×	×	×	×	×	×		×	×	×
Self licking or biting	×	×	×	×	×	×		×	×	×
Wind sucking	×	×	×	×	×	×		×	×	×
Pacing	×	×	×	×	×	×		×	×	×
Head throwing	×	×	×	×	×	?				
Coprophagia				×			×			
Intake reduced	×	×	×	×	×	×	×	×	×	×
Intake increased			×	×	×		×		×	
Drop performance	⊗		×	×	×	×	×	×		
Spooking-shying	×	×	×	×	×				×	
Stopping & Refusing co-operate	×	×	×	×	×	×		×		×
Rearing	×	×	×	×	×				×	×
Bucking	×	×	×	×	×				×	×
Bolting	×	×	×	×	×				×	×
Excessive Sleeping				×					×	
Excessive Lying	×			×				×	×	
Other time budget changes	×	×	×	×	×	×	×	×	×	×
Reduced lying or sleeping	⊗	×	×	×	×		×	×	×	×

High & prolonged light	Low light intensity	Monotonous environment Insufficient stimuli	Monotonous food + nutrient deficits	Absence fibre pelleted food.	Excessive social contact	Weaning	Isolation from social partner	Isolation all contact with conspecifics	Group changing	Absence male	No courtship	Excessive feeding.	Insufficient exercise
	×	×	×	×	×	×	×	×	×	×		×	×
		×	×	×	×	×	×	×	×	×		×	×
		×	×		×	×	×	×	×			×	×
	?						×		?	⊗	⊗	?	
					×			×	×	⊗	⊗		
		×		×	×		×	×	×	⊗	⊗		
	?	×			×		×	⊗			⊗		
					⊗				×				
				?	⊗		×	×	×			×	
					×		?		×			×	
					⊗		×	×	×				
	×	×	×	×	×	×	×	×	×			×	×
	×	×	×	×	×	×	×	×	×			×	×
	×	×	×	×	×	×	×	×	×			×	×
	×	×	×	×	×	×	×	×	×			×	×
	×	×	×	×	×	×	×	×	×			×	×
		×		×	×	×	×	×	×			×	×
		×	⊗	×									
	×	×	⊗		×	×	×	×	×	×			×
		×		×	×	×						×	×
	×	×	×	×	×	×	×	×	×				
	×	×	×	×	×	×	×	×	×			×	×
	×				×		×	×	×	×	×	×	×
		×				×	×	×	×			⊗	⊗
		×				×	×	×	×			⊗	⊗
		×				×	×	×	×			⊗	⊗
	×	⊗	×	×	×	×		×				×	×
	×	⊗	×	×		×		×					
	×	×	×	?		×	×	×	×			×	×
				?		×	×	×	×	×			×

accumulate knowledge that can be used thereafter, and in this way the science can grow.

A perusal of the previous chapters will indicate that behavioural problems in horses are to a very large extent environmentally controlled, and that they may be symptoms of inadequate environments in one way or another. This may relate to the physical environment or to the social environment. There are with horses also problems relating to their riding or working and training. For example, if a horse will not turn to the left, or go on a left circle, this is the result of bad and incorrect riding or handling at some previous stage although it may have become so severe a problem that it appears to have physical origins (for example lack of accurate vision in one eye). The job of the horse psychiatrist is having had the horse cleared from obvious physical defect by a veterinarian, to tease out all the factors that might have given rise to the problem in the first place, and then suggest a solution.

Behavioural problems are very rarely the result of one single factor that can be easily corrected; they are normally the result of a summation of environmental inadequacies. One behavioural problem is the result of many environmental factors, and *vice versa* (*Figure 10.1*).

In this chapter we will only discuss some of the more common problems and their causes. My hope is that owners or trainers will in future think more seriously about their horses' psychological health and design environments that are better adapted to cater for a horse's psychological demands and in this way reduce behavioural problems themselves.

I have outlined (*Chapters 1 to 9*) what is known to date about horse behaviour and consequently the physical and social requirements of his environment. Here we can apply this knowledge to improve husbandry.

Problems relating to eating and feeding

We have looked briefly at the normal behaviour and physiology of the horse in relation to eating and feeding (*Chapters 7 and 8*). Here we will emphasise the behavioural problems that so often arise, particularly in stabled horses.

One of the most important things to understand is that it appears that horses are relatively unselective when fed food in a food bowl or manger or by hand. This is a result of conditioning and can lead them to eat unsuitable or even dangerous foods from the bowl that they would normally not touch. This has been known to cause colic and other problems. The only solution to this is to be very vigilant when feeding horses from food bowls, and make sure that only fresh food is fed and new foods introduced slowly.

Another major problem, which often causes behavioural difficulties and certainly reduces the relaxation of the horse, is that many stabled horses are unable to fulfil their evolutionary allotted time eating because they are fed a limited amount of low fibre food. This may lead to many problems, including an increase in aggression and the development of stereotypes or stable vices (*Chapter 11*). The solution to this problem is to allow animals access to even low quality fibre such as straw at all times. If the amount they eat must be controlled, then the best way is not to ration feed fibre, but feed it in such a way that the horse has to work to obtain it. One successful way of doing this is to give the fibre food in a hay net with very small holes so that the horse can only pull out one strand at a time and hence eats very slowly.

A feeding and eating phenomenon that may have to be confronted is that the horse will not eat enough and does not maintain weight. Many Thoroughbreds and Arabs in particular tend to be very reactive nervous horses who at the slightest opportunity will leave their food to rush to the door, or stand and stare out. One of the most successful techniques to help overcome this is to ensure that an important social partner is with the horse at feeding times. Whether this be another horse, a goat, a person or a cat is not important. At my own stud we find putting two horses in one stable, particularly in a strange place, helps greatly. However the two must, of course, be normally associating social partners. A mare will often relax and eat better if one of her own offspring (even if an adult) is with her. Failing all else, the horse usually eats better if his handler, groom or even rider is with him. Horses tend to eat up better at night; the reason for this is, presumably, because there are fewer disturbances at night, thus less to react to.

Over-eating is encountered with some horses. Even though they have fulfilled their time for eating and have had quite sufficient they will continue to eat. This is easy to control, it simply means that the horse out at pasture must be kept short of grazing. Frequently, horses that have been kept stabled for long periods then released to grass will over-eat and put on too much weight. This is usually because (presumably) the food is good and they cannot stop. Keeping them relatively short of grass is the answer, *not* to shut them up with nothing to eat for long periods. If it is difficult to restrict them outside, then they may have to be brought in but must be offered either straw or some high fibre hay to occupy themselves. Again this can be in a net with very small holes so that the horse takes a great deal of time obtaining a mouthful. Over-eating in stabled animals is easy to control though, again, they must not be kept without food for long periods, but given a not highly palatable high fibre food instead of high quality grains or hay.

Bedding and bed eating

The traditional way of bedding horses on straw and mucking them out every day is appropriate and will encourage them to lie down *only* if the bed is very deep. What in fact usually happens is that the bed is far too thin and the horse spends too much time standing immobile with resulting foot and leg problems. Such bedding is also very expensive in terms of labour and materials. For these reasons other types of bedding have been developed.

One 'problem' that people often have with straw beds is that the horses eat the bed. They will go to endless lengths to ensure that the horse does not 'eat the bed', including changing bedding material. Let us examine why the horse should *not* eat his bed. The reasons given for this are twofold:

1. The horse eats too much and then cannot eat his food, or he prefers the bed to his food.

    If the horse eats much of his bed, and prefers it to his food, then there is probably something wrong with the feeding strategy. The most likely explanation is that the horse is rationed on fibre in his feed and he desperately needs the fibre, so he will eat any he can get. The extreme case is where the horse will seek out and eat even pieces of straw covered in urine and faeces on a muck heap because he has such a need for fibre. Alternatively the horse may start chewing wood in his box and this can lead to crib-biting. In any case if the horse prefers wood to his food, then there must be something wrong with his food, either in terms of content or taste. If, therefore, you do not want your horse to eat his bed, then change his diet. There is, in any case it appears, no reason for a horse doing any work – including training for the Grand National or a 100 mile race – to have to be fed so much carbohydrate that he has to have very restricted fibre. Feeding high protein foods to mature horses who are fit is incorrect. Hard working horses require high carbohydrates for energy, not proteins. Growing horses require more protein. I have been in racehorse stables where they are fed large corn feeds with protein supplements and then a high protein low fibre hay such as lucerne hay, a recipe for many behavioural problems. Often 100 per cent of horses in such stables will show what are classed as abnormal behaviours.

2. The horse will eat poor quality food, dust and mould which will give him colic.

   In some cases eating his bed could be the cause of this behaviour. If the horse has such a restricted fibre diet that he will forsake his corn feed to eat such a poor quality forage, then the answer is to correct the feeding. As we have seen, except when fed from a food bowl, horses are very selective eaters and they will not take in foods that are suspect unless very hungry, conditioned to, or with a, strong dietary deficiency.

   Therefore, provided reasonable straw is used for the bed, it can act as a food 'balancer' and there is no objection to the horse eating it. If he wishes to pick and play around with the straw, eating some, it helps to fill up his time and balance his diet. Only very occasionally does one have a pathological bed-eater who almost exclusively eats his bed and even such horses can be corrected with time. In such cases this behaviour may be an indication of other psychological problems.

TYPES OF BEDDING

Shavings are becoming popular and they are certainly very easy to manage and low in labour costs although, depending on the area, they may be expensive to buy. If horses are fed too little fibre and bedded on shavings or chippings, they will however take to eating them and although small quantities do no harm, too much may be harmful as chippings are very indigestible. Dust can also be a problem with such beds. Again, to avoid the animal standing immobile for too long, it is essential to have a deep bed. One of the disadvantages of shavings is that they break down much more slowly than straw and if, as we have suggested (*Chapter 8*), the system is relatively self-sustaining and the muck returned to the grass after decomposition, then extra muck heaps must be built.

Shavings will take approximately two years to break down. Although they can be applied in thin layers, fresh to the grass, this is not always advisable. The speed of decomposition can be increased by careful management of the muck heaps, introduction of neutralisers such as lime and green materials (for example, weeds and so on), but we cannot go into this here.

Shredded paper is another material that is becoming more common for beds. Paper breaks down faster than chippings. If the animals take to eating it, then it is possible for the ink to have bad effects on health (this is why fish and chip shops had to give up serving in newspaper, an ecologically retrograde step!). Shredded paper is a good bed if it is deep enough, but it is often more expensive than shavings or straw and therefore even less likely to be very generously used.

Rubber mats have also been tried to see how they effect the time the horse spends lying down which is important. Time spent lying is reduced by shallow beds, on rubber and with no bedding.

NO BEDDING

If horses are stalled during the day and out at night, and are healthy it is highly unlikely that they will lie down in the stable. Therefore, there is little point in giving them beds, except to make the stable look good. It is easier and often better for the feet if the horses simply stand on the normal flooring. Concrete and brick floors are not as good as earth or grass, or other slightly giving materials like sand.

On the other hand, the introduction of slats in stalls causes many behavioural problems of many types. For example, intensively reared pigs and cattle are now subjected to slats (so that labour costs can be kept to a minimum), and some European countries are seriously thinking of outlawing them because of resulting behavioural difficulties. Slats would be inappropriate for horses that are stalled all the time, but not for horses which are stalled for a part of the day and out at pasture or yarded at night. Luckily the capital costs of building stables with slats and slurry tanks is still considerable and discourages such ideas. This is one case where traditional horse management which resists change has acted in the interests of the horse and his behaviour. If there is no bed, remember that the horse must be given some other access to fibrous feeding material particularly if he is stalled and tied up all day.

DEEP LITTER

Deep litter beds are creeping into horse management despite the disapproval of the horse establishment. Deep litter straw beds have many advantages.

Firstly, they demand much less labour which means that the owners, grooms or students instead of spending many hours mucking out can be doing something more interesting and important like exercising, schooling or merely talking to their horses.

Secondly, they form a deep mat which is soft and encourages lying down. The time budgeting we did showed that horses lay down on deep litter beds rather more than horses do at grass (the slowly decomposing bottom of the litter gives off heat and makes the bed warm), or on daily mucked out beds.

Thirdly, deep litter beds are economical in terms of the use of bedding material. It would be possible to manage shredded paper as a deep litter, but I have not heard of anyone doing it. The cost of keeping one horse well on a deep litter bed throughout the winter is approximately 1,000 kg worth of straw, as compared to about 3,000 kg for a daily mucked out bed which also requires four times the labour time.

The disadvantages of deep litter is mainly that they must be well drained and carefully managed. New straw must be put down morning and evening and if wet areas develop they must be removed and the drainage corrected. A badly managed deep litter bed, in conjunction with poor ventilation, can be very bad news for the horse's physical and psychological health.

Another possible disadvantage of deep litter bedding is that the horse can have his feet wet much of the time and this might lead to foot problems. However, in the ten years I have been keeping our horses on deep litter beds (12 horses per year; or 120 horse winters) we have never had any foot problems related to thrush or poor stable hygiene. The reason for this may well be that we do not clean out the horse's feet!

The reasoning behind this is that the foot of the horse evolved to be naturally full of earth, gravel and so on in the wild where no person runs around mucking out their feet. Rarely do feral horses develop severe foot problems related to wet and damp even in marshy and wet areas. The hoof has evolved to remain healthy under these conditions. It is not, however, evolved to stand around in slightly acid muck and urine. Cleaning out the foot of a stabled horse results inevitably in the foot filling up with droppings as he moves around, so he has muck next to the sole rather than earth and mud. Of course, if the horse's droppings are always removed straightaway and the foot cleaned out about four times a day this can be avoided, but is all this extra work necessary? Under my own system, the horse's feet are never cleaned before he enters the stable and never in the stable, thus the feet are never full of muck, but of mud or gravel or whatever the horse has been in before entering the stable.

However, this needs further testing and we do not yet have any good data on the actual long term effects of deep litter on the feet of the horse.

Muck eating (Coprophagia)

Foals eat their mother's fresh warm droppings and this is nothing to worry about, it is normal behaviour. The reason for it is that in this way the foal obtains the necessary bacteria to help him digest the cellulose and fibre that he takes into his gut. In fact horses are nothing like as efficient at extracting all digestible material from food as cattle are. The reason for this is that in horses much of the digestion is in the hind gut and done with the help of bacteria. If digestion is primarily in the front part of the gut (as in the stomachs of the cow), then the rest of the digestive tract can concentrate on absorbing all the dead bacteria which have lived on the fibre. But if this happens in the hind gut, as is the case in horses, then the bacteria are expelled before they are absorbed and so full use of them is not made.

If horses were to be really efficient extractors of digestive material then the sensible thing for them to do would be to eat their own faeces! But not many horses do and when adult horses do so it is considered undesirable and a 'behavioural problem'. We must remember that it is important that young foals eat muck in order to obtain the necessary bacteria. Hence the stable must *not* be left so clean (if the horse is in), that he cannot do it.

Adult horses who already have the necessary bacteria will only eat muck if they are confined and, in addition, lack fibre or because they have little else to do in an isolated, monotonous and dull environment. Like many other actions that we have mentioned, this can easily become a habit which may be difficult to stop, even after the apparent cause has been removed.

Another possible cause is a dietary deficiency and I have heard of cases being cured by adding mineral supplements to the food. The cure is, as usual, to think of the horse's total environment and consider how it can be improved in terms of becoming closer to the type of environment that horses evolved to live in.

Distribution of food

Unlike cattle it is necessary to give yarded horses approximately 3 m of space between each individual for feeding. It is better if all animals are able to obtain their fibre ration simultaneously. This means that the food should be placed in well spaced bundles, rather than in continuous racks or troughs. Young horses and family groups will, however, eat close to each other without competition (*Chapter 6*), and less space can be allowed – 1·5 m to 2 m per horse.

Concentrate feeds should be given in separate bowls and it may be necessary to tie individuals until they have finished their own feed, otherwise certain horses may move around taking over the food of others. Mares are usually tolerant of their foals eating their food but the foal may end up as a result having too much and the mare insufficient.

Aggression

I have mentioned aggression in passing. In the first place it has been argued that horses are not by nature aggressive animals since they are social herbivores and therefore behaviour that cements the bonds between individuals, that is affiliative behaviour, is more important than behaviour that is likely to cause the group to split up; that is 'aggression'. Also for the vast majority of time horses do *not* have to compete for any scarce resource.

One situation when stallions do compete is for mares, in order to be able to breed with them. Thus fighting does normally occur between adult stallions in the presence of mares. Sub-adult males will be submissive at such times since they will not be able to compete successfully. The adult stallion may well chase and attack colts (and sometimes sub-adult fillies) if they are with the mares.

Other times when aggression does occur is when a mare has recently foaled and protects her foal from others and when there is a scarce resource like food or water which is not well spaced. Certain individuals will tend to be less tolerant than others of other animals and may well threaten them if they come too close. The introduction of strangers and changing groups tends to increase aggressions.

Aggression towards humans can often be related to inappropriate environments, past experience and handling.

Isolation

When horses are kept isolated in individual stables and not allowed normal social contact with other horses and their family group, the aggression directed towards other horses, people or other species tends to increase. *Isolation induced aggression* is used by experimental psychologists to increase aggression in, for example, laboratory rats and it is well known that isolation does increase aggression in many species. Horses are no exception.

Much of the aggression that one sees in difficult horses is, therefore, the result of their past and present experiences so a thoughtful redesigning of the environment, including keeping the horse in a more social environment more of the time can do much to reduce it. However, this is not always successful; as we have seen horses frequently and easily form habits which become well entrenched and very difficult to change.

It is not difficult however to raise horses that are not aggressive simply by following, as closely as possible, the environmental design that they have evolved to live in. In this instance keeping them in groups, allowing them contact with their families and, for stallions, allowing them to grow up as socially adapted animals in a social group. I would suggest therefore that stud owners think carefully about the way they raise their young stock (in order to try to fulfil these criteria). Several breeders with whom I have discussed these types of problems have had great success in doing this. On my own stud we have, for the last ten years, been experimenting with different husbandry techniques to cut down expense and raise healthier, socially adapted competing horses. This has given us many of the answers.

One of the problems associated with having badly behaved, over-excited and aggressive stallions is that people believe this is the way stallions ought to behave and encourage it, assuming that it indicates 'virility' and 'dominance'. This is unfortunate because if one has a relaxed and socially adapted stallion, mare owners are not impressed; they consider his good manners as 'lack of virility'!

Castration

Castration is normal practice for the majority of colt foals. Is this a sensible and necessary practice? If adult entire males can behave in a relaxed way as do other horses, perhaps it is not always sensible and I would imagine that the owners of very successful geldings such as Arkle and Red Rum are kicking themselves for having had their horses castrated. Indeed, it is becoming more and more evident that castrating horses that are intended for competition is foolish. There are important physical effects of keeping an animal entire, such as an increase in growth and strength as the result of having the male hormone – testosterone – circulating in the body.

There is no doubt that children's ponies and horses that are to be for novices should continue to be castrated. However, experienced breeders, aiming at producing competition horses, hacks and working horses for the knowledgeable, should consider carefully before as a matter of course castrating colts. In the great majority of cases, stallions are 'difficult' because they are made so. Is it right that people should compensate for their own incompetence by surgery?

Early experience

An understanding of the importance of early experience and upbringing is crucial for correcting problems of aggression – one, if not *the* most, undesirable characteristic in horses and almost entirely the result of mismanagement. We have seen (*Chapter 4*) how horses bring up their young and we have made suggestions on how this can be mirrored in modern horse management (*Chapter 6*). One of the most important factors is to allow the foal to associate naturally with other horses.

We have explained how traumatic weaning appears to be for many mares and foals and why; and suggested that it is often at the weaning period that a basis for abnormal and sometimes anti-social behaviour is begun (*Chapter 5*). If weaning is followed by the raising of the young horses isolated in boxes, then there is little chance (since the horse has not had the opportunity of growing up in a normal horse society) that he will be a normal horse able to integrate socially and also behave appropriately with people. Another alternative is for young horses to be placed in groups together, where they grow up having social contact only with their peers. We have explained how abnormal this is (*Chapter 5*), and why it seems that this type of upbringing may cause many handling and disciplinary problems later in their lives (*Chapter 6*).

The answer may well be to bring up horses in a society of mixed ages, as near as possible to the family groups they would naturally be with all their lives. Allowing horses to develop their natural strong and long term relationships with other individuals is also important for a well balanced horse. Sometimes it is possible for people to be substitutes for other horses and where this happens very close relationships will develop. However, if this happens, the human must be aware of the responsibilities he has to the horse in this respect. It may be very satisfying and a very fine relationship, but remember it is a responsibility since you have it for the duration of the horse's life.

Imprinting on the handler by the foal often develops when a foal is hand reared. This can lead to embarrassment thereafter. This '*mal-imprinting*', as it is called, may result in all types of behaviour, including sexual behaviour, being directed at the horse's adopted species, not its own. Discipline problems are also very frequent in hand reared foals. This is normally because, as we have seen, the handlers are not as rough with the foals as other horses are and therefore they do not develop the appropriate manners and proprietories.

There are many other effects of early experience, such as what the horse eats and so on, but perhaps the most important are the effects on social behaviour and this, of course, affects how the horse behaves with people, how he learns and in the end how valuable he is.

Present experience

When I visit stables which have horses with behavioural problems, the fact that one or two horses have stereotypes, or are aggressive or have other behavioural problems, is usually excused by the management on the grounds that 'the horse had a terrible experience, or was badly handled, or unfed before it came to us, but we have done marvels with it'.

Because horses are indeed profoundly affected by early and past experience there may be an element of truth in these statements. However, a sensitive manager who is familiar with how horses behave, will ask himself if all is well for the horse in the environment at the present, or if there is not something that could be done to try and at least reduce the problem.

Restriction

We have seen that horses are adapted to be, above all else, an efficient, fast and far moving species. What is the effect of restricting them, so that they are able to move freely for only a short time every day? Sometimes even this movement is not even free. For example, in riding school or dressage work those horses who are stabled and then taken out for a short time only get to practise highly disciplined movements.

Many stabled horses in particular are, in addition, fed too much concentrate food for the work they are doing. The result is that a horse which is fed high levels of energy giving carbohydrates and has only a short exercise period to let off this energy will leap and cavort around. The handler or rider may then become slightly afraid of the horse and therefore will take him out less and so the problem becomes worse.

Some stable managers cater for this problem of under-exercising stable horses by allowing them free movement in a yard or school (or field which is not reserved for growing grass) for periods each day. This can be a useful and necessary procedure, but it is better if several horses can be placed in the exercise yard together. They then have the opportunity of a social get-together and as a result of imitating each other ('social facilitation' as it is called) they will have more exercise. If the horses are familiar with each other and are normal socially adapted animals this poses no problems. Integrating horses that have never had sufficient social contact can be done, but slowly and thoughtfully.

Horses kept in yards in family groups move around considerably more than horses kept in individual boxes even though the amount of space each has is the same or very similar (*Figure 7·3*). This is another factor in favour of yarding horses if they have to be kept inside.

The anatomy of the horse is also geared for him to be moving much of the time. One of the major physical problems of horses, particularly competition and racehorses is that they tend to 'stiffen up' and their lower legs swell when confined to stables for the majority of the time. This is the result of enforced immobility and for long periods of this to be contrasted with short bursts of hard and often fast work is surely not the most sensible way of ensuring long life and soundness.

In my own experience of long distance riding and racing, I have found that it is essential to allow the horse free movement at all times. However, in a big stable the horse will not move around sufficiently by himself, but with a second horse or out at grass he usually will. This means that when we go to competitions we should put two horses in one stable and ignore the horror of the stable managers.

Some horses are kept stalled, a more restricted system but cheaper and using less space. This has been a traditional way of keeping farm and carriage horses throughout much of history. We have no records of the behavioural problems in the past, but I would doubt that they were much worse than today. The reason being that these stalled horses were normally out at work for at least six hours a day and often more. When they returned to the stall they were, therefore, tired and happy to rest. During these relatively short periods in the stalls they also had all their eating to do. The system of stalling can work well under these conditions. Unfortunately stalled horses these days are usually pleasure horses who are worked far less each day and therefore are in the stalls for much longer periods. They may also be fed low fibre diets because it is easier or because the owners imagine that this is a progressive and modern way of feeding horses. The result is that a great many stalled horses develop behavioural problems of one sort and another – stereotypes, an increase in aggression, bad manners and sometimes lack of co-operation.

Crowding

Horses become more aggressive, not only when isolated, but also when crowded. This is not unique to horses and it is a common consequence of crowding. Under such conditions there is usually a dominance hierarchy established as an artefact of restriction and crowding. This can be rigid in horses and cause animals at the bottom of the hierarchy to be constantly fearful of attack. The consequences of this is that when feeding animals in a group, it is necessary to give them sufficient individual patches of feed so that all can eat simultaneously and to have them sufficiently far apart so that one cannot prevent another from approaching the feed. Keeping horses in yards has this disadvantage, that one does have to ensure that they have plenty of feeding space. It is advisable to have the feed patches no nearer than 3 m. Young horses can, however, eat happily in groups close together with no competition and adult horses will usually be tolerant of young horses up until they are sexually mature allowing them to eat together if they are brought up together.

Crowding can cause other problems which contribute to the development of stereotypes or stable vices such as extreme timidity and lack of confidence in certain individuals.

Reproduction problems

We must remember that infertility may often have its origins in inadequate psychological environments. We know this too from human medicine and it would seem rash and unsatisfactory in the long term to rush in with drugs, particularly treatment using steroids (related to sex hormones) which can have very wide reaching effects on other aspects of both behaviour and physiology, without considering whether we can improve the chances of breeding by changing other environmental conditions, including the social environment.

The following is a list of the most common behavioural problems associated with reproduction found in stallions and mares and what to do about them following the above reasoning.

THE STALLION

Excessive excitement.   This can result in damaging both the mare and himself. Slowly allow the stallion to have free access to mares (non-oestral) in a large yard or field. Depending on the stallion this may involve having to firstly integrate him into the stable yard and allow him to smell, touch and investigate other horses. This can be done initially by keeping both horses on long leading reins or allowing them contact over stable doors. The gradual social reintroduction will be geared towards allowing the stallion to run freely with non-oestrual mares for much of the day in a yard or at grass.

If the horse is very mature and has had this problem for some time, then this period will take much time and patience if injury to him, mares and people is to be avoided. It is possible in most cases however.

Lack of libido. This and/or a low sperm count may be the result of over-using the stallion. A break in covering, if possible allowing him to be run out with non-oestral and the occasional oestral mare will often allow the stallion to recover his interest. Allowing the horse to have longer to court the mare and be courted by her is often helpful in these cases.

A bad experience, such as the stallion being frightened or hurt by bad handling during in-hand covering, can often be the origin of such a problem. In this case, again, the best cure is to allow the horse to re-establish interest and develop bonds with mares in the natural way by giving him free access to them, preferably all the time.

Excessive aggression. Excessive aggression often expressed to the mare or to the handlers is the result of bad management in the vast majority of cases. By thinking about what we have discussed in this book, I hope the reader may be able to isolate the problem. In stallions it is normally related to isolation, lack of social interaction, being handled incorrectly and by people who are inexperienced or experienced and afraid. Normally, social interactions between other horses and with people must be worked towards by developing a suitable retraining strategy.

MARES

As with stallions, mares have similar problems and can be corrected in the same way. Because of the complexity of the female reproductive physiology and behaviour, it is particularly important to allow proper courtship to occur before a stallion is allowed to mount a mare.

The damage to future reproductive performance and the unethical horrors some maiden mares are submitted to as a result of a lack of understanding of these psychological criteria has already been discussed (*Chapter 5*), as have maternal behaviour, maternal rejection, mal-imprinting and problems of hand rearing.

Stimulation

BOREDOM

How varied and 'stimulating' should an environment be for a horse, or a person for that matter? If it is not sufficiently interesting and varied, then there are not enough messages going into the brain and the person or the horse is 'bored'. If there is too much for long periods of time, then a person may become neurotic. As far as we know, animals have the same problem and it appears that there is an 'optimum level of environmental stimulus' (Welsh 1964). In other words, if the horse is kept in dull isolated environments with nothing much going on and is unable to see out, touch or smell other horses or people, then we might expect that it is not stimulated enough – that is, the horse is bored.

Unfortunately, one of the tendencies in modern stable design is towards reducing the environmental stimulation. The result is the development of many behavioural problems. It seems that this is becoming worse. As a thoughtful German magazine, *Freizeit im Sattel* put it recently 'Does your horse have to live in a prison?'

OVERSTIMULATION

The horse can also suffer from over-stimulation, like human beings. Too much and prolonged noise, excitement, exercise, coming and going and too many strange people or horses to mix with socially may cause this.

Stress and distress

For short periods all species seem to be able to adapt to both these extremes of boredom and stimulation. However when either condition is prolonged for a long time, the horse (or person or rat) may not be able to adapt to the conditions without it affecting his physiology or behaviour. These effects appear to be non-adaptive or self-destructive.

The physiological changes which become self-destructive (such as a thickening of the arteries or ulcers in the stomach) are called diseases of 'stress'. It is these physiological changes which can also result in behavioural changes. Some of these are 'self-destructive', and take the form of abnormal behaviours, such as wind-sucking for example. Behaviour may be abnormal in other ways, for example an inordinate amount of time being spent in one activity when compared to the normal non-stressed horse. One of the key problems that is concerning those of us involved in assessing animal welfare at present is how to measure when an animal is under psychological stress perhaps as a result of physical or social factors in his environment. To distinguish this from the physiological phenomenon, it is called 'distress'.

The measurement of behavioural distress is still in its infancy. The performance of abnormal behaviours can be one indicator of behavioural distress. It has also been argued that an inability to perform much or all the behaviour within the animals repertoire will give rise to distress, or perhaps even changes such as in how time is spent could be considered to result in distress.

What I am primarily concerned with is in designing horse environments which *minimize behavioural distress*. These can be called 'ethologically sound' and will prolong the life and 'happiness' of our horses. This involves the minimisation of physiological stress and psychological distress and behavioural problems.

Handling, riding and stockmanship

It is important to understand as far as possible how the horse perceives the world and to act appropriately as a result (*Chapter 3*).

Learning and how and when the horse learns and what it will learn must also be carefully considered.

There are so many problems that arise from not understanding the importance of these things that it is rather meaningless to embark on a list of them. However, because there are some major common problems here we will briefly discuss a few and see what approaches may help with them.

SPOOKING

'Spooking', or shying persistently at objects, is a term used to describe horses that have not been sufficiently handled, have not been brought up in a balanced social contact and have not had an opportunity of learning about new places or objects from their mothers and elders. These horses are more prone to develop severe spooking problems than others.

Superimposed on this however is the fact that young animals will by nature be suspicious of new and strange things or places. In such an event it is very important to let them take their time and gradually gain confidence; for example, by slowly approaching an object. Efforts to speed them up, or hit them or frighten them into moving forward towards the object will only result in reinforcing the behaviour in the first place. Thus, if you are asking a horse to ford a stream for the first time and he is unfamiliar with running water, take the trouble to get off and lead him up to the water slowly until the horse gains confidence and comes across. After crossing go back and do it again and again until the horse does it without a fuss. Failure to do this, especially if the horse is being hit or frightened at the stream, will 'negatively reinforce' him – the horse has learnt streams are dangerous and frightening. It may thereafter take several days before the horse has confidence to approach the water with you on his back, so take your time. This applies too with traffic training, with loading horses into trailers, with tying them up, with going through and opening gates and so on.

The more the young horse is exposed to all these different things and strange places, the more used to adapting to them will he become until he does not bat an eyelid at all sorts of terrifying things. However if the horse is hurt at any time associated with the training then one must return to square one and start again. The golden rule is *never ask a horse to do something you cannot make him do, or have not time to wait until he does it.*

A bit of hunger will work wonders in making a horse more

interested in approaching or boxing, or whatever the problem. He must only be given food when he does the right thing.

Older horses who have become established in doing some inappropriate thing, are more difficult but can be retrained if people have enough time and patience.

Rearing, bucking, head shaking, bolting and so on are all well known and relatively common problems which have to be treated in the same way.

Hygiene

The British people pride themselves on being a nation of animal lovers. As far as horse keeping goes, I have met very many non-British people who volunteer that the British are the 'fussiest horse keepers' they have ever met. If this is the case, then *are* there fewer behavioural problems – and have the British got it right if they take all this extra trouble over their horses? Having travelled in America, Canada, Australia, much of Africa and Europe, I have to admit that there do not seem to be fewer behavioural problems with the horses in Britain than elsewhere, in fact one is tempted to consider there are rather more. If we care so much for our horses, surely this should not be.

The answer must be that the British have got their priorities wrong in terms of horse husbandry. In fact this is quite easy to see. There is a heavy, almost desperate emphasis sometimes on 'turn out', on hygiene and cleanliness of horse and rider, on having the right clothes and having a completely clean horse. Many competitions are really about 'turn out' (showing, driving, even dressage and jumping to a degree). The horse establishment backs this approach to the hilt. There is never a chance of passing a British Horse Society examination unless you have the order of grooming, the exact way to clean a saddle, never mind if you can actually *handle* a horse, or quiet a difficult animal, or mend a fence! Students and grooms must spend many hours brushing and cleaning, washing and hosing. Often the horses are not put out to pasture for periods each day because they will get dirty; or not ridden through soft ground off the road because they will get muddy – or not exercised at all because of the work in cleaning that this creates.

It is of course nice to have well turned out horses and clean tack, but if this means that far more important things – from the horse's point of view – are missed (for example time spent schooling and training, time spent handling and teaching and talking to horses) then it is inappropriate. If you are rash enough to ride your horse muddy, or your tack uncleaned – well, you might as well have leprosy as far as other 'horsey' people are concerned! This approach also means that many who would like to be involved with horses are scared off by the ritual, rigmarole and I am afraid what often amounts to snobbery of people with horses. Many will actually cause very considerable problems to their horses by an over insistence on cleanliness and hygiene, washing off their horse's legs every day in detergent causing tender sore skin; oiling hooves so that they become so soft that they wear away. Clipping and blanketing animals that are then at risk from cold and sometimes mud fever and for which there is often little reason other than ease of cleaning. Worst of all is not spending enough time looking at the horses and their behaviour to be able to spot behavioural problems before they become serious.

An over emphasis on hygiene and cleanliness can be a bad thing and perhaps we should think a little about priorities in our modern horse management. The horse has, after all, managed to look after himself and survive for 35 million years without interference from us except for the last 5,000 so there is a real possibility that the horse got it right and can survive without us, if we can only give him the option!

Appropriate environments

One of the modern trends in horse stabling, particularly in Europe and America but growing now in England, is to build stables within one building with a passage down the centre and horses in individual boxes with sliding doors and grated tops so that the horses are isolated and exposed to few other environmental changes. There are even boxes that slide in and out of the walls for food and water so it becomes virtually unnecessary to enter the stables. The building may be kept immaculate and it can make it easier for management and be more labour saving, but it does *not* necessarily make it better for the horse.

One way of considering if this is the case is to measure the number of abnormal behaviours, or stereotypes that are performed by horses in such an environment. I found in one such barn breeding Hanovarians that 26 per cent of the horses (100 horses in the sample) were performing a stereotype of one sort or another and that was within a period of half an hour! One could reasonably suggest that during the 24 hour period practically every horse would be performing a stereotype of one sort or another.

It is quite possible to design appropriate practical labour saving environments for horses and with the growth of the 'urban' horse for riding indoors in cities, it is becoming more and more important. However the treatment of behavioural problems and the designing of appropriate environments for horses has to be thought of on an individual basis. Some years ago as a result of a survey of the behavioural problems of farm animals, including horses (Kiley-Worthington 1977), I found that most of the problems that were encountered in intensive management and 'over management' of horses were the same problems as psychologists are encountering in urbanised people whose environments are often very restricted and in many senses deprived.

Ethologically sound environments

A few suggestions can be made at this point with a more 'ethologically sound' environment in mind.

1. Keep horses outside as much as possible and allow them free access to other horses and free movement as much of the time as is possible.
2. Feed horses a high fibre diet, whatever their exercise programme and make sure that they can fulfil their time they have for eating (at least twelve hours a day).
3. If horses have to be kept inside, then it is much better to keep them in family groups. Groups of unrelated animals can be kept together if they are integrated slowly.

4. Weaning should be avoided.
5. Allow courtship and wherever possible, natural 'pastural' mating. Owners should send mares to stallions who are allowed to cover naturally.
6. If horses have to be kept individually housed in stables, ensure that the environment is varied enough and that the horse can see, touch or smell other horses and other activities going on in and around the yard. The more isolated the horse, the more inappropriate, so reduce the walls between loose boxes, or simply have kicking boards. Good views from stables also help here.
7. During birth and after birth do not interfere or disturb mother and foal except in very extreme circumstances. Go away on holiday while your horses are foaling if you cannot resist this.
8. Do not under-estimate your horse's learning speed or potential. What you may call a stupid horse may be one that has learnt only too fast not to do what you want him to because of incorrect reinforcements. Remember your elementary learning theory and apply it *always*.
9. Obtain your horse's co-operation, do not set out to 'dominate' and 'overcome' and 'break' him, it will not lead to the best relationship. Mutual respect is what is required. Remember that the horse is stronger than you – he has great potential for co-operation, so use, do not abuse, this. However there is no reason why your horses should not be obedient and quiet.

   In this way we can raise horses that are far less likely to develop behavioural problems; it is a *preventive equine psychiatry* if you like.

I must stress that these suggestions are not only for the pony breeders, but are for *all* horses. Where misguided over-management has created the problems and costs in terms of horse welfare, as well as money, the horses particularly at risk from behavioural problems as a result are thoroughbreds and other competition and racehorses. Following suggestions of this type is often much more practical than it seems as the main objections are often that it 'breaks tradition'. Try asking yourself sometimes before doing a traditional horse management practise 'why' or even 'why not?' and see if you can figure out a biological rational reason why doing it is a good idea. If not, think carefully if there is not a better way of doing it, from the horse's point of view – or if it needs doing at all.

11 Stereotypes

What are stereotypes?

The dictionary definition of a stereotype is 'An aberrant behaviour, repeated with monotonous regularity and fixed in all details'. A couple of hours spent observing practically any group of stabled horses will reveal many examples of stereotypes. To date the emphasis in the treatment of recognised stereotypes, such as cribbing and wind-sucking, has been on preventing them from being performed. This has been traditionally done by fitting the horse with muzzles, straps and cradles so that he is physically unable to perform the activity. Lately surgical techniques involving cutting the appropriate muscles to prevent the animal being able to contract the muscles in the neck to swallow air (an integral part of the activity) have been developed. These techniques are, firstly, unreliable in physically preventing the activities; and, secondly, they do not attempt to attack the *cause*. The result is that the animal may well develop some other stereotype or abnormal behaviour. Obviously we must try and understand their causes, their function and in particular their prevention. This is an approach which should prove rather more successful than the hit and miss attitude of applying surgery or gadgets.

Of the stereotypes that are encountered all can be related to their motivational origin. (*Figure 11.1*).

The external factors in the environment together with internal ones in the mind of the horse, can also combine to cause the stereotype. The remarkable thing is how so many environmental factors can contribute, and add up to cause the behaviour (*Figure 11.2*). It is not therefore a simple thing to determine the cause.

Those in Origin Related:			
To Eating	To Locomotion	To Cutaneous Irritation	To Aggression
Chewing	Pacing	Box-kicking	Head-extending,
	Weaving	(hind feet)	ears back and
Lip-licking	Pawing	Rubbing self	nodding
	Tail-swishing	Self-biting	Kicking stall
Licking	Door-kicking	Head-tossing	(hind feet)
environment	(front feet)	Head-circling	
Crib-biting		Head-shaking	
Wind-sucking		Tail-swishing	
Wood chewing		Head-nodding	

Figure 11.1
A list of stereotypes classified in relation to their origin

Apart from these there are many other stereotypes, each horse usually developing his own variety.

It has often been suggested that animals that perform stereotypes are suffering from various forms of brain damage. This could be the case, but it is likely in only a very small minority of cases since the animals that perform them are quite normal in all other behaviour. Stereotypes can however, have an effect on brain function and development in children and probably other species.

Another important cause that has been suggested for the performance of stereotypes is dietary deficiency. Again this is possible in a small minority of cases, but with the care taken in providing balanced diets in modern horse husbandry, it is unlikely. It is often the animals that are apparently best fed and 'looked after' which develop them. The amount of fibre and time available for eating does have much effect however.

Causes of stereotypes

HEREDITABILITY

All behaviour is the result of both genetics and environment (*Chapter 9*) Many people believe that the performance of stereotypes is inherited. Actually there is no direct evidence of

Contributory Factors	Possible genetic tendency to develop stereotype	High sensitivity and/or or reactivity of horse	Frustration situation. Animal requires something and is unable to obtain it. (Anticipation here)	Conflict between motivations (e.g., approach & avoidance)	Fear, either innate or conditioned
Persecution (from other individual)			√	√	√
Conditioned response (e.g., sight of handler/vet)			√	√	√
Group changing too frequently			*√	√	√
Homogeneous group			√	√	√
Group too small			√	√	√
Group too large			√	√	√
Lack females			√	√	√
Lack males			√	√	√
Lack sub-adults			√	√	√
Crowding			√√	√	√
Isolation from mother/foal			*√	√	√
Isolation from social partner			*√	√	√
Isolation from other species			*√	√	√
Environmental stimulus too low			√√		√
Environmental stimulus too high					
Noise – too much			√√		√
Noise – not enough					
Light – too much			√√		√√
Light – not enough					
Routine – too rigid			√		

Drafts		✓
Ventilation – too poor		✓
Temperature – too low		✓
Temperature – too high		✓
Changes – not enough (monotonous)	✓	★ ✓
Changes – too many		★ ✓
Bedding – inappropriate		✓
Bedding – insufficient		✓
Exercise – too little		✓
Feeding – overfeeding		★ ✓
Feeding – underfeeding		★ ✓
Feeding – restricted feeding		★ ✓
Feeding – insufficient roughage		✓
Feeding – nutrient deficiency		✓
Feeding – monotonous diet		✓
Physical restriction – tied		★ ✓
Physical restriction – other stabling		★ ✓
Water – restricted access	✓	★ ✓
Water – dirty or flavoured		✓

The environmental variables are not mutually exclusive and normally summate to cause the stereotype. Based on 252 cases.

Figure 11.2
The environmental variables that affect the performance of stereotypes and the important situations that give rise to them.
Those marked★ are particularly important

this. A *tendency* to develop a stereotype may well be inherited though. Also, it is clear that horses learn to perform them by imitation. Thus foals with their mothers may well develop a stereotype by watching their mother performing it.

Although it is disputable, the performance of stereotypes does seem to be related to temperament. Thus, animals often considered particularly reactive and sensitive are more likely to develop them. Certainly we see more stereotypes in the 'warm bloods', Thoroughbred and Arab type horses, rather than in the cobs and heavier 'cold blooded' horses. But this may not be related to the breed since it is usually the warm blooded horses which are kept restricted in the types of environments likely to give rise to stereotypes.

EXTERNAL ENVIRONMENTAL CAUSES

All stereotypes can be described as the results of frustration (an environmental imperfection where something is required and not received) or a mis-match between the environment that is expected and that observed. However, also important are fearful situations and approach avoidance conflict (a type of frustration), a result of conditioning (for example, the appearance of a rough handler or a vet indicating probable pain) as well as innate fears (sudden loud noises or bright lights). A conflict between approaching or going and avoiding or stopping is often the cause of stereotypes in the ridden horse. This is the result of the rider giving conflicting aids, either intentionally or not. The horse is unable to work out what is required and resists; for example, he may then throw up his head, or swish his tail.

As we shall see, established stereotypes may bear little relationship in cause or function to their origins. For example, a series of non-pathological stereotypes were performed by a mare when anticipating food (*Figure 11.3*). However, if she was stabled for even a few hours, she would perform them more generally. She never developed a stereotype to the point where her health, performance or condition was affected as she was rarely kept stabled, although she clearly had a tendency to develop them. Her mother was a pathological generalised crib-biter which indicates how both genetical tendencies and environment

Figure 11.3
A series of non-pathological (not harmful) stereotypes in an Anglo-Arab mare: A, head out, reaching with the nose pointing and head nodding; B, prolonged lip licking; C, head circling around and around; D, pronounced chewing repeatedly

interact to cause or control a stereotype. Even horses that have a genetical predisposition to perform such behaviour will not develop them if kept in appropriate environments.

Physical and social effects are superimposed on the genetic tendency for the animal to perform a stereotype. Some animals are more likely to perform them than others in the same conditions. So it is, as we all know, quite possible to keep some animals stalled for 23 hours daily without stereotypes occurring. However, if, for example, the light is inappropriate, the noise level too high, the animal too socially isolated, then these factors will add up to the point where the environment is so inadequate that the animal develops a stereotype. The horse may, of course, adapt in another way rather than performing a stereotype; for example, by becoming exceedingly aggressive. The most important factors in the external environment influencing the development of stereotypes can be divided into those of the physical environment, and those of the social environment.

PHYSICAL ENVIRONMENTAL FACTORS

Feeding and time budgeting—If horses are fed a low fibre diet which is presented to them in a form which allows them to eat their entire daily ration in one to two hours, what are they going to do with the extra 14 or so hours normally spent feeding?

Horses kept in these conditions tend to spend a great deal more time simply standing. These are the animals most at risk of developing a stereotype, and the majority of them perform one although it may not be pathological. Increasing eating time and a more usual distribution of time in different activities can prevent them developing.

Restriction—This is perhaps the most important single cause of stereotypes that has been recognised. Stabled horses (restricted) are more likely to develop stereotypes than horses at pasture and if the animal is stalled rather than in a loose box, then this becomes even more likely. This is true of calves, pigs, sheep, hens and children as well.

Several stereotypes of horses develop from behaviour related to 'frustrated' movement, for example weaving which can become very elaborate.

Dull environments—In the previous chapter I pointed out the importance of too much or too little environmental stimuli in causing behavioural problems. I also pointed out that it was often in the most modern, lavish, cleanest and best organised stable (from a human point of view) that conditions were worst in this respect for horses. The isolation of horses in barn type blocks where they are unable to see out and have bars all around tends to increase the chances of the horses developing stereotypes.

Evidence from studies of children and captive animals in zoos shows that stereotypes can be reduced by providing toys or objects in the environment to look at or to manipulate. Increasing the interest of the environment in stables may be difficult but not impossible. For example, instead of the horse being restricted further when found performing a stereotype, objects to manipulate can be given to him – something as simple as straw to eat or play with, or his stable top door opened to allow a little more contact with other animals. If the horses are in groups in busy yards this helps. 'Occupational therapy' like more exercise, or teaching the animal to do something extra such as working the land he lives on, or harrowing the school he works in, can help.

However, the causes and the organisation of stereotypes is more complex than this. Although novel objects or environmental changes will initially reduce how much the stereotype is performed, this only lasts as long as the object remains novel. In fact, when the animal has an *established* stereotype the novel object may actually increase the performance of it. It is important to realise that a monotonous environment may be an important contributory cause for the development of stereotypes – therefore always ensure that the environment is changing and complex particularly for the young horse.

Frustration, conflict and fear—If the horse is hungry but unable to obtain food, or socially frustrated by being isolated from a stable mate, then he may develop a stereotype and this may become established. He may also perform the stereotype when he experiences a slight conflict as to whether to approach or avoid something.

Frightened chickens also perform more stereotypes and this can be reduced by the use of tranquillisers and sedatives. In the same way stereotypes in horses can sometimes be reduced by these drugs, but since the horse will continue to perform them once the drug has ceased working and the drug itself can have undesirable side effects they are clearly not a solution to the problem.

SOCIAL ENVIRONMENTAL FACTORS

Weaning—When case histories of established stereotype performers are known the development of the behaviour can very frequently be traced back to the weaning period. This is not surprising; as we have seen (*Chapters 5 and 6*) the association between mother and foal is very strong and long lasting. Enforced separation of both causes psychological trauma and to the foal who is developing both physically and behaviourally very rapidly at this stage, such traumatic experience is irreversible. It seems as though the effects are seen in later behaviour particularly in the development of stereotypes.

Since nearly all modern domestic horses are weaned, it is difficult to obtain a large sample of unweaned horses. However, although many of the 15 horses I have bred have a genetical tendency to develop stereotypes, none have been weaned, and none have developed stereotypes. This is far too small a sample, but it is suggestive.

It may be that weaning is the single most important factor governing the development of stereotypes.

Social contact—Horses that have social contact for the majority of time either at pasture or, if inside in yards, with free association in family groups – or even in stables where much contact is possible across partition bars – are less likely to develop stereotypes than those kept in isolated individual stables. In the latter there is no touch possible between individuals and little smell or visual contact. We have seen that contact between individuals is relatively common when the horses are able to form the relationships they like (*Figure 5.3*) It appears that deprivation of social contact is another factor in the development of stereotypes.

Crowding—On the other hand, crowding and excessive social contact may equally be important in developing stereotypes in some animals. There is considerable evidence that in birds a reduction in the area for each increases the chance of stereotypes occurring. Nobody has measured this in horses yet but anecdotes suggest this does seem to happen. Thus, horses in groups in large paddocks rarely develop stereotypes whereas horses confined in small paddocks in groups sometimes do.

These are the factors which at present we know are important in causing stereotypes to develop. Normally several of these factors will be present however, and will summate to cause the *development* of the stereotype. An *established stereotype* will however be performed in almost every situation, and is not therefore a good indicator of the cause. In addition, even if all these factors are corrected, because of the *habit strength* of an established stereotype, it will not necessarily stop or even be performed less than before.

Stereotypes and learning theory

Stereotypes show many of the characteristics of learnt behaviour. For example it is possible to develop stereotypes (in the rat at least) through 'operant conditioning' (Type II conditioning where the animal has to consciously *do* something).

This behaviour may then *generalise* and occur in many different situations. For example an activity such as head tossing is initially evoked by some mild stimulus, such as nasal irritation. It becomes accidently reinforced (that is, the horse obtains some reward from it; for example, he is returned home from a ride out), thereafter it becomes associated with that particular situation. Subsequently, however, the stereotype may generalise and be performed in many different situations which show no apparent relationship to the original cause.

HABIT STRENGTH

Another very important factor which has led to much confusion in the literature on stereotypes is habit strength. Apparently the more an activity of this type is performed, the more it is likely to be performed. It is self-rewarding. In this way it can eventually occur in situations quite different from the type of situation which gave rise to it. We usually see *established stereotypes* which have generalised and therefore occur in many different situations because they are recognised as a problem. They are of 'high habit strength' (the more they are performed, the more they are likely to be performed). But the situation in which they are reported may *not* relate to the situation in which they arose. Thus, if we want to know about their cause, then we must look at that particular animal, its history and background and unravel the conditions that gave rise to the stereotype.

It is therefore useful to make a distinction between *developing* stereotypes and *established* stereotypes. The latter will be more general in their appearance, and therefore will not tell us about their original cause. It must be appreciated that to change the environmental conditions may well not cure an established stereotype although it may have an effect on preventing its further establishment.

It is quite possible to design environments that prevent young horses developing stereotypes – by being aware of the type of environment the horse has evolved to live in and in particular considering the physical and social factors which have been outlined here. In this way it would be possible to drastically reduce the number of stereotype performers within one generation. However this is not to say that all the horses with established stereotypes will be cured by changing the environment.

AVERSIVE CONDITIONING

If stereotypes are similar to learnt behaviour, then it might be possible to condition the animal *not* to do them; that is, use aversive conditioning by negatively reinforcing them every time they attempt to perform the stereotype. This technique has been

Figure 11.4

A pathological crib-biter. This horse has worn away the top of the stable door by his crib-biting. The causes at this stage were: a restricted access to fibre; 20 to 23 hours confinement per day to an individual stable with no contact (other than visual) with other horses; a high nutritional plane (he is a advanced level dressage horse). The neck muscles are characteristically contracted. This has given rise to people using straps around the upper neck and to the cutting of the muscles to prevent the horse crib-biting. Neither solution attacks the *cause*, so does not cure the behavioural syndrome giving rise to it. In the case of this horse the stereotype had generalised, and was therefore performed in practically any situation. Correction of all these factors above, allowing the horse access to others, access to pasture and as much fibre as he could eat (but presented in a hay net with a very small hole) resulted in a considerable cutting down of the crib-biting, but not its total extermination

successfully used, for example, to stop alcoholics drinking. In horses it has been tried by giving them electric shocks when they try to perform the stereotype. However the treatment has not been standardised and the samples are far too small for any conclusive results. I am currently engaged on a project to test this further.

IMITATION

Another characteristic of stereotypes is that they are sometimes apparently learnt by imitation. Imitation is, of course, a type of learning. It is therefore unwise, for example, to allow young horses close and prolonged association with crib-biters (*Figure 11.4*) as they may learn to do it themselves by imitation. On the other hand it is unlikely a horse will learn to do this behaviour unless he has an innate tendency to develop it or, more likely, he has other things wrong or unacceptable in his environment.

Why are stereotypes performed?

We have considered the cause of a stereotype, but what is its function?; why does the animal do it instead of something else?; what is to be gained from doing it?

I don't think these are very difficult questions to answer. I suggest that stereotypes are performed in order to switch the animal's attention from outside himself, which for one reason or another is unacceptable. For example, either there is too much stimulation and the horse's nervous system is 'overloaded', or there is insufficient stimulation from outside, and he is 'bored'. In the latter case the system needs stimulation. Thus the horse switches attention onto stimulating himself which he can control, in one way or another. It is, if you like, a safety valve which enables the horse to cope with an insupportable environment by switching out of it onto himself.

If this is so (and you can see how difficult this would be to test) then the performance of stereotypes are adaptive; that is, they may prevent the horse from perhaps becoming psychotic or neurotic. Recent work which has found that endogenous opiates are excreted by stereotypic performing pigs tends to back up this hypothesis. It seems as if the endogenous opiates are excreted to give the animal a mild 'high' during the performance of the stereotype.

If these behaviours are adaptive, it may not be a good idea to prevent them being performed because, if so, the horse may no longer be able to support the environment; and other behavioural problems which may be even more serious could result. For example, horses that are prevented by various gadgets from performing a stereotype often become much more aggressive. We do not yet know what are the behavioural effects of modern surgery techniques, which cut the muscles to prevent the performance of crib-biting or wind-sucking.

If stereotypes are adaptive, then they will also serve as a sign of bad environmental design. If it is necessary for horses, or even one horse in a stable, to perform them, then there must be something wrong with the stables. They might therefore become a useful index of when the environment is adequate and when it is not. However this is complicated because stereotypes are of high habit strength and even improving the environment will not cure the stereotype once it is established.

Prevention

The prevention of the development of stereotypes with appropriate environmental redesign is relatively easy. This is surely what we must aim for. It involves a clear appreciation of the type of social and physical environment the horse has evolved to live in. An effort to match this is superimposed on a detailed understanding of the animal's past experience. This will lead to 'ethologically sound environments'. We have an accumulation of knowledge on these factors now and are in a position to be able to advance in the treatment of psychological disease in horses.

On the other hand the cure of established stereotypes is not fully understood but with a knowledge of individual case histories we can often improve the situation.

What is quite clear, however, is that in the vast majority of cases stereotypes in horses, as in other species, are psychological problems and the use of surgery, drugs or gadgets may prevent them being performed, but will not cure the cause – they may in fact worsen the problem if we are correct in believing that stereotypes are the way horses and other species adapt to unacceptable environments. (Further references to stereotypes and their causes can be found in the bibliography.)

12   Horse Welfare

No subject concerning animals arouses so much emotion and illogical argument as that of animal welfare. This is particularly so in relation to house pets and horses. Every horse owner believes he is right, he knows all the answers and that is all there is to be said. Alas, what does one find when one turns to scientific colleagues? Often, I'm afraid, exactly the same emotional response, usually laced with arrogance.

With such arguments each side becomes entrenched in their position. Often shrouded by ignorance, they do not understand or keep pace with the arguments flowing from the very few who remain open minded enough to contribute constructively to these debates. Despite this, in the last decade there has been a gradual trickle of new ideas and approaches to the debate.

In this chapter I intend to examine various arguments which are of direct relevance to animal welfare – particularly horse welfare which many people may be unfamiliar with. I shall then continue by outlining my own approach to what is 'cruel' to horses, what is acceptable and what is not in terms of designing horse husbandry and why.

Many of these ideas undermine the very basis of some of our cultural beliefs and perhaps some considerable advances in our thinking and changes in our culture as well as attitudes to animals may result from these debates. Thus the subject is an exciting, if exacting, one to study and there is a very real need for better informed people on these issues. Many countries are drawing up guidelines on animal welfare which in some cases has become legislation.

In order to understand the majorities' present attitude to horse welfare, we must take a step back from ourselves and look at Western culture. We find immediately that our attitude to animals, including horses, is coloured very largely by the Judeo-Christian belief that animals are essentially inferior to humans. This is demonstrated by apparently simple ideas such as: animals do not have souls, humans do; animals do not have a language, humans do; animals are less intelligent than humans.

At first glance this all seems so obvious that there is surely no argument – or is there? The result is that most of us 'nice' people have a responsible patronising attitude to animals. We realise that we must be kind to these creatures and treat them like children or mentally defective human beings. If we are nasty and unkind to them, then this harms not only them but ourselves – it is bad for us – we become less 'good' people.

However, animals are not human beings so we do not have to treat them with the same respect. Indeed we may kill them and eat them and, should our religion demand it, we are entitled to cause very real suffering to an animal provided this will benefit people in the end; suffering that our culture will not permit for any humans. This allows us ethical justification in doing practically anything to animals, provided it is done in the name of our current gurus: science and religion. For example, it is well known that there are some controls in Britain on the treatment of animals in scientific research; but, provided arguments for the performance of operations, possibly involving a great deal of pain and suffering for the animals, are based on the possibility of benefiting *people* then almost anything is permitted to be performed. In Australia and in some parts of the United States and Europe, scientists who wish to perform such operations on live animals must defend their reasons for so doing in front of a committee, not only composed of their peers but including philosophers and laymen. In Britain no university or institute has such a committee and the suggestion that they should be instigated has often met with derision.

The religion of Jews and Mohammedans demands that animals should have their throats cut while still conscious, and despite the fact that this is against the law in Britain, nevertheless an exception is made because of human religion. This is then rendered quite acceptable to many people, provided it is of course not done in public. Again it is the effect on *people* that is considered, not the effect on the animal concerned.

Arguments for intensive animal husbandry are based on the same premis: that by raising animals in this way it is possible for more people to be better fed and to make money. After all the poor farmers could not survive economically unless they practise such modern more 'efficient' practices. The ground for these particular arguments has become particularly shaky in the last few years. It is evident that firstly more people are *not* getting better fed by the intensive husbandry in the West. What is in fact happening is that the very well fed West (whose main health problems often rotate around diseases as a result of overeating), is actually causing the growing rates of malnutrition and starvation in the developing world by encouraging the people there to grow cash crops instead of food crops (George 1976). In addition as a result of these practices we have beef mountains, milk lakes, butter swamps, egg beaches, chicken moors and so on. Such practices are causing the rich to become richer, the poor even poorer, and even the Western farmer still has to have large handouts from the government to survive economically! Should we not recognise that agriculture is a service, not an industry (in 1976, the last date for which I have any figures, agriculture cost the country only slightly less than education)?

There are many arguments to think about here, but the central point is that almost the only concern of our culture is the amelioration of the lot of human beings involving, fundamentally, an increase in the standard of living (this means having more material goods).

But what of the animal? In recent years particularly, the large scale use of animals for drug testing, vivisection and factory farming has caused some people to consider whether we can be 'right', whether it is ethically acceptable to allow some practices, although they may eventually benefit humans (Singer 1976, Ryder 1979, Reagan 1982, Clarke 1983).

To understand these arguments, it is important to take a step backwards from our own cultural enclave, to try to follow rational arguments instead of defending entrenched irrational positions, and therefore to try and look at the living world as if one were outside it. If we do this honestly, we may all discover that we have certain niggling doubts of our often long held beliefs, whatever side of the fence we are on.

In the first place we might consider that animals may have an *intrinsic value of their own*, to the living world, and to themselves, rather than just be considered in so far as they are of value to humans. If one considers they do have some intrinsic value, then it is necessary to consider more carefully what will in the end benefit them.

A look at the living world and a little knowledge of biology will remind us that there are many millions of species of animal life and each is uniquely different from every other, not only in its anatomy and body form, but in its behaviour. But not only this, each species has its own strengths and weaknesses: its own fields of excellence, and areas of incompetence. Whales cannot fly, but they can communicate over enormous distances in a way which we cannot and which we do not even understand. Bats can catch prey by echo-location, but they are almost blind. Dogs can track people by using smell, but we cannot. Horses can pick up very slight visual cues and are superb at running fast and far over rough ground. Humans are very bad at smelling, not much good at running, no great guns at hearing, but good at manipulative skills. To consider humans 'superior' to other mammals then begs the question.

Apart from this why should we believe that only humans have 'souls' unless we have some evidence to prove this? In a recent court case, discussing distress in veal calves, when the witness was asked if he *really* believed that calves had souls, he replied by asking the questioner what he meant by a 'soul'. The subject was immediately dropped. First define what you mean by a soul, then we can consider if it is rationally likely that both men and animals have one.

The question of language and whether other species have a language or not we have already discussed (*Chapter 3*) and seen that horses fulfil five of Hockett's criteria for language and some chimps and a gorilla fulfil all seven. Language it appears can only be defined 'as that which only humans do' a circular and meaningless state of affairs.

Humans are said to be superior in intelligence to any animal. It is true that they are the only species that can build space rockets.

But they are not the only species who use tools: chimps, ants and some birds also use tools. Humans learn fast, but they do not always learn faster than other species. Dogs for example will learn complex mazes using smell cues, and horses can learn very fast if motivated (*Chapter 9*). Pigeons can learn 300 slides. It is doubtful that all humans considered mentally normal can do this.

Perhaps then the argument that we are more 'intelligent' and 'superior' is a little arrogant. We may come off with the highest score for achievement in the technological field, but it is surely possible that other animals have elaborate mental experiences that we cannot imagine. There may be no proof of this, but a rational person must admit that such an idea cannot be rejected out of hand.

If then there does not seem to be a very clear division between man and the rest of creation, should we discriminate between how we treat, and think about, animals and about people?

Richard Ryder (1979) was the first person to consider this idea very seriously and he coined the term 'speciesism'. This is the discrimination of one species in favour of its own species. The majority of twentieth century people who are educated and brought up within a Western type culture, where they are taught to be philanthropic, are also brought up to be 'speciests', to discriminate in favour of their own species. Peter Singer, in his absorbing book *Animal Liberation* (1976) takes this one step further and, as a philosopher, he asks the question 'Should one be a speciest, is it ethically any more acceptable to be a speciest than it is to be a racist or a sexist?' He concludes that it is not. Rationally, if you find it ethically unacceptable to be a racist or a sexist, then you cannot accept being a speciest.

Others have countered this idea by saying that even though the above distinctions between animals and man may not be clear there is one distinction and this is that only people are 'self-aware' or conscious of themselves and their existence. Griffin (1976) suggested that in fact this is not true and that throughout the animal kingdom there is evidence which suggests many animals are self-aware. Recently in America, Gallop *et al* (1977) designed experiments to see if chimps recognise changes to their own appearance. This would be one way of finding out if they have some self-recognition. He finds that they do, but his results are controversial.

As a scientist, however, I feel that we cannot reject out of hand the hypotheses that animals are not self-aware. It seems that we might be more likely to be correct by assuming that other mammals are more likely to be similar to humans and have some degree of self-awareness or consciousness; rather than assuming that such a development arose only once in evolutionary history even though it has obvious survival advantages.

If then, animals may have some idea of self-awareness and there is no easy way to make a distinction between animals and people, some argue that animals then must have certain 'rights'. In particular many will argue, as have Regan (1983), Clarke (1983), Rollin (1983) and Narveson (1983) that animals have *the right to life*.

This then very briefly outlines the way much of the argument goes for 'animal rights', or for equal consideration of animals. We cannot go into depth here regarding these arguments, but for any reader who would like to follow them up, the Bibliography has the references.

If, at least, some animals are self-aware then surely they should not be treated with so much lack of consideration? But where do we draw the line – what about insects and fish for example? This question revolves around the idea of 'sentience'.

It is suggested that as one descends the animal kingdom, so the degree of 'sentience' or the amount of self-awareness and ability to 'feel' declines. Thus, most people will consider that mammals have feelings and emotional responses very much like humans. However, the lower vertebrates perhaps feel less and invertebrates even less. What is ethically acceptable to do to which species is at present very much an individual decision. Some, like the Buddhists, maintain that all animal life is sacred. Peter Singer (1976), a purist, says that because speciesm is unacceptable as a philosophy and an honest life style, then it is not acceptable to use animals or animal products in any way, but rather animals must be left free to roam unmolested in wildlife parks. Sadly, however, the wildlife parks are too small and surrounded by human populations. There is no way this can happen in this age without human beings having to 'manage' wild animal populations.

Apart from this objection to the purist argument there is another which may well be more important for the readers of this book. Such an approach would mean that we humans have no animals around us, that we are thrown more and more into the exclusive company of humans. This might suit certain urban people who know no animals as their personal friends or have never had any intimate contact with animals, but to me it conjures up an empty world. Many of my closest friends are animals, and how very dreary it would be without them!

How can we justify keeping animals and using them if we are not speciests? It seems to me we can indeed do this in accordance with the natural laws of 'nature' – use and be used – provided we remain within certain bounds and apply the same approach to our fellow humans. This means that we are ethically entitled to have animals and to live with them just so long as our relationship remains symbiotic (of mutual advantage). If, on the other hand, it should become a parasitic relationship (to the advantage of the humans, and the disadvantage of the animals) then it is ethically unacceptable since it may cause suffering and distress to the animals. Slavery was abolished because it was disadvantageous to the slaves – the owners were parasitic. However, servants are more acceptable because it is a symbiotic relationship.

The next problem we are then faced with is how to define 'suffering'? In the natural way of things there is always some suffering; animals are cold, hungry and in pain from time to time and we all have nervous systems which are designed to cope with such emergencies. It would not be appropriate to eradicate all such pains and stresses. On the other hand, when these stresses are prolonged, then the body is no longer as able to cope with them, and health and behavioural problems occur. Perhaps it is there that we should draw the line.

If there are signs of distress or suffering we may consider that the way animals are kept and utilised is unacceptable. Signs of physical distress are relatively easy to spot; for example, physical abuse, illness, malnutrition and so on. Less easy to define and recognise are signs of psychological distress, but it is nevertheless possible to do this.

This then is what 'cruelty' is – keeping animals in environments where they are physically or psychologically distressed. Physical distress is very much easier to identify, but we must not over emphasise this at the cost of psychological distress. As I have pointed out throughout this book, there are mentally distressed horses in the least expected places and we are, I think, guilty of having ignored psychological demands and in this way caused much suffering – 'cruelty' if you like.

That there is a difference between normal functioning human beings and other species is of course true, but then there is also a difference between cats and dogs and horses, ducks and other species. Certainly too, even if one considers that the technological ability of humans indicates this species superiority, then what about humans such as the mentally retarded and infants, they demonstrably do not have this ability, should they then be treated like animals?; if not why not?; or, put it another way, should we treat animals like animals?

Surgery

It can be argued, and frequently is, that one way of ensuring animals are not in 'distress', even though the environment may be inadequate in many ways, is to use surgery to 'prevent the animal hurting itself, or others'. Thus, hens in intensive units peck each other, so beaks are cut back; pigs bite each others' tails so tails are cut off; stallions can be aggressive, so they are castrated unless required for breeding; horses crib-bite so their neck muscles are cut – children suck their thumbs, so cut their thumbs off!

These solutions I find both irrational and extraordinary. Let us look at the various reasons why surgery is used other than to cure a physical malfunction.

VETERINARIANS AND SURGERY

The first thing to realise is that veterinary surgeons are, as their name suggests, trained surgeons. They have developed surgical techniques, often to a remarkable degree of sophistication, and are very good at applying them. One only needs to look at any veterinary journal to see the emphasis on surgery and new surgical techniques. Thus they tend to favour surgery and often it must be mentioned, this is one of the major ways in which they make their money. They are not disinterested. By contrast they rarely have any thorough training in ethology or behaviour and if they are taught any, it is usually taught by a veterinarian who himself has no good grounding in the discipline. Vets therefore tend to emphasise and encourage surgery.

COSMETIC SURGERY

This is the type of surgery to make the animal look 'better' which may well follow fashion. The cutting off of tails in certain breeds of dogs or the trimming of their ears is in this category. As far as horses go, cosmetic surgery is becoming more common in at least some countries. Morgan horses in the United States for example often have their tails denervated in order to prevent them raising them since the show Morgans must have a low tail carriage. The cutting off of the whiskers of the British show horse or pony is also in this bracket. I have already pointed out that since these whiskers are important for the normal functioning of the horse, it must be distressing not to have them. It is not irreversible however since the whiskers grow back, but one might suggest, nevertheless, that it is unnecessary.

This raises the problem of what is acceptable in the area of external trimming and cutting. Is mane trimming or hogging acceptable (from the horses point of view) or not?; and similarly is the cutting of feather off the legs?; or should the horse be totally untouched with the scissors? If the cutting, trimming or clipping will be in the interest of the horse as far as benefiting him physically for the task he is to perform, then one might argue that it is acceptable. On the other hand if it is merely cosmetic and has little disadvantage from the horse's point of view, should it then be left? There is an argument to suggest that the horse has evolved with his particular physique and (taking an evolutionary position) all structures have some function. It is worth thinking about.

BEHAVIOURAL OR PERFORMANCE SURGERY

I have already briefly discussed (*Chapter 11*) the use of surgery to 'cure' behavioural problems such as stereotypes, in particular crib-biting and wind sucking. This is becoming an increasingly popular operation. It often involves general anaesthetics, prolonged and painful aftercare (Stekel 1982) and there is no evidence that it always 'cures' the problem. In any event since the problem is behavioural, if surgery is performed without environmental redesign in order to try and remove the cause the inability of the horse to be able to perform this behaviour may disturb him further. I would suggest that such practices are quite unethical and unacceptable, from the horse's point of view.

Another form of surgery that is frequently in the news is the denervating of the lower leg. This prevents the horse feeling pain and thus allows him to go sound. Again this is surely an ethically suspect practice. Pain is after all a mechanism to prevent further exertion or use of a particular part of the body, in order to help survival.

Thus to denervate the animal may endanger his survival and is not in his interests, therefore is not ethically acceptable; on the other hand, if it prolongs his life, it could be justified. Firing and blistering and other such antedeluvian practices which cause considerable pain, distress and suffering to the animal for the possibility of human gain are, for the same reason, ethically very suspect.

Various people argue, like Descartes, that animals cannot feel pain, but I doubt whether many people who read this book believe such an argument – and I will leave it here to be argued more fully by others.

CASTRATION AND BREEDING

Surgery is of course also used in castration, and the vast majority of male horses in Britain today are castrated. It is worth examining if this is really necessary, bearing in mind that this prevents the animal from fulfilling all his natural behaviours and breeding. It radically changes his behaviour and probably his personality. Should castration ever be considered necessary?; why and when?

The first reason why castration is universally practised in Britain, and is very widely encouraged by the horse establishment is that it then allows more controlled breeding. It allows the breed societies or the establishment to have a very real control on how horses are bred. This, the establishment argue, is necessary for 'improvement' of the breed and of horses in general. It is difficult to reach a consensus of opinion even within the horse world of what this 'improvement' might be. There are numerous worthy ladies (usually with a smattering of army officers) in tweeds who breed show ponies and appear to dominate the horse establishment in Britain. They are often outraged by the 'rubbish' that is, they maintain, constantly being bred, often by single mare owners who love their mare and wish to breed her foal; or by others further outside the establishment such as gypsies.

What is meant by 'rubbish' depends on who you are talking to. The show judge will find many top long distance horses 'rubbish' judged on her criteria of, primarily, conformation. The show jumper judge may find the champion hack 'rubbish' according to his criteria, the shire breeder any horse with light bones 'rubbish', the racehorse owner anything that cannot win a race 'rubbish'. Rubbish is after all in the eye of the beholder. The only essential criteria, perhaps, is that the animal has four functioning legs and characteristics which qualify him as a horse or pony and no hereditary diseases. In the Western Isles of Scotland, for example, any horse that is not a Highland pony is considered 'rubbish', and in Sussex, the Highland pony is considered an ugly slow thing compared to the Arab. In Egypt the Arab has been selected to have a very typy head and fast speed, he may be narrow chested, herring gutted and have weak looking hocks, but at the same time he may well be able to out gallop and out endure any of the soft heavier straight legged British Arabs. Which is 'improved'?

Surely the only measure of 'improvement' must be in performance. There the truth is that in racing, where records have been kept for sometime, there has been no significant improvement in the speed of horses over the last half century, despite increasing knowledge of physiology, nutrition and genetics of the horse (Snow 1984). In the showing world, the 'improvement' simply follows the fashions of the day. One thing is clear, horses are becoming less able to breed themselves and survive adequately on their own. Biologically speaking this is certainly no 'improvement'.

If then, 'rubbish' and 'improvement' are in the eye of the beholder, surely we are all entitled to our own judgement, and should not be bullied by the equine establishment, or anyone else. If we have a well loved mare that we would like to breed to a well loved stallion, then why not?; provided they too want to breed, and there is no history of hereditary diseases. Surely the single mare owners' valuation in terms of affection, attention and delight is as valid as the establishment's nebulous fashions? Or would we be happy to apply the same criteria of breeding to human populations? At present it is generally accepted that even those humans with hereditary diseases and those who are mentally defective should not be castrated, or their breeding prevented.

If then there is no particular reason in regard to the prevention of breeding should no horses be castrated, except those with hereditary disease?; or are there occasions when castration might be in the general interest of horse and human? Perhaps the latter. As we have seen, stallions do have complex sex lives and, if they are not handled by experienced people when mares in season are also around, they can prove dangerous to humans. So, I would suggest that in the first place horses and ponies that are intended to be ridden and worked by novices and children should continue to be castrated.

On the other hand as we have also seen, stallions can be relaxed gentle animals if kept in appropriate social environments and handled sensibly. If the animal excels at some sport or art of equitation then, if we are selecting on the grounds of performance, we will have missed out if he has been castrated. The owners of such geldings as Arkle and Red Rum must be kicking themselves that they had them castrated! So, it would seem that if horses are intended to work in competition, or be used and handled by competent people and kept in appropriate environments, they should not be castrated.

The almost universal castration of colts is a particularly British characteristic; for example, Mohammedans have never believed in castrating any male animal and they had a very effective cavalry. They also work their stallions in draught, ride them and so on. In Britain it is only very recently that permission has been given to take part in any competition on a stallion (other than racing) though it is still not possible to enter for all competitions.

To conclude then, it would seem that the ethical use of surgery in horses can be confined to its use to cure or overcome physical disease, and in some cases castration.

The use of drugs

Advances in modern science have allowed us the choice of a veritable plethora of drugs for psychological and physical diseases in humans and in animals. Tranquillisers, sedatives, desensitisers, growth promoters, antibiotics, steroids and hormone treatments are some of them. There has recently been some debate on the use of Butezanodole (a desensitiser) to suppress pain and therefore lameness in competing horses. The use of all drugs is prohibited in racehorses, and it is difficult to see why any should be permitted for other equine sports. If a top competitive horse is not sound, then he cannot compete, no matter how many years he has been trained – this after all is the name of the game. From the horse's point of view, until such time as he can be consulted concerning whether he would take a drug or not, he should not be given drugs other than those to reduce suffering in normal day to day living, according to the ethical position taken here which considers what is in the best interest of the *horse*.

The use of drugs for horse breeding, to bring the mare into oestrus and so on, is biologically unsound. In this way we are not selecting for natural fertility. This shows in Thoroughbred figures which have relatively low fertility rates, even with the use of a battery of drugs. This is not in either horse, or human long term interest.

The use of tranquillisers and sedatives to try and overcome the incompetence of handler or trainer would also be considered unacceptable. A careful rethink and a retraining programme can often be used instead.

Using negative reinforcement and punishment

I read an extraordinary letter to a horse magazine recently in which the correspondent outlined a 'scientific conditioning procedure' she had seen put into effect when a horse misbehaved in the show ring. It consisted of a particular number of beatings spaced at particular intervals. As a scientist, I shudder and blush with embarrassment when I hear such stories though it is hardly the fault of the horse keeper today who has been sold the idea of the God Science being able to cure all ills, and about using the 'scientific method' or 'mechanistic approach' to cure horses of undesired behaviour.

I have already pointed out (*Chapter 9*) the grave dangers with a rigid interpretation of the conditioning process and, I hope, stressed the importance of the handler and the method of using conditioning; in particular stressing how important positive reinforcement (reward) is in learning.

Of course conditioning can be misused, and wrongly used, and indeed can cause distress and suffering to the horse. Let us hope that this explanation of how it works will make some small contribution to reduce this.

Measuring suffering and distress

What behavioural criteria can we use to assess whether or not an animal is suffering? There are several, the most important being:

1. We can look for abnormal behaviours, such as the performance of stereotypes, or an excessive increase in aggression.
2. We can see if the horse is permitted to perform *all* the behaviours within his repertoire that he would normally do in a free ranging type of environment. He may, for example, have insufficient space to lie down with ease, to scratch all parts of his body, or to move around the required amount. He may also not be able to perform certain behaviours, like courtship (if only bred in hand) or copulation (if castrated). If a mare she may not have the opportunity to breed and be maternal.
3. The way the time is spent can also be an indicator of 'distress' in some cases. This applies particularly where food is relatively low in fibre and can be eaten rapidly. So, large differences in the amount of time eating and standing around

in stables, although perhaps not necessarily in itself distressing, can be an indicator of possible distress.

4. Another way of assessing distress is by the development of the young horse, both physically and socially. If horses grow up socially inept, unable to mix normally or to perform the normal behaviours of their age group, we can suggest that something is wrong.

We cannot say that the animal *is* in distress because he performs one of these. However all these indicators could be used. On the other hand can we argue that some behavioural deprivations or abnormalities are ethically acceptable, and some not? If so why? These are problems that bear considering.

These arguments are based on an evolutionary assumption which is that the horse has evolved to live in a certain way both socially and physically, and that a gross change from this is likely to cause the horse distress.

Another way of considering this question is to ask the horse to choose what type of environment he would like to live in by giving him choice tests. These experiments take a long time to do, and much money and there are also problems with interpreting the results. For example, a horse may choose an environment simply because it is familiar, not because it is in the long run the best for him. Marion Stamp–Dawkins (1980) argues strongly for such tests; I feel that we need much more pragmatic ways of assessing distress in animals *now* not in a number of years when the tests have been done.

These then are some of the ways we can identify animal suffering, and no doubt there will be further methods developed as we learn more about behavioural changes.

There are, of course, obvious cases of neglect and malnutrition in horses and several welfare organisations are concerned with this, as with the export of live horses. However, it is difficult to argue logically that horses must not be exported live, but cattle, sheep and pigs can be. Why should this be so? Clearly the interest in preventing the export of live horses stems not from logic but from the original taboo of eating horse flesh. The question worth asking is should *any* of these animals be exported live?

Some practices have already come under public scrutiny and perhaps it is time to examine some of the traditional practices of horse husbandry using the criteria of 'suffering' which are being used on animals raised for food. As I have already mentioned some of the most distinguished competitive and (even worse) teaching establishments, have blatant examples of 'animal suffering' in terms of these definitions.

In particular the following common practices need a very critical eye:

1. Inhand covering of maiden mares, in particular, but other mares too.
2. Isolation of horses in fields or boxes, however big, with little or no contact allowed between individuals.
3. Feeding of horses restricted amounts of fibre which prevent them having anything to eat for long periods, particularly when confined or restricted.
4. The weaning of youngsters by separating them from their mothers and raising them either in groups or in isolation in stables.
5. The overuse of negative reinforcement and punishment in training.

Horses are adapted to withstand great variations in temperature and nutritional levels, so bear in mind that just feeding and keeping your horse warm and apparently physically healthy may not be keeping him in ideal conditions. It is too easy to pass judgement on others without having a critical look at what we do ourselves!

In this chapter we have just touched on the various arguments associated with horse welfare. There is no doubt that this will be considered highly controversial, but I hope it will at least make everyone think about the environments in which they keep their horses, in order to reduce their behavioural problems and psychological suffering. The Bibliography gives references to several publications which the keen reader might like to refer to in following these arguments.

I hope that the reader has gained some insight into horse behaviour through reading my book and I hope too that the seeds of the science and art of Equine Preventitive Psychiatry have been sown. Nobody knows all the answers but gradually we are gaining some knowledge and as a result of the efforts of a small number of people our thinking is gradually advancing.

From the point of view of the horse the great enemies are the traditionalists who know all the answers, who resist rational argument and whose firmly held opinions will never be shaken. Let us hope that these issues will gradually be discussed in a rational way and that more people who have anything to do with horses or other animals for that matter, will develop more open minds.

Appendix

Details of the methods and subjects of the experimental and observational work

MARE AND FOAL OBSERVATIONS

These were done from the day of birth to nine months old. The observations were conducted for half-hour periods once a day for the first seven days, and then twice a week thereafter. They were done between 0900 hrs and 1300 hrs. All the activities performed during the observation time were recorded for the mother and the foal. These were: stand, eat, graze, lie, walk, trot, gallop, rush around, buck, kick, head toss, head shake, head rub, scratch, rub or lick object, contact make, contact break (involving non-interrupted movement towards or away from the other for at least 10 metres and all the activities listed in *Figure 6.5*).

In addition, every 5 minutes the distance between mothers and foals and their next nearest neighbours were recorded.

553 horse hours of continuous observation were made on 14 mare and foal diads from 7 different mares. The observations were conducted between 1973 and 1982.

TIME BUDGETS

A group of 10 horses in a yard and 3 in single stables where they could see, smell and touch each other were the subjects of this work. Both groups were simultaneously recorded for two 24-hour periods in February. Each horse's activity was recorded every 15 minutes as were the distances apart, and who the neighbours were. Both groups were fed *ad libitum* hay and straw. Data for comparison with the ration-fed single-stabled isolated horses was collected from the literature and observations in other stables. The work was done in 1982.

INTERACTION BETWEEN INDIVIDUALS

All the activities in *Figure 6.5* were recorded for both the performer and recipient. The group of 13 horses of mixed ages and sexes were recorded between May to August 1981, and January–February 1982. 288 hours observation were made in 3 different field locations (2,880 horse hours an average of 10 horses there at any one time). A total of 8,177 interactions were scored. The data was analysed using the SPSS package on University of Sussex Computer.

GRAZING AND CARRYING CAPACITY ON GRASS

Data for this was collected between 1972 and 1982 at Milton Court Ecological Farm and Stud, East Sussex. The details of management procedures etc., are given in Kiley-Worthington (1981 and 1984) 'Ecological Agriculture. A case study of an ecological farm in the South of England', *Biol Agric & Horti* 2. p 101–33.

FLEHMEN

This was done at the South African Equestrian Centre in 1971. Each horse was tested twice with a solution of the substance and his or her reaction recorded. 43 horses, including 10 stallions were tested with 11 different substances. The test involved presenting the solution on a piece of cotton wool to the nostrils of the horse (smell) or gently rubbing the cotton wool on the tongue (taste).

STEREOTYPES

Work on the cause and function of stereotypes was begun in 1967 and continues, recently with a grant from the University Federation of Animal Welfare. The data has been recorded from visits to approximately 100 stables, and a returned questionaire from 59 owners. People with horses who perform such behaviours, or veterinarians who know of them are asked to get in touch with the author if they are willing to co-operate in the on-going research.

LEARNING AND TRAINING

The effects of weaning on training work was done on the home-bred herd and other related horses sent to us for training over an 8-year period. The work on training a red deer, and a South Devon bull was carried out simultaneously. All animals were trained in the same way by the same trainer.

DETAILS OF THE MANAGEMENT PRACTICES AT THE STUD

The reasons and thinking behind the design and running of the stud and ecological farm have been published elsewhere, e.g. Kiley-Worthington (1980, 1981 and 1984) and articles in *Horse and Driving* (1979 and 1980). Here is a brief resume.

1) It was evident after literature search and visits to innumerable studs and stables that many conventional stud and stable practices were unlikely to be acceptable to the horse as there were many behavioural problems.

2) It was considered necessary to set up and run an establishment to keep horses in ecological, ethological and ethically sound environments. In the first place this meant that the horses should *have the opportunity to perform all the behaviour in their repertoire* including social behaviour, sexual and maternal behaviour. This involves allowing them to live in social groups, the stallion to court the mares and copulate naturally, mares allowed to raise their own foals in groups and youngsters not forcibly weaned by humans. Thus the system was designed to allow the horses to live and mix in their preferred social groups (which are family groups) and to allow the youngsters to grow up in these groups.

For the majority of time the horses are at pasture. When, for reasons of weather, or ease of management, they are inside, they are kept in custom-designed yards and rarely single stables.

The horses are Arabs and part-breds and they are tested in competition to see if horses raised in this way are able to compete and win. At present they take part in most equestrian disciplines: Arab flat racing and endurance, harness working, showing, jumping, gymkhanas. They also teach, give displays, work at liberty and give buggy rides. We have now one international long-distance horse, two national level horses, four horses working at medium dressage level and one advanced.

Another of the ideas behind the stud was to see if these well-bred hardy and tough Arabs and part-breds could again be fitted into an agricultural system and contribute to it rather than being a drain on it.

List of the horses and their details who are the subjects of the observation and experimental work

Name & stud book	Type	Sex	Breeding sire	Dam	Height (in hands)	Date born	Place	Date sold/ gone	Skills
*Syringa AASB	Anglo–Arab	F	Nimran ASB	Kathiawar GSB	15.2	1963	C.G.	1972	General riding, dressage
*Baksheesh AASB	Anglo–Arab	St	Harwood Asif ASB	Syringa AASB	15.2	1971	M.C.	1985	L.D. Racing dressage, jumping liberty, etc, teaching
Aderin Welsh sec A. Sheeba	Welsh mountain	F	unknown		12.2	1970	Wales		Pony club, etc., teaching
Sheeba	Irish cob	F	unknown		15.2	1958	1950 ±	1982	Riding, etc, teaching
*Achmed PBASB	P.B. Arab	G	Baksheesh	Aderin	13.3	1973	M.C.	1983	Riding, pony club, teaching
*Amey PBASB	P.B. Arab	F	Baksheesh	Aderin	13.2	1974	M.C.	1976	
*Alia PBASB	P.B. Arab	F	Baksheesh	Aderin	13.3	1975	M.C.	1977	Riding, teaching
*Aisha PBASB	P.B. Arab	F	Baksheesh	Aderin	13.3	1976	M.C.		L.D. Riding teaching, dressage
*Acacia PBASB	P.B. Arab	F	Omani	Aderin	13.2	1982	Druim.	1986	Backed
*Alpha PBASB	P.B. Arab	G	Omani	Aisha	14	1983	Druim.	1986	Backed
*Shiraz PBASB	P.B. Arab	F	Baksheesh	Sheeba	15.2	1973	M.C.		L.D. Racing, harness, riding, dressage, liberty
*Marhleesh PBASB	P.B. Arab	G	Baksheesh	Sheeba	16	1974	M.C.		
Mahleesh PBASB	P.B. Arab	G	Baksheesh	Sheeba	16	1974	M.C.		Riding, jumping
*Koombyar PBASB	P.B. Arab	G	Baksheesh	Sheeba	15	1976	M.C.	1978	
*Shereen PBASB	P.B. Arab	F	Baksheesh	Sheeba	15.3	1977	M.C.		L.D. Racing harness, teaching,

Name	Breed	Sex	Sire	Dam	Height	Born	Place	Acquired	Use
Sugar Shaker	Cob	F	unknown	Sugar Shaker	15	1973	M.C.	1975	Lunged
★ Nobbley-Nosh PBASB	P.B. Arab	G	Baksheesh		15	1970	?	1982	Harness, riding
Melanie	Thoroughbred	F	unknown	Melanie	15.3	1978	M.C.	1982	Riding, showing
★ Bakini PBASB	P.B. Arab	F	Baksheesh	Melanie	15.1	1979	M.C.	1982	
★ Masad PBASB	P.B. Arab	F	Baksheesh		16				Lunged
Omeya ASB	ASB	F	Genji	Zumana	15.1	1976	Devon		L.D. Harness, teaching, dressage, liberty, etc.
Omani ASB	ASB	G	Hassani	Omeya	15.2	1981	M.C.	1984	L.D. Riding dressage, etc.
Crysthannah Royal ASB	Pure Arab	F	Crystal King	Hannah of Fairfield	15	1977	Hamps		L.D. Dressage, teaching, etc.
★ Carif ASB	Pure Arab	St	Cherif	Crysthannah Royal	15	1983	M.C.		L.D. Dressage teaching, racing
★ Osnan AASB	Anglo-Arab	G	Baksheesh	Omeya	15	1984	Druim.		
★ Bosanji PBASB	P.B. Arab	G	Baksheesh	Shiraz	15	1982	M.C.		Riding, L.D.
Shabat	P.B. Arab/Trekhener	G	Trekhener	Shereen	15.3	1983	M.C.		L.D. Dressage
★ Astra PBASB	P.B. Arab	F	Baksheesh	Aderin	13	1985	Druim.		
Snip	P.B. Arab	F	Baksheesh	unknown	16	1979	M.C.	1982	Riding, jumping
Jim HPS	Highland	G	unknown		15	1972 ±	?	1983	Riding
Stardust	Welsh type Cob	F	unknown		12.3	1973 ±	?	1982	
Willow	Cob	F	unknown		15	1970	?	1982	Riding

★ home bred.   M.C. = Milton Court Sussex.   Druim. = Druimghigha, Mull.   AASB = Anglo-Arab Stud Book.   PBASB = Part-Bred Arab Stud Book.
L.D. = Long Distance.   ASB = Arab Stud Book.

Thus, the majority of the horses do appropriate work in chains (harrowing, muck-carting, haymaking, etc). Much of their fitness exercise is done in this way. They also are invaluable for sheep-gathering, cattle-herding, taking food to the stock on the hill, and many other chores. We could not run the farm without them. The advantages of having these types of horses doing these types of jobs is that they can be used, and enjoyed by any horse-owner who wishes to have fun, compete and get to know their horses better by working them and having them contribute to their costs.

Our horses breed and we sell young horses to bring on at around three years backed and bitted.

The horses are not fed bought-in concentrates, added proteins or supplements, but rather given well-made organically produced and licensed foods made and grown on the farm (hay, silage, barley and oats). They have high-fibre diets and are never fed more than 10 lb of corn a day even when in flat race or long-distance training.

ECONOMICS

The economic soundness of this approach has been tested over the last ten years (see Kiley-Worthington and Rendle 1984) and the horses have proved an economic asset to the farm. The main income is from the sale of young stock. Their costs are very low due to the home production of the majority of their food, and the low veterinary bills. In addition the pastures have increased in their yield and carrying capacity as a result of having the horses and their muck to help to upgrade the system. The carrying capacity in Sussex was estimated at 1 bovine unit per acre with no fertiliser treatment from bought-in sources. The horses' teaching commitment is only three hours per week per horse.

Perhaps the most important asset has been the privilege of sharing life and work with a small herd of adaptable relaxed horses able to turn their 'hoof' to anything and apparently enjoy it. The close relationship built up between species in this way is the greatest payment of all. The preceding table lists the subjects and their details.

Bibliography

Archer, M. (1973), The Species Preference of Grazing Horses. *J. Brit. Grassland Soc. 28,* 123.

Archer, M. (1977), Grazing Patterns in Horses. *Brit. Vet. J. 133,* 98.

Bareham, J. R. (1972), Imprinting and Neonatal Behaviour. *Soc. Vet. Ethol.,* Bristol. *Appl. Anim. Ethol.* Abstract.

Berger, J. (1977), Organizational Systems and dominance in Feral Horses in the Grand Canyon. *Behav. Ecol. Sociobiol. 2,* 91–119.

Blake, H. (1975), *Talking with Horses.* Coronet, London.

Blake, H. (1975), *Thinking with Horses.* Coronet, London.

Blaxter (1967), *The Energy Metabolism of Ruminants.* Hutchinson, London.

Carson, K. and Wood-Gush, D. G. M. (1983), The Nursing Behaviour of Thoroughbred Foals. *Equine Vet. J. 15,* 257–262.

Carson, K. and Wood-Gush, D. G. M. (1983), A review of the literature on feeding, eliminative and resting behaviour in horses. *Appl. Anim. Ethol. 10,* 179–190.

Carson, K. and Wood-Gush, D. G. M. (1983), A review of the literature on social and dam-foal behaviour in horses. *Appl. Anim. Ethol. 10,* 165–178.

Clutton-Brock, J. H., Greenwood, P. J. and Powell, R. P. (1976), Rank and Relationships in Highland Ponies and Highland Cows. *Zeit. Tierpsychol. 41,* 202–216.

Clarke, S. (1978), The Rights of Wild Things. *Inquiry* 22, 1–2, 171–188.

Clarke, S. R. (1983), Humans, Animals and 'Animal Behaviour' in H. I. S. Miller and W. H. Williams *Ethics and Animals,* 169–182. Humana Press, Clifton, New Jersey.

Darwin, C. (1859), *The Origin of Species.* Reprinted 1950 Watts & Co., London.

Dawkins, M. S. (1980), 'Animal Suffering' in *The Science of Animal Welfare.* Chapman and Hall, London.

Dawkins, R. (1976), *The Selfish Gene.* Oxford University Press, Oxford.

Dawson, F. L. C. (1984), 'Equine Reproduction' in J. Hickman *Horse Management*, 1–54. Academic Press, London.

Dixon, J. C. (1970), Pattern Discrimination, learning set and memory in a Pony. *The Thoroughbred Record*, 192.

Duncan, P. (1980), Time budgets of Camargue Horses. *Behav*. 72, 26–47.

Duncan, P. and Vigne, N. (1979), The effect of group size in horses on the rate of attacks of bloodsucking flies. *Anim. Behav*. 27, 623–625.

Edwards, P. J. and Wallis, S. (1982), The Distribution of Excreta on New Forest grassland used by cattle, ponies, and deer. *J. Appl. Ethol*. 19, 953–964.

Estes, R. D. (1966), Behaviour and Life History of the Wildebeeste. *Nature*. 212, 999–1000.

Estes, R. D. (1972), The role of the vomeronasal organ in mammalian reproduction. *Mammalia 36*, 315–341.

Feist, J. D. and McCullogh, D. R. (1976), Behaviour patterns and communication in feral horses. *Tierpsychol*. 2, 41, 337–371.

Fiske, J. C. (1979), *How Horses Learn*. Stephen Green, Vermont.

Fouts, R. S. and Mellgren, R. C. (1976), Language, signs and cognition in chimpanzee. *Sign language studies 13*, 319–346.

Fraser, A. F. (1968), *Reproductive Behaviour in Ungulates*. Academic Press, London.

Frisch, K. von (1967), *The Dance language and orientation of Bees*. Oxford University Press, Oxford.

Gallup, C. G., Boren, J. C., Gregg, J. G. and Wallnau, L. B. (1977), A mirror for the mind of man, or will the chimpanzee create an identity crisis for *Homo sapiens*? *J. Human Evol*. 6, 311.

Gardner, K. A. and B. (1969), Teaching sign-language to a chimpanzee. *Science 165*, 664–672.

Goldsmith-Rothchilde, B. von (1976), *Sociale organization und verhalten eines Camargue-Pferde-Bestandes*. Lizentiat, Bern.

Griffin, D. R. (1976), *The question of animal awareness*. The Rockefeller University Press, New York.

Groves, C. P. (1974), *Horses, asses and Zebras in the Wild*. David & Charles, Newton Abbot.

Hafez, E. S. E. and Wierzbowski, S. (1961), Analysis of copulatory reflexes in the stallion. *4th. Int. Cong. Anim. Rep*. The Hague 2, 176.

Hafez, E. S. E., William, M. and Wierzbowski, S. (1962), on 'The behaviour of horses' in *The Behaviour of Domestic Animals*, (ed. E. S. E. Hafez), Baillière Tindall, London.

Harrison, R. (1964), *Animal Machines*. Stuart, London.

Harlow, H. F. (1959), The Development of learning in the Rhesus monkey. *Amer. Sci* 47, 459–479.

Hockett, C. F. (1958), *A course in modern linguistics*. MacMillan, New York.

Houpt, K. A. (1979), The Intelligence of the Horse. *Equine practise 1*, 20–26.

Houpt, K. A. and Keiper, K. R. (1980), Dominance hierarchies in feral and domestic horses. *31. Jahrestagung der Europ. Verein fur Tierzucht.*

Janis, C. (1976), The evolutionary strategy of the Equidae and the origins of rumen and caecal digestion. *Evolution 30*, 757–774.

Janis, C. (1982), Evolution of horns in ungulates. Ecology and paleoecology. *Biol. Rev. 57*, 261–318.

Jerison, H. (1973), *Evolution of the brain and intelligence*, Academic Press, London.

Jewell, P. and Anderson, G. G. H. (1978), Genetic conservation in domestic animals: purposes and actions to preserve rare breeds. *Proc. Roy. Soc. Arts* 693–710.

Jost, H. (1897), *Die Assoziationsfestigkeit in ihrer Abhängigkeit von der Verteilung der Wiederholungen.Z. P5*, 14, 436–72.

Kare, M. R. and Bauchamp, G. K. (1977), 'Taste, smell and hearing' in *Duke's physiology of domestic animals* (ed. M. J. Swenson), 713–730.

Kellog, N. N. and Kellog, L. A. (1933), *The Ape and the Child*, McGraw-Hill, New York.

Kiley, M. (1972), The vocalisation of ungulates. Their cause and function. *Zeit. Tierpsychol.* 31, 171–222.

Kiley-Worthington, M. (1976), The tail movements of ungulates with particular reference to their causation and function as displays. *Behav.* 6–115.

Kiley-Worthington, M. (1977), *The behavioural problems of farm animals*. Oriel Press, Stockton.

Kiley-Worthington, M. (1981), Ecological Agriculture. What it is and how it works. *Agric. Envir 6*, 349–81.

Kiley-Worthington, M. (1983), Stereotypes in horses. *Equine practise 5*, 34–40.

Kiley-Worthington, M. and de la Plain, S. (1983), *The Behaviour of Beef Suckler Cattle*, Verlag Bukhauser, Basel.

Kiley-Worthington, M. Horse language. *Proc. Int. Ethol. Congr.* Toulouse.

Kiley-Worthington, M. (1984), Ethology and Ethics in Animal Husbandry. *Proc. IFOAM*, Witzenhausen.

Klingel, H. (1968), Socialorganization and verhaltensweisen von Hartmann und Bergzebria. *Zeit. Tierpsychol.* 24, 76–88.

Klingel, H. (1969), Reproduction in the plains Zebra in 'Behavioural and ecological factors' (ed. E. B. Brehmi). *J. Reprod. Fertil. Supp. 6*, 339–395.

Linden, E. (1974), *Apes, men and Language*. Penguin, Harmondsworth.

Mariner, S. (1982), The grazing of ragwort by horses. *Proc. Soc. Vet. Ethol.*

Marler, P. (1967), Animal Communication signals. *Science*, 157–724.

Miller, H. B. and Williams, W. H. (eds.) (1983), *Ethics and Animals*. Humana Press, Clifton, New Jersey.

Miles, F. (1969), *Excitable cells*. Heinemann, London.

Mohr, E. (1971), *The Asiatic Wild Horse*. J. A. Allen, London.

Navreson, J. (1983), 'Animal Rights revisited' in H. B. Miller and W. H. Williams, *Ethics and Animals*, 45–60. Humana Press, Clifton, New Jersey.

Negus, V. G. (1966), *Comparative anatomy and physiology of the larynx*. Wagner, New York.

Oldberg, F. O. and Francis Smith, K. (1977), Studies on the formation of ungrazed eliminative areas in fields used by horses. *Appl. Anim. Ethol. 3*, 27–34.

Ostrander, S. and Schraeder, L. (1980), P. S. I. *Psychic discoveries behind the Iron Curtain*. Abacus, London.

Patterson, D. A. and Ryder, R. (1979), *Animal Rights: A symposium*. Centaur Press, London.

Rees, Lucy (1983), *The Horse's Mind*. Stanley Paul, London.

Reagan, T. (1982), *All That Dwell Therein*. University of California Press, Berkeley, California.

Rollin, B. E. (1983), 'The Legal and Moral basis of Animal Rights' in H. B. Miller and W. H. Williams *Ethics and Animals*, 103–120.

Rossdale, P. D. (1968), Modern stud management in relation to the oestrus cycle and fertility of thoroughbred mares. *Equine Vet. J.* 1.2, 65–72.

Rossdale, P. D. (1983), *The Horse from Conception to Maturity*. J. A. Allen, London.

Rossdale, P. D. and Mahaffrey, L. (1958), Parturition in the thoroughbred mare with particular reference to blood deprivation in the newborn foal. *Vet. Rec.* Feb. 15th.

Rubenstein, D. I. (1981), Behavioural ecology of island feral horses. *Equine Vet. J. 13*, 27–34.

Ryder, R. (1975), *Victims of Science*. Davis-Poynter, London.

Schafer, M. (1975), *The Language of the Horse*. Arco, New York.

Schjelderup-Ebbe, T. (1913), Housenes stemme. Bidrag til housenes psykologi. *Naturen* 37, 262–276.

Scott, J. P. and Maistron, M. V. (1950), Critical periods affecting the development of normal and maladjusted social behaviour in puppies. *J. genet Psychol* 77, 25–60.

Singer, P. (1976), *Animal Liberation*. Jonathan Cape, London.

Sissons, S. and Grossman, J. D. (1953), *The Anatomy of Domestic Animals*, W. B. Saunders, Philadelphia.

Smyth, R. H. (1966), *The Mind of the Horse*. Stephen Green, Vermont.

Steckel, R. (1982), Can Surgery cure Cribbing? *Equus 1982*, 16–18.

Swenson, M. J. (ed.) (1970), *Duke's physiology of Domestic Animals* (8th. ed.), Cornell University, Ithaca, New York.

Tyler, S. (1972), *Behaviour and Social Organization of New Forest Ponies*. *Animal Behav*. Monograph 5, 85–196. Baillière Tindall, London.

University Federation of Animal Welfare, Dawkins, M. & Wood-Gush, D. G. M. (eds.) (1982), *Workshop on Animal Awareness*, Oxford University Press, Oxford.

Walls, G. L. (1963), *The vertebrate eye and its adaptive radiation*. Hafner, New York.

Waring, G. (1983), *Horse Behaviour*. Noyes Press, New York.

Wells, S. M. and Goldsmidth-Rothchilde, von B. (1979), Social behaviour and relationships in a herd of Camargue horses. *Z. Tierpsychol*. *49*, 363–380.

Welsh, B. L. (1964), Psychopsyciological response to the mean level of environmental stimulation: a theory of environmental integration in *Medical aspects of stress in a Military Climate*. US Govt. Print. Washington.

Welsh, D. A. (1973), *The Life of Sable Islands Wild Horses*. PhD. Thesis, Dalhousie, USA.

Wierkowski, S. and Hafez, E. S. E. (1962), on 'The behaviour of horses' in *The Behaviour of Domestic Animals*, (ed. E. S. E. Hafez), Baillière Tindall, London.

Williams. M. (1976), *Horse Psychology*. J. A. Allen, London.

Zeuner, F. E. (1963), *A History of Domestic Animals*. Hutchinson, London

Index